CW00428239

The Caribbean

must SEES

Chief Editor	Cynthia Clayton Ochterbeck
Senior Editor	Gwen Cannon
Contributing Writer	Janis Frawley-Holler
Production Coordinator	Allison M. Simpson
Cartography	Peter Wrenn, Alain Baldet
Photo Editor	Brigitta L. House
Photo Research	Martha Hunt
Documentation	Julie Howle, Doug Rogers
Proofreader	Margo Browning
Production	Octavo Design and Production
	Apopka, Florida
Cover Design	Paris Venise Design
	Paris, 17e
Printing and Binding	Banta Book Group
	Spanish Fork, UT

Contact us:

Michelin North America
One Parkway South
Greenville, SC 29615
USA
800-423-0485
www.michelin-us.com
email: TheGreenGuide-us@us.michelin.com

Special Sales:

For information regarding bulk sales, customized editions and premium sales, please contact our Customer Service Departments:

USA – 800-423-0485   **Canada** – 800-361-8236

Manufacture française des pneumatiques Michelin
Société en commandite par actions au capital de 304 000 000 EUR
Place des Carmes-Déchaux – 63 Clermont-Ferrand (France)
R.C.S. Clermont-FD B 855 800 507

Note to the reader:

While every effort is made to ensure that all information in this guide is correct and up-to-date, Michelin Travel Publications (Michelin North America, Inc.) accepts no liability for any direct, indirect or consequential losses howsoever caused so far as such can be excluded by law.

Admission prices listed for sights in this guide are for a single adult, unless otherwise specified.

Welcome to the Caribbean

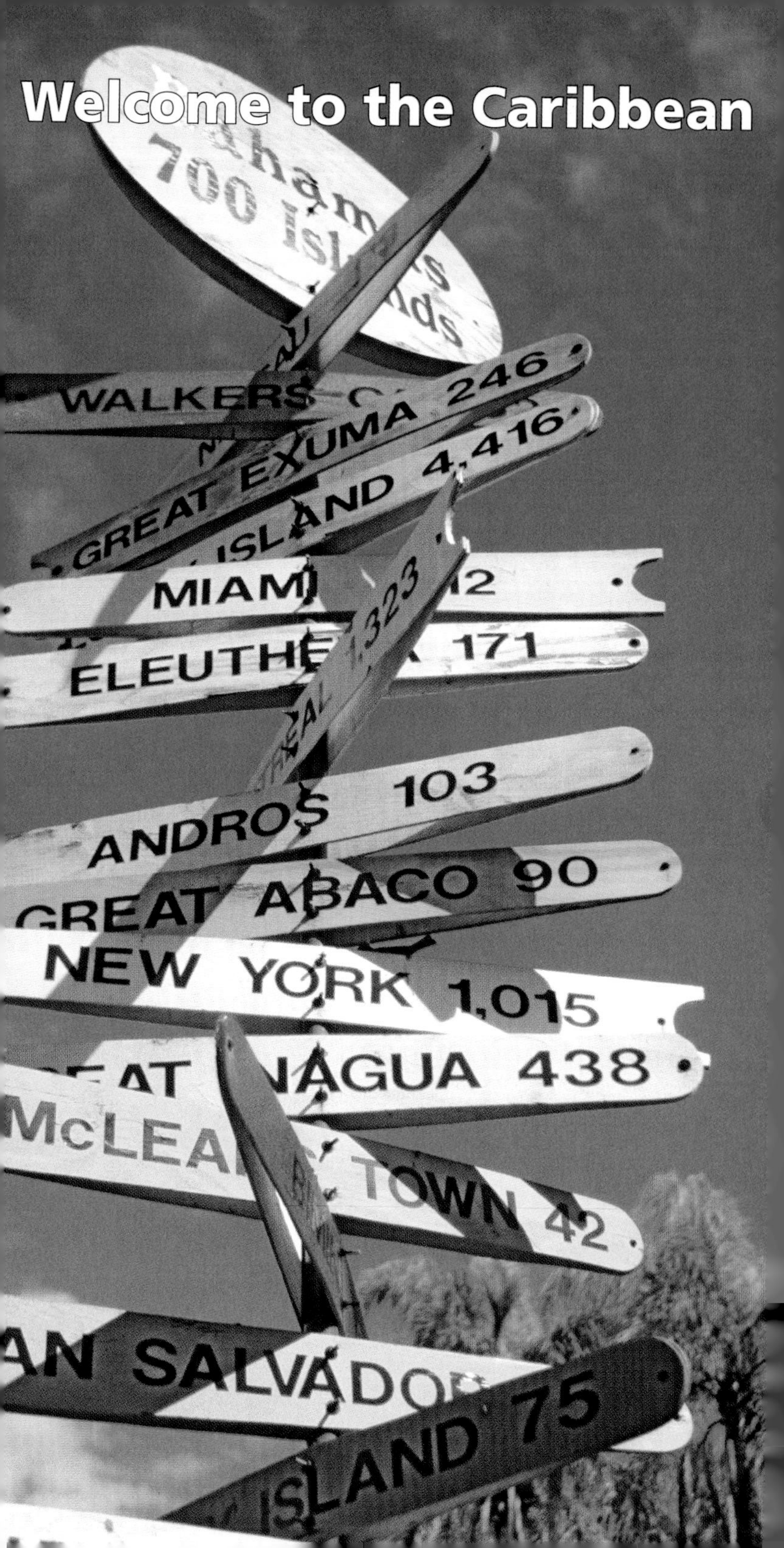

Table of Contents

Table of Contents

THE MICHELIN STARS

For more than 75 years, travelers have used the Michelin stars to take the guesswork out of planning a trip. Our star-rating system helps you make the best decision on where to go, what to do, and what to see. A three-star rating means it's one of the "absolutelys"; two stars means it's one of the "should sees"; and one star says it's one of the "sees" – a must if you have the time.

★★★ Absolutely Must See
★★ Really Must See
★ Must See

Three-Star Sights

The Baths★★★ (BVI)
Botanical Garden
  of Nevis★★★ (K&N)
Réserve Naturelle
  de Bouillante★★★ (GUA)
British Virgin Islands★★★
Buck Island Reef NM★★★ (USV)
The Chikuzen★★★ (BVI)
Curaçao★★★
Deadman's Bay★★★ (BVI)
Fuerte San Felipe
  del Morro★★★ (PR)
Grace Bay Beach★★★ (T&C)
Great Harbour★★★ (BVI)
Guadeloupe★★★
Guánica Biosphere
  Reserve★★★ (PR)
Îlets de Pigeon★★★ (GUA)
La Soufrière★★★ (GUA)
Les Saintes★★★ (GUA)
Magens Bay Beach★★★ (USV)
Martinique★★★

Museo de Arte de
  Puerto Rico★★★ (PR)
Museum Kurá
  Hulanda★★★ (ABC)
Old San Juan★★★ (PR)
The Painted Walls★★★ (BVI)
Pink Sands Beach★★★ (BAH)
Puerto Rico★★★
Rendezvous Bay★★★ (ANG)
Rose Hall
  Great House★★★ (JAM)
Salomon Bay Beach★★★ (USV)
Stingray City★★★ (CAY)
Stingray Sandbar★★★ (CAY)
St. John★★★ (USV)
Trace des Crêtes★★★ (GUA)
Whim Plantation
  Museum★★★ (USV)
Willemstad★★★ (ABC)
The Wreck of the
  R.M.S. Rhone★★★ (BVI)

Two-Star Sights

Anse Dufour★★ (MAR)
Anse du Grand
  Cul-de-Sac★★ (BART)
Asa Wright
  Nature Centre★★ (T&T)
Balneario de Luquillo★★ (PR)
Bloody Bay Beach★★ (T&T)
Bloody Bay
  Marine Park★★ (CAY)
Booby Pond
  Nature Reserve★★ (CAY)
Boston Bay Beach★★ (JAM)
Brimstone Hill
  Fortress NP★★ (K&N)
Cane Garden Bay★★ (BVI)
Carib Indian
  Reservation★★ (DOM)

Cas Abao Beach★★ (ABC)
Castara Beach★★ (T&T)
Cayman Islands★★
Chutes du Carbet★★ (GUA)
Crane Beach★★ (BAR)
Diamond Rock★★ (MAR)
Domaine deBloody Bay
  Valombreuse★★ (GUA)
Dunn's River Falls★★ (JAM)
Firefly★★ (JAM)
Fort Saint-Louis★★ (MAR)
Fuerte San Cristóbal★★ (PR)
Garden of the Groves★★ (BAH)
The Grenadines★★
Habitation Clément★★ (MAR)
Jamaica★★

Two-Star Sights *continued*

James Bond Beach★★ (JAM)
Jardins de Balata★★ (MAR)
Klein Curaçao★★ (ABC)
La Fortaleza★★ (PR)
La Soufrière★★ (V&G)
Marigot Bay Beach★★ (LUC)
Montagne Pelée★★ (MAR)
Mudjin Harbour Beach★★ (T&C)
Nelson's Dockyard★★ (A&B)
Nevis★★
Observatorio de Arecibo★★ (PR)
Palm Beach★★ (ABC)
Paradise Beach★★ (BAH)
The Pitons★★ (LUC)
Plage de Grande Anse★★ (GUA)
Plage de la Feuillère★★ (GUA)
Queen's Park Savannah★★ (T&T)
Rincón Beach★★ (PR)

Saint-Martin★★ /
  Sint Maarten★★
Sand Bank Bay Beach★★ (K&N)
Sapphire Beach★★ (USV)
Seven Mile Beach★★ (CAY)
Shoal Bay East★★ (ANG)
Smith's Cove Beach★★ (CAY)
Southern Beach★★ (A&B)
Saint-Barthélemy★★
St. George Village
  Botanical Garden★★ (USV)
St. Kitts★★
St. Kitts Scenic Railway★★ (K&N)
St. Lucia★★
Tillett Gardens★★ (USV)
Tobago★★
Turks and Caicos★★
US Virgin Islands★★

One-Star Sights

Anse Canot★ (GUA)
Anse des Flamands★ (BART)
Antigua★
Aruba★
Baie Orientale★ (STM)
Barbuda★
The Beach at Rum Point★ (CAY)
Belmont Estate★ (GRE)
Bird Sanctuary★ (A&B)
Boiling Lake★ (DOM)
Bonaire★
Bottom Bay Beach★ (BAR)
Cable Beach★ (BAH)
Caicos Conch Farm★ (T&C)
Caroni Bird Sanctuary★ (T&T)
Cayman Brac
  Parrot Reserve★ (CAY)
Cayman Turtle Farm★ (CAY)
Crystal Cay Marine Park★ (BAH)
Dickenson Bay Beach★ (A&B)
Doctors Cave Beach★ (JAM)
Dominica★
Fort Christian★ (USV)
Fort Saint-Louis★ (STM)
Grande Anse du Diamant★ (MAR)
Greenwood Great House★ (JAM)
Grenada★
Hadicurari Beach★ (ABC)
Half Moon Bay Beach★ (A&B)

Jardin Botanico★ (PR)
Laventille★ (T&T)
Manchebo Beach★ (ABC)
Marigot Museum★ (STM)
Maunday's Bay★ (ANG)
Mullins Beach★ (BAR)
Musée de la Banane★ (MAR)
Musée Gauguin★ (MAR)
Museo de Arte de Ponce★ (PR)
National Museum
  and Art Gallery★ (T&T)
Negril Point
  Lighthouse★ (JAM)
Pinney's Beach★ (K&N)
Pirates Bay Beach★ (T&T)
Plage de la Caravelle★ (GUA)
Plage de Pompierre★ (GUA)
Saba★
Silver Sands Beach★ (BAR)
South Friar's
  Bay Beach★ (K&N)
Store Bay Beach★ (T&T)
Saint Vincent★
Straw Market★ (BAH)
Sulphur Springs★ (LUC)
Taino Beach★ (BAH)
Trinidad★
Wallilabou Beach★ (V&G)

The following abbreviations appear in the Star List:
A&B Antigua & Barbuda; ANG Anguilla; BAH Bahamas;
BAR Barbados; BART St-Barthélmey; BVI British Virgin Islands;
CAY Caymans; DOM Dominica; GRE Grenada; GUA Guadeloupe;
JAM Jamaica; K&N St. Kitts & Nevis; LUC St. Lucia; MAR Martinique;
PR Puerto Rico; STM St-Martin; T&C Turks & Caicos; T&T Trinidad &
Tobago; V&G St. Vincent & the Grenadines; USV US Virgin Islands.

Calendar of Events

Listed below is a selection of the Caribbean Islands'
most popular annual events. Please note that dates
may vary from year to year. For more detailed information, contact the Caribbean Tourism Organization
at 246-427-5242 or www.doitcaribbean.com.

January

LaSource Sailing Festival   473-440-4809
St. George's, Grenada   www.grenadasailingfestival.com

St. Barts Music Festival   590-590-27-87-27
Various locations,
    St. Barthelémy   www.stbartsmusicfestival.org

February

Aruba's Carnival   297-582-3777
Various locations, Aruba   www.aruba.com

Carnival   868-675-7034
Port of Spain, Trinidad   www.visittnt.com

Carnival   596-596-61-61-77
Island-wide, Martinique   www.martinique.org/festivals

March

BVI Spring Regatta and Sailing Festival   284-494-3286
Road Town, Tortola,
    British Virgin Islands   www.bvispringregatta.org

International Regatta Cup   787-785-2026
Fajardo, Puerto Rico   www.gotopuertorico.com

April

Sailing Week   268-462-8872
St. John's, Antigua and Barbuda   www.sailingweek.com

Sint Maarten Carnival   599-522-337 or 800-786-2278
Philipsburg, Sint Maarten   www.st-maarten.com

May

Calabash Intl. Literary Festival   876-965-3000
St. Elizabeth, Jamaica   www.calabashfestival.org

Crop Over Festival (5-week festival)   246-427-2623
Bridgetown, Barbados   www.barbados.org

Curaçao Jazz Festival   599-9-465-8043
Willemstad, Curaçao   www.curacaojazz.com

St. Lucia Jazz Festival   758-452-4094
Various locations, St. Lucia   www.stluciajazz.org

Calendar of Events

June

Grand Turk Conch Carnival   649-946-1128
Grand Turk, Turks and Caicos   www.oasisdivers.com

Vincy Mas (Carnival)   784-457-2580
Kingstown, St. Vincent   www.carnivalsvg.com

July

4th of July Carnival Parade   800-372-8784
Cruz Bay, St. John,
    U.S. Virgin Islands   www.usvitourism.vi

Saba Carnival   599-416-2231
The Bottom, Saba   www.sabacarnival.net

August

Anguilla Summer Festival   264-497-2759
Landsome Bowl in the Valley, Anguilla   www.festival.ai

Festival of Women Cooks   590-05-90-82-09-30
Pointe-a-Pitre, Guadeloupe
            www.antilles-info-tourisme.com/guadeloupe

September

Cayman Madness Dive Vacation   345-949-2022
(diving festival) George Town,
Grand Cayman Island   www.caymanislands.ky

October

Pirates Week (national festival)   345-949-5859
George Town,
    Grand Cayman Island   www.piratesweekfestival.com

World Creole Music Festival   767-448-2045
Roseau, Dominica   www.worldcreolemusicfestival.net

November

Statia Day (cultural festival)   599-318-2433
Various locations, St. Eustatius www.statiatourism.com

December

Crucian Christmas Festival   877-840-1815
St. Croix, U.S. Virgin Islands   www.st-croix.net

Foxy's New Year's Eve Party   284-495-9258
Jost Van Dyke, British Virgin Is.   www.b-v-i.com

Junkanoo Festival   242-302-2000
Nassau, New Providence Island,
    The Bahamas   www.junkanoo.com

St. Kitts and Nevis National Carnival   869-465-4040
Basseterre, St. Kitts and Nevis www.stkittscarnival.com

Area Codes

To call between the French Isles, dial 0 and the area code and the 6-digit number. To call between Saint Martin and Sint Maarten, dial 00 + area code + local number. Except in Puerto Rico (dial 1 + area code + number) and the French Isles, it is not necessary to dial the area code to make a local call in the Caribbean.

Anguilla 264	Dominica 767	St. Kitts & Nevis 869
Antigua 268	Grenada 473	Saint Lucia 758
Aruba 297	Guadeloupe 590	Saint-Martin 590
Bahamas 242	Jamaica 876	Sint Maarten 599
Barbados 246	Martinique 596	St. Vincent & the
Bonaire 599	Puerto Rico 787 & 939	Grenadines 784
British Virgin Islands 284	Saba 599	Trinidad & Tobago 868
Cayman Islands 345	Saint-Barthélemy 590	Turks & Caicos 649
Curaçao 5999	Sint Eustatius 599	US Virgin Islands 340

PLANNING YOUR TRIP

Before you go, contact the following organizations to obtain maps and information about sightseeing, accommodations, travel packages, recreational opportunities and seasonal events.

Anguilla
Anguilla Tourist Board
Coronation Ave., The Valley, Anguilla, BWI
264-497-2759 or 800-553-4939;
www.anguilla-vacation.com

Antigua and Barbuda
Antigua and Barbuda Department of Tourism
Corner of Nevis Street and Friendly Alley
P.O. Box 363, St. John's, Antigua, West Indies
268-462-0480; www.antigua-barbuda.org

Aruba
Aruba Tourism Authority
L.G. Smith Blvd. 172, Eagle, Aruba
297-582-3777 or 800-862-7822;
www.aruba.com

Bahamas
Bahamas Ministry of Tourism
P.O. Box N-3701, Nassau, Bahamas
242-302-2000; www.bahamas.com

Barbados
Barbados Tourism Authority
Harbour Rd., Bridgetown, Barbados
246-427-2623 or 800-221-9831;
www.barbados.org

Bonaire
Tourism Corporation Bonaire
Kaya Grandi #2, Kralendijk, Bonaire,
Netherlands Antilles
599-717-8322 or 800-266-2473;
www.infobonaire.com

British Virgin Islands (Tortola, Virgin Gorda, Jost Van Dyke, Anegada)
British Virgin Islands Tourist Board
P.O. Box 134, Road Town, Tortola,
British Virgin Islands
284-494-3134 or 800-835-8530;
www.bvitouristboard.com

Cayman Islands (Grand Cayman, Little Cayman, Cayman Brac)
Cayman Islands Department of Tourism
The Pavilion, Cricket Square
P.O. Box 67GT, Grand Cayman, British West Indies
345-949-0623; www.caymanislands.ky

Curaçao
Curaçao Tourist Board
19 Pietermaai
P.O. Box 3266, Willemstad, Curaçao,
Netherlands Antilles
5999-434-8200 or 800-328-7222;
www.curacao-tourism.com

Dominica
Dominica Tourist Board/National
Development Corporation
P.O. Box 293, Roseau,
Commonwealth of Dominica
767-448-2045; www.dominica.dm

Grenada
Grenada Board of Tourism
Burns Point, P.O. Box 293
St. George's, Grenada, West Indies
473-440-2279 or 800-972-9554;
www.grenadagrenadines.com

Must Know: Practical Information

Guadeloupe
Guadeloupe Tourist Office
5, Square de la Banque,
B.P. 1099, 97181 Pointe-à-Pitre, Guadeloupe, FWI
590-590-82-09-30 or 800-391-4909;
www.antilles-info-tourisme.com/guadeloupe

Jamaica
Jamaica Tourist Board
64 Knutsford Blvd., Kingston 5,
Jamaica, West Indies
876-929-9200 or 800-233-4582
www.visitjamaica.com

Martinique
Comité Martiniquais du Tourisme
Immeuble Le Beaupré - Pointe de Jaham,
97233 Schoelcher
596-596-61-61-77; www.martinique.org

Puerto Rico
Puerto Rico Tourism Company
La Princesa Bldg. #2 Paseo de la Princesa
P.O. Box 902-3960, San Juan, Puero Rico,
00902-3960
787-721-2400 or 800-866-7827;
www.gotopuertorico.com

Saba
Saba Tourist Bureau
P.O. Box 527, Windwardside, Saba
599-416-2231; www.sabatourism.com

St-Barthelémy
St. Barthelémy Municipal Office of Tourism
Rue Gén. de Gaulle 97133 St. Barthelémy
590-27-87-27; www.st-barths.com

Sint Eustatius
Sint Eustatius Tourism Development
Foundation
Fort Oranje, Oranjestad, Sint Eustatius,
Netherlands Antilles
599-318-2433;
www.statiatourism.com

St. Kitts and Nevis
St. Kitts Tourism Authority
Pelican Mall, Bay Rd.
P.O. Box 132, Basseterre, St. Kitts, West Indies
869-465-4040 or 800-582-6208;
www.stkitts-tourism.com and
www.nevisisland.com

St. Lucia
St. Lucia Tourist Board
P.O. Box 221, Sureline Building, Vide Bouteille,
Castries, St. Lucia
758-452-4094 or 800-456-3984;
www.stlucia.org

Saint-Martin
St-Martin Tourism Office
Route de Sandy Ground, 97150
Marigot, St-Martin
590-87-57-21; www.st-martin.org

Sint Maarten
Sint Maarten Tourist Bureau
Vineyard Office Park, WG Buncamper Rd, #33,
Sint Maarten, Netherlands Antilles
599-542-2337 or 800-786-2278;
www.st-maarten.com

St. Vincent and the Grenadines
St. Vincent Ministry of Tourism and Culture
Cruise Ship Terminal, Harbour Quay,
Kingstown, St. Vincent and the Grenadines
784-457-1502 or 800-729-1726;
www.svgtourism.com

Trinidad and Tobago
Tourism and Industrial Development
Company/Trinidad and Tobago Tourism
P.O. Box 222, Maritime Centre, 29 Tenth Ave.,
Barataria, Trinidad, West Indies
868-675-7034; www.visittnt.com

Turks and Caicos
Turks and Caicos Tourist Board
P.O. Box 128, Front St., Grand Turk,
Turks and Caicos Islands, BWI
649-946-2321 or 800-241-0824;
www.turksandcaicostourism.com

US Virgin Islands
(St. Thomas, St. John, St. Croix)
United States Virgin Islands Division
of Tourism
78-123 Estate Contant,
Charlotte Amalie, St. Thomas 00804
800-372-8784; www.usvitourism.vi

Must Know: Practical Information

TIPS FOR SPECIAL VISITORS

Disabled Travelers – Businesses and attractions in the Caribbean have little or no accommodations for disabled travelers. Puerto Rico and the US Virgin Islands are the exception, since they must adhere to US federal law regarding access for the disabled. National parks in Puerto Rico and the US Virgin Islands have facilities for the disabled; check the National Park Service Web site *(www.nps.gov)*.

Senior Citizens – Some hotels, attractions and restaurants in the Caribbean, including national historic sites and parks in Puerto Rico and the US Virgin Islands, offer discounts to visitors age 62 or older (proof of age may be required). AARP (formerly the American Association of Retired Persons) offers discounts to its members *(601 E St. NW, Washington, DC 20049; 202-434-2277 or 888-687-2277; www.aarp.com)*.

WHEN TO GO

Winter is the best time to travel to the Caribbean islands. **Peak season** is mid-December through mid-April, when mainlanders rush to the islands to cure their winter blues. Generally, you'll find the best lodging discounts from late September until about mid-December. The months of April through July are hot and humid with many sudden showers.

Weather on most Caribbean Islands is consistently warm and humid throughout the year, with regular northeasterly trade winds bringing moisture from the Atlantic Ocean. Air temperatures hover around 82°F (28°C) in summer and 75°F (24°C) in winter. The average water temperature is 83°F (28°C) in summer, and 79°F (26°C) in winter. Rain tends to fall in the late afternoon and early evening, often with thunderstorms. For most islands, the **rainy season** begins in May and ends in the fall.

Hurricanes normally occur from June through November; the peak month is September. Recovery efforts are well under way after the devastating 2004 hurricane season; for updates, check online with the Caribbean Disaster Emergency Response Agency (CDERA) at www.cdera.org.

GETTING THERE

By Air – The majority of flights to the Caribbean depart from Atlanta, Georgia; Charlotte, North Carolina; and Miami, Florida, often with a transfer in San Juan, Puerto Rico.

By Cruise Boat – Most cruises to the Caribbean embark from and return to Miami, Florida. Cruises to the **Bahamas** usually begin from and end in Fort Lauderdale, Miami or Port Canaveral, Florida and stop in Nassau or Freeport. Major cruise companies include **Carnival** *(800-CARNIVAL; www.carnival.com)*; **Celebrity** *(800-722-5941; www.celebritycruises.com)*; **Holland America** *(877-SAIL HAL; www.hollandamerica.com)*; **Norwegian Cruise Line** *(800-327-7030; www.ncl.com)*; and **Royal Caribbean** *(866-562-7625; www.rccl.com)*. For additional information, visit the industry's Cruise Lines International Association online at: www.cruising.org.

Major Caribbean Airports

Airport	Web site/Phone
Anguilla Wallblake Airport (AXA) The Valley	http://anguilla.caribbeanway.com/airport.asp 264-497-2719
Antigua V.C. Bird International (ANU) St. John's	www.antigua-barbuda.org/Agtsp01.htm 268-462-0358
Aruba Queen/Reina Beatrix International Airport (AUA) Oranjestad	www.airportaruba.com 297-582-4800 ext. 241
Bahamas Nassau International Airport (NAS) Nassau, New Providence Island Freeport Airport (FPO) Freeport, Grand Bahama Island	http://bahamas.caribbeanway.com/ airport.asp 242-377-7281 242-352-6020
Barbados Grantley Adams International Airport (BGI) Bridgetown, Christ Church Parish	www.barbados.org 246-428-7101
Bonaire Bonaire Flamingo Airport (BON) Outside of Kralendijk	www.infobonaire.com/travel.html 599-717-5600
British Virgin Islands Terrence B. Lettsome International Airport (EIS) Beef Island, Tortola	www.bvitouristboard.com 284-494-3701
Cayman Islands Owen Roberts International Airport (GCM) Georgetown, Grand Cayman Island Gerrard Smith International Airport (CYB) Cayman Brac	www.caymanislands.ky/vacation_essentials/ air.asp 345-949-7811 Same Web site Same phone number
Curaçao **Curaçao** International Airport (CUR) Willemstad, Netherlands Antilles	www.curacao-airport.com 599-9-839-3100
Dominica Canefield Airport (DCF) Roseau Melville Hall Airport (DOM) Near Marigot on the northeast coast	www.ndcdominica.dm 767-449-1199 767-445-7109
Grenada Point Salines International Airport (GNO) St. George's	www.grenada.org 473-444-4150 or 473-444-4101
Guadeloupe Point-à-Pitre Le Raizet International Airport (PTP) Point-à-Pitre	www.guadeloupe.aeroport.fr/ 590-21-14-00
Jamaica Norman Manley International Airport (KIN) Palisadoes/Kingston Donald Sangster International Airport (MBJ) Montego Bay	www.manley-airport.com.jm 876-924-8452 or 1-888-247-7678 www.sangster-airport.com.jm 876-952-2712 or 1-888-247-7678

Must Know: Practical Information

Airport	Web site/Phone
Martinique International Lamentin Airport (FDF) Lamentin	www.martinique.org/transportation.htm 596-42-16-00
Puerto Rico Luis Muñoz Marín International Airport (SJU) San Juan Rafael Hernandez International Airport (BQN) Aguadilla	http://welcome.topuertorico.org/tinfo.shtml 787-319-9262 787-891-2286
Saba Juancho E. Yrausquin Airport Flat Point	www.sabatourism.com/gettosaba.html 599-4-62255
St-Barthélemy Aéroport de St-Barthélemy (SBH) Bale de St. Jean	www.st-barths.com 590-27-65-41
Sint Eustatius Franklin Delano Roosevelt Airport (EUX) Concordia	www.statiatourism.com 599-318-2887
St. Kitts/Nevis Robert L. Bradshaw International Airport (SKB) Basseterre, St. Kitts Newcastle Airport (NEV) Newcastle, Nevis	www.stkitts-tourism.com/DiscoverSK/ Airlines.asp 869-465-8972 869-469-9040
St. Lucia Hewanorra International Airport (UVW) or (UVF) Vieux Fort George F. L. Charles Airport (SLU) Castries	www.slaspa.com 758-454-6355 758-452-1156
St-Martin and Sint Maarten Princess Juliana International Airport (SXM) Philipsburg, Sint Maarten	www.pjiae.com 599-545-2060
St. Vincent and the Grenadines E. T. Joshua Airport (SVD) Kingstown, St. Vincent	www.svgtourism.com 784-458-4011
Trinidad and Tobago Trinidad Piarco International (POS) Port of Spain, Trinidad Tobago Crown Point International (TAB) Crown Point, Tobago	www.tntairports.com 868-669-5196 868-639-0509
Turks and Caicos Providenciales International Airport (PLS) Providenciales	www.provoairport.com 649-941-5670
U.S. Virgin Islands Cyril E. King International (STT) Charlotte Amalie, St. Thomas Henry E. Rohlsen Airport (STX) 13 miles from Christiansted, St. Croix	www.viport.com 340-774-5100 www.viport.com 340-778-0589

GETTING AROUND

Island Hopping

For the names of air carriers between the islands, check the Web site of your destination's airport (*see chart above*). Some island airlines offer island-hopping fares for flights between several islands within a specific time period.

The Bahamas Out Islands – Departing from Potters Cay (*under Paradise Island bridge*) in Nassau, Bahamas Ferries (*242-323-2166; www.bahamasferries.com*) services Harbour Island/Spanish Wells, Andros, the Exumas, the Abacos and North Eleuthera. The "slow boats," mail boats also depart from Potters Cay (*for schedule, contact the dock master's office 242-393-1064*).

Cayman Islands – There is no ferry service from island to island, only air service. Island Air offers daily charter flights to Little Cayman from Grand Cayman (*345-949-5252; www.islandaircayman.com*).

The French Isles – Ferries regularly run between Guadeloupe, Martinique and Dominica; and between Guadeloupe and les Saintes and Marie-Galante.

Grenada's Out Islands – A ferry departs Saint George's for Carriacou 5 days weekly; return ferry departs 4 days a week.

Lesser Antilles – Ferries from Saint-Martin service Saba and Saint-Barthélemy. Basse-Terre (*Bay Rd.*), St. Kitts is connected by ferry with Charlestown, Nevis.

Trinidad and Tobago – A once-daily (*except Sun*) ferry departs Port of Spain for Scarborough, Tobago (*an approx. 5-hour crossing*).

The Virgin Islands – Ferries from St. Thomas in the US Virgin Islands depart from Charlotte Amalie and Red Hook for Tortola and Virgin Gorda. Ferries from St. John reach Tortola, Jost Van Dyke and Virgin Gorda. Ferries from Tortola service Peter Island. Check with the tourism office about other boat services.

By Car – Cars can be rented at most island airports. Rates are generally higher than in the US; a credit-card deposit may be required. The following are some of the major rental car agencies with locations in the Caribbean:

Alamo	www.alamo.com	800-462-5266
Budget	www.budget.com	800-472-3325
National	www.nationalcar.com	800-227-7368

By Public Transportation – **Puerto Rico** has extensive bus service throughout the island; a free trolley runs within Old San Juan (*see p 63*). **Saint-Martin** operates mini-buses daily between Grand-Case, Marigot, and Philipsburg (in the Dutch side); mini-buses also operate in Dominica. **St. Thomas** in the US Virgin Islands, **Barbados**, and **Aruba** offer regular bus service. Contact the tourism office (*see listing p 10*) of your island destination for specific information.

By Taxi – Travel by taxi is common in the Caribbean. In most cases, taxis are regulated and fares are established by the government; many drivers carry a fare chart. Agree on a rate and the type of currency with the driver before you enter the cab.

Must Know: Practical Information

VISITING THE CARIBBEAN

Before you travel, contact your destination's tourist office for entry requirements. Information is also available from the **Caribbean Tourism Organization,** 80 Broad St., New York, NY 10004; 212-635-9530; www.doitcaribbean.com.

Entry Requirements – US and Canadian citizens should carry a valid passport as proof of citizenship. Visas are not normally required, but a round-trip transportation ticket is mandatory.

Caribbean Customs – Check in advance with the tourist office of your destination for items you can bring into the Caribbean for your personal use. If you are planning to buy items such as tortoiseshell jewelry or other articles made from threatened or endangered animal species (whalebone or ivory, skins or fur), contact the US Fish and Wildlife Service (*www.fws.gov; 800-344-9453*). Keep **receipts** for all purchases you make while in the Caribbean.

Travelers to countries in the **Caribbean Basin Initiative** (CBI) generally have a $600 duty-free exemption on their return to the US (CBI countries included in this guide: Antigua and Barbuda, Aruba, Bahamas, Barbados, British Virgin Islands, Dominica, Grenada, Jamaica, Netherlands Antilles, St. Kitts and Nevis, St. Lucia, St. Vincent and the Grenadines, Trinidad and Tobago). For US citizens returning from the US Virgin Islands, the duty-free exemption is $1,200. For Canadian citizens who have been out of Canada a minimum of 7 days, the limit is $750 Canadian dollars. For other information about what you can bring back to the US, contact the US Customs Service (*877-287-8867; www.customs.gov*). For Canadian customs: Canada Revenue Agency (*800-461-9999; www.cra-arc.gc.ca*).

Languages – English is spoken on most of the islands described in this guide. English is the official language of all US- and British Commonwealth-affiliated islands in the Caribbean. French is the official language in the French isles, and Dutch is the official language of the Netherland Antilles.

Money and Currency Exchange – *Unless otherwise noted, all prices shown in this guide are in US dollars.* US dollar bills are accepted on many Caribbean islands. Currency can be exchanged at most banks and airports. For cash transfers, contact **Western Union** (*800-325-6000; www.westernunion.com*). Banks, stores, restaurants and hotels accept travelers' checks with photo identification. To report a lost or stolen credit card: **American Express** (*800-528-4800*); **Diners Club** (*800-234-6377*); **MasterCard** (*800-307-7309*); **Visa** (*800-336-8472*).

Driving in the Caribbean – A US driver's license is valid in some, but not all Caribbean islands. Check in advance with the tourism office of your destination. Inquire about International Driver's Licenses with the American (*800-463-8646; www.aaa.com*) and Canadian (*613-247-0117; www.caa.ca*) Automobile Assns.

Duty-Free

"Duty-free" means that the store owner doesn't pay duties when importing merchandise to sell in his store. However the owner is not required by law to pass that savings on to customers—some do; some don't. Before you go, research the cost of jewelry, electronics, linens, liquor and other merchandise you're interested in purchasing, so you can compare prices in the islands. Duty-free is not always a good deal in terms of price—and ease of return.

Some islands require a local permit, obtainable from rental-car companies. Drivers must carry vehicle registration and/or rental contract, and proof of automobile insurance at all times. Gasoline is usually sold by the gallon (1 gal=3.8 liters) and is generally expensive (about $3 per gallon). Vehicles are driven on the left-hand side of the road on British Commonwealth countries.

Electricity – Voltage in Puerto Rico, the Cayman and the Virgin Islands is 110 volts AC 60 Hz, the same as in the US and Canada. On other Caribbean islands, it can range from 110 volts to 230 volts. Foreign-made appliances may need AC adapters and North American flat-blade plugs.

Taxes and Tipping – All the Caribbean countries included in this guide impose a hotel or occupancy tax of 6% or higher (10% is common). Some governments tax meals and alcoholic beverages, as well as rental cars. Except in the US Virgin Islands, a **departure tax** *($5–$25)* is charged at the airport; it's advisable to have cash available when you depart. Many Caribbean hotels and resorts automatically add a service charge (the average is 10% to 15%) to your bill.

Time Zones – Islands in the Western Caribbean *(see map inside front cover)* are in the **Eastern Standard Time** zone. Islands in the Eastern Caribbean *(see map inside back cover)* are in the Atlantic Standard Time zone.

Drinking Water – In most of the islands, the water is potable at major resorts and hotels, and restaurants in the major cities. You may prefer to drink bottled water, which is generally available at convenience stores and hotels. .

Measurement Equivalents

Degrees Fahrenheit	95°	86°	77°	68°	59°	50°	41°	32°	23°	14°
Degrees Celsius	35°	30°	25°	20°	15°	10°	5°	0°	-5°	-10°

1 inch = 2.5 centimeters   1 foot = 30.48 centimeters
1 mile = 1.6 kilometers   1 pound = 0.45 kilograms
1 quart = 0.9 liters   1 gallon = 3.78 liters

ACCOMMODATIONS
For a list of suggested accommodations, see Must Stay.

Web Sites
Here are some additional Web sites to help you plan your trip:
Caribbean Hotel Association: www.caribbeantravel.com
Caribbean Home Page: www.caribinfo.com
Carribbean Tourism Organization: www.doitcaribbean.com
US Department of State's travel advisory: http://travel.state.gov/travel/warnings.html

The Caribbean

The Caribbean: So Many Islands, So Little Time

Soothing offshore waters reflect infinite shades of turquoise, cerulean and azure. Soft sea breezes amplify island rhythms of local patois, Goombay and reggae. Miles upon miles of seductive, often secluded, beaches entice you to walk barefoot in the warm, glistening sand. This is the Caribbean.

Also known as the West Indies, the Caribbean Islands form a long, curled tail off the coast of Florida, stretching southeastward roughly 2,500 miles toward Venezuela. The islands edge the vast Caribbean Sea on their south shores, and the immense Atlantic Ocean on the north (the Bahamas and the Turks and Caicos lie entirely within the Atlantic). Beneath these waters, wondrous reefs, created over centuries, lie waiting to be explored. A colorful mix of islanders—more than 30 million of them—add their traditions and place names.

From lush rain forests, accented by brightly colored tropical flowers, to arid deserts, the islands owe their natural beauty to a series of violent underwater volcanic eruptions which, about 50 to 70 million years ago, hefted a submarine mountain chain to the surface. Black-sand beaches serve as present-day reminders of such volcanic activity.

The earliest inhabitants in the Caribbean, the Stone-Age **Ciboneys** lived peacefully as hunters and gatherers. Daring seafaring people with Asiatic features, the **Arawaks** set sail for the islands in large canoes, around the time of Christ's death, from northern Brazil and Venezuela. Their peaceful fishing villages, reached from Trinidad to Puerto Rico and later the Bahamas, until the warring **Caribs** invaded the island chain, leaving death and destruction in their wake.

First sighting land in the Bahamas in 1492, **Christopher Columbus** stepped forth on the island he called San Salvador, greeted by the gentle Arawaks, who called themselves the "Lukku-cains" (island people). Thinking he had discovered a trade route to the East Indies, Columbus called them "Indians." Columbus' discovery of the New World opened the doors for two centuries of domination by Spain, who emptied the Americas of their gold and silver, destroyed the islands' native peoples through disease and mistreatment, and imported African slaves to mine ore and harvest crops.

The Caribbean: So Many Islands, So Little Time

Spain's tight grip on the Caribbean gave rise to the Golden Age of Piracy, when English buccaneers and French corsairs from Normandy attacked Spanish treasure ships and port settlements. Attracted by salt and tobacco, the Dutch entered the Caribbean as pirates and smugglers in the late 1500s, ushering in a flourishing trade with Spain's colonies there. By the 1620s, the Dutch, English and French were founding their own colonies on Caribbean shores in search of profits from tobacco, sugar and cattle.

Battling each other at home, European powers raised their flags over Caribbean ports when victorious, and ceded their island possessions when vanquished. Most of the islands changed hands many times among the Spanish, British, French, Dutch, Danes, and Swedes—St. Lucia alone changed hands 14 times. Emancipation of the slaves beginning in the 1830s brought the arrival of indentured servants from Ireland, Scotland, Portugal, China and India.

Tired of serving as cheap labor for foreign-owned enterprises, islanders launched independence movements in the 1950s and 60s. Today most of the islands are independent countries, or are autonomous within a commonwealth.

The sum of its history—a seesaw sequence of colonization and trade—makes the Caribbean one of the most distinctive regions of the world. Because each island perpetuates its own culture, customs and cuisine, and revels in its own music, dance and natural beauty, you can island-hop forever and never come close to repeating an experience.

Columbus's Controversial Landing

As we learned in school, the *Pinta*, the *Nina* and the *Santa Maria* first dropped anchor on October 12, 1492 at "Guanahani," the Lucayan name for the island Columbus christened San Salvador, in the Bahamas. In recent decades, this "fact" has come under fire. Computerized research published in 1986 by the National Geographic Society provides evidence that Columbus actually sailed into Samana Cay (today's Atwood Cay), about 60 miles southeast of San Salvador. Others believe he first made landfall on Grand Turk in the Turks and Caicos. And so the debate goes on.

The Bahamas

Laid-back island attitude with a British accent—that's what you'll find in the **Bahamas★★**. Sitting 55mi off Florida's coast, these coral islands splay across 100,000 square miles of the Atlantic Ocean. Some 3.5 million visitors a year flock to the beaches and casinos of Nassau, Paradise Island and Freeport.

Bahamas Breakdown

We can't cover all 700 Bahamian islands, of course (only about 20 of which are inhabited), but here are the archipelago's major ones described in this guide: **New Providence Island★**, the governmental and commercial hub of the islands, boasts the famed city of **Nassau★★**. Known for stunning, white-sand beaches, **Paradise Island★** is home to modern resorts like Atlantis. **Grand Bahama Island** claims the touristy cruise ports of **Freeport** and **Lucaya**.

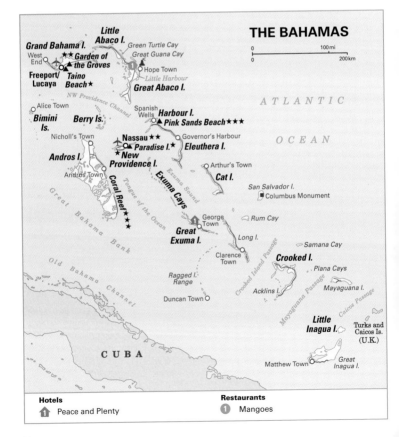

Out Islands

Pure magic for those seeking serenity, the Out Islands boast the best in sailing and boating, enviable fishing and endless stretches of deserted beaches where only your own footprints decorate the sand. With fewer people and amenities, these less-developed outposts draw a different type of tourist. Their pristine beaches and amazing underwater worlds appeal to sailors, fishermen, snorkelers, divers and birders. The Out Island roster includes the Abacos, Acklins, Andros, Berry Islands, Bimini, Cat Island, Crooked Island, Eleuthera, Harbour Island, the Exumas, the Inaguas, Long Island, Mayaguana, Ragged Island Range, Rum Cay and San Salvador. Island-hopping is a must, and is extra-easy via ferries between islands with names like Green Turtle Cay and Man-O-War Cay.

The sailing capital of the Bahamas, the **Abacos** are a cluster of dreamy isles surrounding the Sea of Abaco. Their signature site is the Hope Town Lighthouse, a red and white candy-striped beacon that still burns a kerosene flame to guide sea captains away from the shallows.

The largest island in the Bahamas chain, and the least charted, **Andros** is a haven for underwater adventurers, who come to explore the 140mi offshore **coral reef★★★** that parallels the island's eastern edge.

The **Berry Islands** are known for bonefishing. The **Biminis**, the big-game fishing capital of the Bahamas, lure the international champion anglers, as well as amateurs, to their waters and tournaments.

Cat Island, the birthplace of actor Sidney Poitier, is known for its friendly locals and for the highest point of land in the Bahamas: Mount Alvernia, topped with a medieval monastery. Divers, snorkelers and others looking to wind down will find an off-the-beaten-path experience at **Crooked Island**, with its 45 miles of eye-popping barrier reefs.

Eleuthera's unspoiled beaches and sweet pineapples are what make it famous, but next-door neighbor **Harbour Island** owns the title of most beautiful Bahamian island: three miles of powdery, pink sandy beach and gingerbread clapboard houses framed by bougainvillea-covered white picket fences swayed the judges.

The waters of the **Exumas** offer more shades of aqua than an artist could imagine, quirky island characters, and little cays with pristine beaches. But one of the most memorable natural sights belongs to primitive **Little Inagua**. If you're lucky, you'll witness 20,000 flaming-pink flamingos taking flight into the clear blue sky all at once. That makes roughing it worth it!

Must Shop

Shopping's the thing to do in Nassau on New Providence Island. Along historic Bay Street, a block from the harbor, lots of duty-free shops—not to mention the **Straw Market** *(below)*— cater to cruise-ship passengers and other tourists. *No sales tax is charged, and 11 categories of goods are available duty-free.*

Straw Market★

Prince George Wharf, behind Rawson Sq., Nassau. 242-322-7500. Open year-round Mon–Sat 9am–5pm.

Nassau's famous Straw Market is a maze of small stalls where vendors, most of them women by tradition, hawk inexpensive straw goods, T-shirts, local wood carvings and other items. Straw-plaiting and straw work have long been done by Bahamian women, particularly on the Out Islands. Don't think you have to pay the price as marked; haggling with the market's vendors over the price of goods is part of the fun here.

Doongalik Studios

18 Village Rd., Nassau. 242-394-1886.

You'll find the best exhibit of Junkanoo Festival artifacts at this brightly colored gallery. Bahamian paintings and giant sculptures for sale here focus on the popular annual festival *(see p30)*. This islandy "home" is filled with impressive original art inspired by Bahamian culture, from hand-painted canvases and furniture to Junkanoo masks and shell collages. Stroll the sculpture garden, and peek inside the traditional Bahamian house next door, where the **True-True Shop** is filled with unique gifts.

Shopping Tip

Duty-free shopping can save you 25-50% off US prices on merchandise in 11 categories. Great bargains on cashmere sweaters, and perhaps the best bargains on watches, jewelry, clocks, china, crystal, leather goods, perfumes, linens and liquor await you in Nassau. Local goods such as Bahamian weavings, shell jewelry, art, rum liquors, Old Nassau liqueur, hot sauces and vanilla rum tea make great souvenirs.

Look for a **pink flamingo decal** on store windows, which signifies that the owners have met the strict government guidelines and that all brands stocked within are authentic.

A Special Souvenir

Take home some of the colorful Bahamian batik called **Androsia**, made by hand on Andros Island. You can buy Androsia at these places:

- The Royal Palm Trading Company – Bay St., downtown Nassau.
- Androsia of Cable Beach – Next to Crystal Palace Casino on Cable Beach.
- Royal Palm Beach Trader – At the Atlantis Resort on Paradise Island.
- Androsia of Port Lucaya – Port Lucaya Marketplace, in Freeport.

The Plait Lady

Corner of Bay & Victoria Sts., Nassau. 242-356-5584.

Filled with unique basketry and weavings, this three-story shop is a step above the Straw Market. The owner regularly visits all of the Out Islands—each one of which has its own style of weaving—and brings the best of their handmade products, such as baskets, floor mats and hampers, to sell in her shop. The baskets on hand are most unusual and artsy, especially the baskets made in Red Bay on Andros by descendants of Seminole Indians and escaped slaves. Their straw water pitchers are woven so tightly that they never leak a drop.

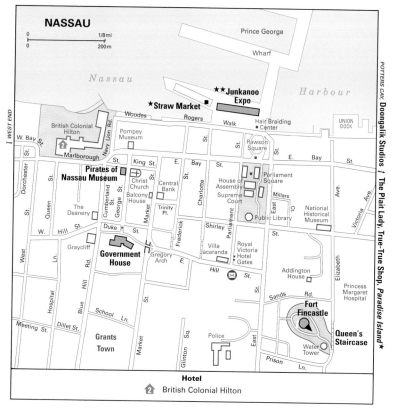

NASSAU map

Must-See Historic Sites

The Cloisters

Off Paradise Island Dr., at Cloister Dr., Paradise Island. Open daily year-round.

What's a medieval French relic doing in the Bahamas? These stone structures, once part of a 14C monastery in Montréjeau, France, were shipped here in crates. In 1962 millionaire Huntington Hartford, who developed Paradise Island, had the pieces reassembled on this rise overlooking Nassau Harbour. Now a favored spot, The Cloisters are especially beautiful at night when illuminated.

Changing of the Guard

Can't make it to Buckingham Palace? You can still watch the Changing of the Guard at Nassau's Government House every other Saturday at 10am. The formal ceremony comes complete with music by the acclaimed Royal Bahamas Police Force Band, the members of which are decked out in crisp white tunics and outrider helmets topped with ostrich plumes.

Government House

Blue Hill Rd. & Duke St., Nassau, New Providence Island. Not open for public tours.
242-322-1875.

This white-columned pink mansion (1932) atop Mount Fitzwilliam has hosted famous residents. In the 1940s, the Duke and Duchess of Windsor lived here when the Duke served as governor general of the Bahamas. A nod to Nassau's British colonial past, a statue of Queen Victoria fronts the building. Make a reservation for the last Friday of the month *(4pm–5pm)*, when the governor general hosts a British tea party *(Jan–Nov; reservations and proper attire required; 242-323-1853)*.

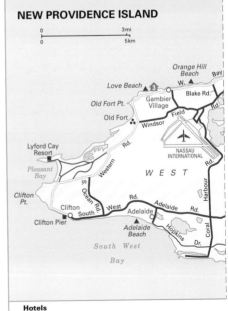

NEW PROVIDENCE ISLAND

Hotels	
🏠	Compass Point
🏠	Dillet's Guest House
🏠	Nassau Beach Hotel

Fort Fincastle

At the top of the Queen's Staircase, Nassau, New Providence Island. 242-325-2212. Open year-round daily 8am–5pm.

From its vantage at the top of the town's highest point, this small fort, shaped like a paddle-wheeler steamboat, was built in the 1790s. Though it never saw battle, the fort proved useful, serving as a lighthouse and then a signal beacon. The best view is from the 126ft water tower nearby.

St. Augustine Monastery

East End, off Bernard Rd., Nassau, New Providence Island. 242-364-1331.

If you're seeking peace and quiet, come to this home of the Benedictine monks, who have occupied it since 1946. You'll get a tour of the chapel, the garden, and the old cemetery.

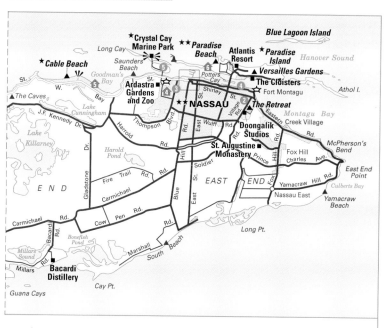

6 Sivananda Ashram Yoga Retreat

Restaurants

2 Sun and...

3 Buena Vista Restaurant

4 The Poop Deck

5 Goldies

Must-See Beaches

Pink Sands Beach★★★

Harbour Island, off northwest Eleuthera Island. 30min flight from Nassau to North Eleuthera Airstrip. From there, take a taxi to the ferry dock for a ferry to Harbour Island.

One of the Travel Channel's top 10 beaches worldwide, Pink Sands lives up to its name—all three miles of it. At the edge of the powdery, pale pink sand, the warm waves of the Atlantic Ocean are invitingly calm, protected by a coral reef. The rays of the sun and the sound of the gentle waves are sure to lull you into a bit of beach napping.

Paradise Beach★★

Northwest Paradise Island, between Colonial Beach & Hog Point.

You'll think you've found paradise indeed when you spread your beach towel on these sands and look out over Atlantic waters the color of blueberry popsicles. Lined with towering Casuarina trees, this beautiful, two-mile stretch is aptly named.

> **Casuarina Trees**
>
> Native to Australia and Malaysia, Casuarina trees bear leaves that resemble weeping pine needles. When a breeze blows through their lacey needles, they mimic the sound of the sea.

Cable Beach★

West of Nassau, on New Providence Island.

Once you get past the towering hotels of Cable Beach, you'll reach this four-mile stretch of white sand backed by palm trees. Sometimes called the Bahamian Riviera, Cable Beach is lined with snack bars, restaurants and watersports rentals, and filled with sunbathers, parasailors, jet-skiiers and swimmers—as well as locals hawking assorted wares.

Taino Beach★

Grand Bahama Island. Take Midshipman Rd. east to West Beach Rd.

You'll find a quieter, less crowded beach here, east of Port Lucaya. White sands, unruffled waters and relative tranquillity (compared to nearby Lucayan Beach) make Taino popular with families.

Must-See Gardens

Garden of the Groves★★

On Magellan Dr., northwest of the intersection of E. Sunrise Hwy. & Midshipman Rd., Grand Bahama Island. 242-373-5668. www.gardenofthegroves.com. Open year-round daily 9am–4pm. Closed Dec 25. $9.95.

You'll get an idea of what the Garden of Eden must have looked like when you visit this 12-acre botanical preserve, begun in the 1970s. Waterfalls, a hibiscus garden, a lush fern gully, a hanging garden of exotic potted plants, and walkways lined with plants like crotons, crown-of-thorn bushes and towering palm trees surround a winding man-made lagoon. The small chapel, similar to a Bahamian church, is a clue that lots of weddings take place here.

The Retreat

Village Rd., south of the intersection with Shirley St. & Eastern Rd., Nassau, New Providence Island. 242-393-1317. Open year-round Mon–Fri 9am–5pm. Closed holidays & Dec 25–Jan 1. $2.

This is the place to go for palms. The 11-acre botanical preserve features 176 rare and exotic **palm trees**★, including species from Asia, Africa, Australia, and North and South America. The Retreat offers you a journey through the best of the tropics, from brilliant red gingers and flowering hot-pink shaving brush trees to tropical orchids growing on tree trunks and wispy ferns flourishing in the

shade of giant tree canopies of mahogany and cedar. The charming mid-19C Bahamian cottage on the grounds serves as the headquarters for the Bahamian National Trust, which now owns the property.

Versailles Gardens

Paradise Island Dr., Paradise Island.

Don't miss the seven-tiered gardens of Versailles across Paradise Island Drive from the Cloisters *(see Historic Sites)*. Wander among vivid flowers of all kinds and beneath stately, shady trees. Gaze at the fountains, waterfalls and statues of French Emperor Napoleon, his wife Josephine, Greek hero Hercules, and other notables from history, and you'll see why the gardens are a popular place for weddings. There's even a lily pond that's home to turtles. The grounds slope down to a private swimming pool for guests at the exclusive Ocean Club.

Must-See Museums

Junkanoo Expo★★

Prince George Wharf, Nassau, New Providence Island. 242-356-2731. Open year-round daily 9am–5pm. Closed major holidays. Call for admission price.

If you're not in town over the Christmas holidays to experience the Junkanoo festivities *(see sidebar, below)* first-hand, catch a bit of the Goombay spirit at this display. Here, you'll find enormous, lavishly designed Junkanoo costumes sculpted of cardboard and crepe paper, and embellished with bright beads and sequins. It takes teams up to a year to complete the intricate works, which follow themes that remain a secret until parade day. Winning entries from each parade are added to the museum's collection each year as older pieces are retired.

Pirates of Nassau Museum

King & George Sts., Nassau, New Providence Island. 242-356-3759. www.pirates-of-nassau.com. Open year-round Mon–Sat 9am–5pm. $12.

This museum is a real favorite of children. Inside, youngsters can make believe they're back in the early 1700s, living life as a buccaneer. Back then the city's wharf was a haven for lawless pirates who appointed Blackbeard magistrate of Nassau, the "Privateers Republic." There's even a reenactment of a ship-to-ship cannon fight with Blackbeard himself!

Jumpin', Jivin' Junkanoo

In the wee hours of December 26 (Boxing Day in England) and on New Year's Day each year, Nassau's streets snap to attention with the beating of goatskin drums, the clanging of cowbells and the blaring of brass horns. The music heralds the annual Junkanoo parade, with its costumed participants dancing in the streets. An Afro-Bahamian holi-

day tradition that began in the 17C when island slaves celebrated their few days off at Christmastime, the parade, which now attracts thousands of spectators, can be heard across the island. The revelry begins at 2am and ends at dawn, so if you're staying in Nassau on December 26, don't plan on getting much sleep! *For more information, visit www.junkanoo.com.*

Must Be Pampered: Spas

The Mandara Spa at Atlantis Resort

*Casino Dr., Paradise Island. 242-363-3000
or 800-722-7466. www.atlantis.com.*

This spa is all about the fragrance of
tropical flowers, tropical rain
showers, a water wall, and 24 treatment rooms designed to melt away
tightness and tension. Expect a
variety of exotic treatments with an
Asian accent.

The Ocean Club Spa

*Paradise Island Dr., Paradise Island. 800-
321-3000. www.oneandonlyresorts.com.*

So long, stress! This legendary hideaway offers spa therapies based on Asian
secrets for healing, beauty and rejuvenation—but using indigenous Bahamian
ingredients. Tension simply vanishes as facials, scrubs, wraps or massages are
done in your own luxury villa, rather than your moving to separate rooms. Try
the Boreh hot-spice therapy. True to Balinese custom, a foot-washing initiates
each treatment.

Sivananda Ashram Yoga Retreat

Near Atlantis resort, Paradise Island. 242-363-2902. www.my-yoga.net.

Practice yoga facing the sea, meditate amid palm trees and flowers, and nibble
vegetarian meals cooked by a Bahamian chef. Though not a spa, this retreat
provides a haven from the hectic by offering a shady yoga platform set on
pure white sands overlooking the crystal blue-green sea. The compound centers upon a meditation temple surrounded by art and hibiscus flowers.

Pirates of the Caribbean

The kooky character played by Johnny Depp in the film adaptation of Disney's
famous ride is a far cry from the real rogues who plagued sailors on Caribbean waters
in the 18C and 19C. Born Edward Teach, probably in England, Blackbeard began his
dubious career in the early 18C. In 1717 he commandeered a British ship off the coast
of the Bahamas. After nearly doubling her armament to 40 guns, the pirate terrorized
the Caribbean, inspiring fear with his large stature, long unkempt black beard, and
bright red waistcoat, with two swords hanging always at his side. His career came to
an abrupt halt in 1718, when the British Royal Navy caught up to him off the coast of
North Carolina. Blackbeard's bloody death—he was shot and stabbed—essentially put
an end to the "Golden Age of Piracy."

Musts for Fun

Visit Bacardi Distillery

Southwest side of New Providence Island on Bacardi Rd. (off Carmichael Rd.). 242-362-1412. Free tours available year-round Mon–Fri 10am–4pm; reserve in advance. Hospitality center closed weekends.

Rum and the islands go hand in hand (where do you think the line "yo-ho-ho and a bottle of rum" came from?), and Bacardi's Nassau outpost is a great place to learn about the sugarcane-based spirit. Five rums, a vodka and a liqueur are produced here, most of it shipped to European markets. The tour of the facility ends at the hospitality center, where you'll be treated to samples of Bacardi rums.

Spend a Day at Blue Lagoon Island

3mi northeast of Paradise Island. 242-363-3333. Reservations required. $85 (boat ride, lunch, water sports). Reserve dolphin encounters separately: 242-363-7150; $75. Boat ride only, $25 round-trip. For details, access www.dolphinswims.com.

A 20-minute boat ride whisks you away to this beautiful island for a day. Once called Salt Cay, the isle is famous for its natural lagoon, drop-dead gorgeous beach and coconut palms, where double hammocks are strung at water's edge—perfect for long siestas. Pet the rays at Stingray City, or have a close encounter of the dolphin kind. It's a day for swimming, sunning, dancing in the sands to the Goombay band or relaxing in this ultra-tropical setting, where the beach scenes were filmed for the movie *Splash*, starring Darryl Hannah and Tom Hanks.

Take a Carriage Tour

Departing from Bay St. at Woodes Rogers Walk, Nassau, New Providence Island. 242-326-9781. $10 per person for 20-minute tour.

The best way to see Old Nassau is the romantic way—in a handsome **horse-drawn carriage**, or surrey, as the locals call it. Sit back and listen to the clip-clop of a horse wearing a straw hat, while your friendly driver navigates the streets and gives you a good orientation to the city, plus the local lore. For a few dollars more, you can extend your tour.

Musts for Kids

Crystal Cay Marine Park ★

1mi west of downtown Nassau, New Providence Island. 242-328-1036. Open year-round daily 9am–6pm. Call for admission price.

Sure, you've been to above-ground aquariums, but have you ever been to one that's *under* the water? Here's your opportunity to see undersea life from a diver's point of view—without getting wet. Simply walk into the observation tower and down the stairs 20 feet to windows that open onto an underwater park. Here you'll be eyeball to eyeball with parrotfish, turtles, stingrays, moray eels, Caribbean lobster and all kinds of tropical fish swimming in the untamed ocean around an actual reef.

Ardastra Gardens and Zoo

Off Chippingham Ave., west of Botanic Gardens, New Providence Island. 242-323-5806. www.ardastra.com. Open year-round daily 9am–5pm. Closed Dec 25. $12 (adults), $6 children (ages 4-12).

Kids will enjoy the 59 animal species, including tropical birds, monkeys and reptiles, at this small commercial animal park. The highlight here is the troupe of marching Caribbean flamingos—the national bird—that perform several times daily.

Atlantis Resort

Casino Dr., Paradise Island. 242-363-3000 or 800-722-7466. www.atlantis.com.

Atlantis is for kids of all ages! The Aqua Tots Program has the three-and-up set hand-feeding fish. At **Discovery Channel Camp**, youngsters 4–12 become pirates for a day searching for buried treasure, astronomers viewing stars through a telescope, scientists eyeballing tiny critters under a microscope, and adventurers touring **The Dig**, an eerie Indiana Jones-like space that depicts the Lost City of Atlantis. You can even get up close and personal with sharks—without getting wet—and see giant grouper in Predator Lagoon; you'll scream with glee as they zip down the waterslides.

Touring Tip: Atlantis Day Pass

One of the islands' best-kept secrets: you can buy a day pass to Atlantis and spend the day enjoying the resort's 11 lagoons, 5 waterslides, the beach bars, restaurants, shops and most of all, The Dig View Window, or The Dig as it's affectionately known. *$25 per person for one day. For details, call 242-363-3000.*

Must Be Seen: Nightlife

Atlantis Resort's Casino and Discotheque

Casino Dr., Paradise Island. 242-363-3000 or 800-722-7466. www.atlantis.com.

Gambling and the Bahamas are synonymous. The grandest casino on these islands is Atlantis, all aglitter with colorful glass sculptures by master artisan Dale Chihuly. You'll think you're in Las Vegas when you see the size of this gambling palace, with its 78 gaming tables and 1,000 slot machines. The payout is said to total more than $35,000 every hour! Don't miss the fabulous Las Vegas-style floor show.

The King and Knights Club

In Nassau Beach Hotel, Cable Beach. 242-327-5321. Shows performed year-round Sun–Mon 8:30pm, Tue–Sat 8:30pm & 10:30pm; $25; reservations suggested.

Be prepared for a grand time when you go to King Eric's Native Calypso Show. A tradition in Nassau, this club is known for its popular evening shows featuring native dance and music. The stage glows with fire dancers, limbo kings, steel drummers and costumed entertainers, all moving to the beat of island rhythms. If you opt for the dinner show, expect fresh Bahamian fish and rum punch.

Bahamaian Cocktails

An icy-cold Kalik, the light, wheaty beer of the Bahamas, chases away the day's heat, and Bahamian bartenders try to outdo themselves with their own unique version of an islandy rum punch or Bahama Mama. But Sky Juice is the historical cocktail of the Bahamas, always stirred up when locals get together to have good times. In days of yore, you climbed up a coconut palm, whacked off a green coconut, chopped off the top to open a hole, and mixed in gin and a little condensed milk with the green coconut water. That's the easy version of the refreshing, power-packed Sky Juice. Today, it's usually served in a glass, but it's a lot more fun to sip it from a coconut, island-style. Be careful. It's a creeper!

Out Island Beach Bars

For transportation, see Practical Information.

Nippers Beach Bar & Grill – *On Great Guana Cay, Great Abaco.* www.nippersbar.com. Perched on a 40-foot dune above a pink-sand beach, this two-level pool bar is a great place to toast sunsets. Nippers is the hippest spot in the Abacos for beach-bar hoppers. The Nipper Mobile picks you up at the settlement dock.

Miss Emily's Blue Bee Bar – *On Green Turtle Cay, Great Abaco. 242-365-4181.* This bar keeps yachters coming back for Miss Emily's famous Goombay Smashes. Her daughter continues the tradition with her mother's secret recipe, as well as a powerful rum punch.

Cracker P's Bar & Grill – *Lubbers Quarters, Great Abaco. 242-366-3139.* www.crackerps.com. The bar poses above a long dock at the old homestead of Paul J. Simmons, alias Cracker Pinder. Take a seat and listen to the legend about him.

Pete's Pub – *Little Harbour, Great Abaco. 242-366-3503. www.petespubandgallery.com.* Sitting on the crescent-shaped shores of Little Harbour, the pub is constructed of flotsam that washes ashore. Visitors add to the decor by donating T-shirts to hang from the rafters.

The Compleat Angler Hotel – *Alice Town, Bimini. 242-347-3122.* This bar is a must if you're in Bimini. The likes of Hemingway *(see sidebar, below)* and Isak Dinesen have partied at the combination museum, trophy room and 1930s-style lounge.

End of the World Bar – *Alice Town, Bimini.* Go barefoot to feel the sandy floor of this tiny bar between your toes. Walls are covered with underwear, cards and sayings. You might just rub shoulders with congressmen, movie stars and generals who drop in after a day of bonefishing.

How Hemingway Got Hooked

Pulitzer Prize-winning author Ernest Hemingway got hooked on the Gulf Stream and big-game fishing when the owner of Key West's Sloppy Joe's bar introduced him to Bimini. From 1935–1937, he fought blue marlin and bonefish by day, and imbibed at **The Compleat Angler**'s bar by night. Bimini still considers Papa Hemingway its adopted son. At a time when it was difficult to get to outposts like Bimini, Hemingway lured his wealthy friends here and put the isle on the map as a fishing destination. An entire room next to the old bar is lined with photos and memorabilia of his fishing trips to Bimini. Today the bar is the rowdy hot spot of Alice Town, drawing international fishing champions after a day of chasing tuna and wahoo as well as marlin and bonefish. *King's Hwy., Alice Town, North Bimini.*

Turks and Caicos

You may as well surrender on the spot. The oh-so-clear waters, blue-blue skies and deserted white-sand beaches of the **Turks and Caicos★** will overpower the cares and complexities of a life lived elsewhere. Lying just 28 miles southeast of the Bahamas, the eight limestone islands and dozens of cays that make up the Turks and Caicos form a loose arc in the Atlantic Ocean some 100 miles north of Haiti. Having lured divers, sailors and anglers for years, these low-lying islands and cays are gradually attracting a wider audience as tourism develops apace. If you're seeking escape but don't care much about sizzling nightlife or trendy shops, come enjoy the pristine landscape and relative serenity of these islands now, while you can.

What's in a Name?

The Turks are likely named, not for inhabitants of Turkey, but for the red top of the Turk's-head cactus found on the island. The top resembles a fez, the cone-shaped hat worn by eastern Mediterranean men.

Caicos (KAY-kos) most likely derives from the Lucayan Indian term *caya hico*, meaning a string of islands. The Spanish word *cayos* for cay (KEY), a low-lying island or reef of sand or coral, is similar.

Divided to Conquer

Divided into the Caicos Islands (West, North, Middle, East and South Caicos, and Providenciales) and the Turks (**Grand Turk** and **Salt Cay**), these islands and cays individually or collectively captivate all who step ashore. Tourism centers on **Providenciales**, more commonly called Provo, one of the world's best dive sites.

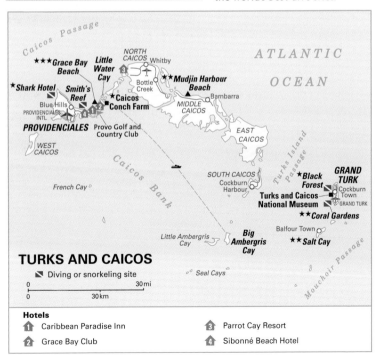

TURKS AND CAICOS

⬎ Diving or snorkeling site

0 ————————— 30mi
0 ————————— 30km

Hotels
1. Caribbean Paradise Inn
2. Grace Bay Club
3. Parrot Cay Resort
4. Sibonné Beach Hotel

Must-See Beaches

Grace Bay Beach★★★

North shore of Providenciales, off Leeward Hwy., east of the airport.

Despite a backdrop of hotels, this gorgeous pairing of sand and sea gets a vote as "Best Beach" by *Condé Nast Traveler* magazine, and *Caribbean Travel & Life* hails it as one of the best beaches in the Caribbean. Families tend to gravitate here for the calm waters and rockless shore. Leisurely stroll along the 12 miles of magnificent white, powdery sand to claim a quiet, private spot of your own. But keep your eyes peeled for JoJo, the local dolphin who lives in the wild and swims among snorkelers and swimmers in the bay.

Mudjin Harbour Beach★★

Middle Caicos, northwest of the airport.

It's no wonder this off-the-beaten-path beach has served as a backdrop for many photo shoots of major magazines: the white sands of its crescent-shaped lagoon—sitting within the Atlantic Ocean—are picturesque and dramatic. Day-trippers love the unusual sandy  expanse, especially its overhanging limestone cliffs and rocky outposts. Caves host stalagmites, stalactites, bats and a salt lake.

Salt Cay★★

6mi southwest of Grand Turk.

This most remote isle is small in size (2.5 square miles), but huge in stature. It serves as a time capsule of the days when Salt Cay was king of the Bermudian salt trade. Ruins here range from windmills to plantation houses, and relics from its heyday as a whaling port can still be found. The tiny cay is protected as a UNESCO World Heritage Site.

Musts for Outdoor Fun

Diving

Scuba diving is the main draw in the Turks and Caicos. Depending upon the tides and currents, the waters offer optimum visibility for exploring a 7,000-foot wall off Grand Turk and Providenciales. The archipelago is noted for spectacular corals, dramatic drop-offs and and hundreds of nurse sharks that converge in French Cay two months of the year. *(For diving etiquette, see p 40.)* Here's only the tip of the iceberg for diving sites:

Coral Gardens★★ – *Off the west-central shore, Grand Turk.* This popular 60-foot-deep dive site offers lush and healthy coral beds (especially hard coral), populated by overly friendly fish like the yellowtail snapper and large Nassau grouper, which follow divers around without mercy. Don't forget your underwater camera!

Black Forest★ – *Off the west-central shore, Grand Turk.* Just a few fin kicks from the boat put you at the wall and the drop-off. The uniqueness here lies in the shadows, created by the wall's ledges, that harbor all sorts of creatures. Prize sightings include incredible sponges, octopus dens and three kinds of black coral.

Shark Hotel★ – *North West Point, Providenciales.* Caution: for experienced divers only. Off Provo's north shore, a 17-mile barrier reef beckons seasoned divers. A short swim from the dive boat brings you to the edge of the wall, where you'll begin what has become a popular deep dive. Be careful—the wall slopes steeply. Be ready for eye-candy that includes elkhorn and staghorn coral *(see sidebar above)*, stovepipe sponges, and the shark hotel itself: a composite of sand chutes that serves as bed chambers for dozing nurse sharks.

Caribbean Coral

Anchored to the Caribbean's many barrier reefs, the tiny marine animals called coral cling together with the help of the calcium carbonate they produce—the same substance used in antacid tablets. Because they look like elk and deer antlers, elkhorn and staghorn coral are easy to recognize. These corals are on the endangered list, however. The best approach is to "look but don't touch," and leave the coral as you found it for others to enjoy as well.

Snorkeling at Smith's Reef

East of Turtle Cove, Providenciales.

Fan corals, parrot fish, sea anemones and turtles await you. Watch for underwater panels attached to orange floats that describe the marine life and the reef's ecology. Wade in where the floats begin, at the 5-foot water level (the reef's deepest point is 22 feet). Abundant ledges and clefts on the reef make the perfect habitat for spider crabs, moray eels and eagle rays. Bring your own snorkeling gear, or rent equipment, and take classes, from Art Pickering's Provo Turtle Divers *(Turtle Cove Marina, 649-946-4232; www.provoturtledivers.com).*

Dive Shops

Before you dive into Davy Jones' Locker, visit a local dive shop. They offer customized dive trips and diving instructions, certification and equipment rental. Here's a sampling:

Dive Provo – *649-946-5029; www.diveprovo.com.* This shop offers some 20 different dives to five areas within the Turks and Caicos.

Big Blue Unlimited – *649-946-5043; www.bigblue.tc.* Big Blue has been cited for its eco-tours.

Caicos Adventures – *649-941-3346; www.caicosadventures.tc.* This outfit has located 100 unchartered dive sites for its customers. Dives vary by week.

Salt Cay Divers – *649-946-6906; www.saltcaydivers.tc.* This company specializes in dive sites around Salt Cay.

Provo Golf and Country Club

Grace Bay Rd., Providenciales. 649-946-5991. www.provogolfclub.com.

If you want to play golf in the Turks and Caicos, this 18-hole course is your best—and only—bet (for now). Tropical flowers and palm trees border greens and fairways that seem to end in turquoise waters and billowy white clouds. You can rent clubs (carts are required) in the pro shop. After your game, relax with a drink in the Fairways Bar and Grill.

Diving Etiquette

To help preserve the Caribbean's diverse underwater worlds, be sure to keep the health of the reefs and the marine life in mind when you snorkel or scuba dive. Coral structures may take hundreds of years to form. Here are some ways to protect sea life:

- Shower off before getting into the water: oil from human skin weakens the delicate mucous membranes that protect coral from disease.
- Never walk or stand on coral: the weight of a human can diminish the reef-building ability of coral. If you're not a strong swimmer, wear a flotation device; it will keep your feet from getting planted on the coral if you need to adjust your mask.
- Practice good body control. Always swim well clear of any reef; never brush up against a reef. Secure your equipment so it doesn't snag the coral.
- Practice good finning. Be mindful of where you kick; your flippers could damage or destroy the coral.
- Look, but don't touch, pick up or hold coral or other reef marine life. Never pull an octopus or any other sea creature from its habitat. Never take anything living or dead from the sea—except garbage.
- Never chase or try to ride any sea creature.
- Ask dive guides about local laws, customs and taboos, so you can be respectful of them.

Musts for Kids

Caicos Conch Farm★

Leeward Hwy., east of Leeward Marina, Providenciales. Open year-round Mon–Sat 9am–4pm. $6 adults, $3 children.

Kids will be intrigued by these large mollusks, snug in their yellowy white shells with pink interiors. At the farm's commercial hatcheries, conchs can mature safely, free from ocean predators, before they are sold to markets of the world for delicious eating. You can purchase fresh conch here for the makings of your own salad. Today the Conch Farm is one of the Turks and Caicos' major tourist attractions. Its hatchery, nursery, and grow-out areas may look a little strange, what with all the vessels, domes and turrets.

With a handful of grants, Caicos Conch Farm owner Chuck Hesse first attempted conch mariculture in 1984. He sold memberships in his organization Protection of the Reefs and Island from Degradation and Exploitation (PRIDE), which, over the years, has successfully blended conch farming with nonpolluting wind generators. Hesse has succeeded, not only in maturing 700,000 juvenile conchs at a time, but also in introducing conch to the taste buds of famous chefs, who are creating their own conch concoctions.

What Exactly *is* a Conch?

There's nothing that says Caribbean like a Queen conch (say "konk"). It's quite a sight to see the bright pink and pale yellow mollusk moseying ever so slowly along the sandy bottom of the sea. Her beautiful shell is coveted by tourists, and her sweet, yummy meat is ordered up by all with island appetites. The meat is so tasty that human consumption of this Caribbean staple has reached extraordinary proportions: the Queen conch's stocks are either depleted or endangered in much of the Caribbean. That's why conch-lovers have their eye on the Caicos Conch Farm: it turns out about one million conchs a year, and has plans to expand. Now everyone's asking for conch, from Miami to LA, in the trendiest of restaurants. You can too. Enjoy it cooked up island-style, diced raw into conch salads, served as crunchy-crusted cracked conch, fried up as conch fritters or stirred into chowders.

Turks and Caicos National Museum

Duke St., Cockburn Town, Grand Turk. 649-946-2160. Open year-round Mon–Fri 9am–4pm; Sat 9am–1pm. Closed Sun. $5.

Want to see a real shipwreck? A magnet for treasure-seekers, the waters off the Turks and Caicos are said to hold what's left of many a ship that went aground. At this museum you can see the remains of a shipwreck that dates back to 1513, the *Molasses Reef* wreck—probably the oldest in the Western Hemisphere. Also on hand are artifacts from early island inhabitants, including a 1,000-year-old paddle used by the Lucayan Indians. A marine exhibit and a space gallery round out the displays. Next door, aloe vera, sea grape, sea-island cotton and other native and imported plants fill the museum's arboretum.

Must Be Pampered: Spas

Shambala Spa at Parrot Cay Resort

On Parrot Cay. US reservations: 904-288-0036. www.parrot-cay.com. Parrot Cay is a private island. If you're not a guest at the resort, you will need advance reservations for the spa. The resort has its own ferry from Provo to Parrot Cay.

The ultimate stressbuster! A reigning sense of calm embraces all of Parrot Cay, but bodies and spirits get an extra dose of nurturing at Shambala (translation: center of peace), an Asian-inspired spa and healing retreat that seduces the world's best known celebrities. Balinese therapists melt away stress with an extensive range of massages, wraps and body treatments based on ancient therapies from Japan, Bali, Thailand and China. Yoga is offered daily, and special healing weeks feature visiting instructors like Rodney Yee. After your treatment or yoga class, reserve a private mini-pavilion at the end of the boardwalk overlooking the sea. You'll drift off and sleep like a baby to the soothing lullaby of gentle waves.

The Pirates of Parrot Cay

Believe it or not, the pirates of Parrot Cay were female—and known for their ferocity. Island legend says, in the days of yore, Parrot Cay was called Pirate Cay for the daring and violent-tempered pirates Ann Bonny and Mary Read, who stayed here in the 1720s. The adventurous Bonny hooked up with Calico Jack, a roguish buccaneer. Disguised in men's clothing, she became part of his crew (all of whom admired her bravery). Onboard, she discovered Mary Read, also dressed as a man. When the Bahamian governor's pirate hunter attacked the ship, Calico Jack and his crew were drunk below, leaving Bonny and Read to fight them off alone. Alas, they were no match for their adversaries. To escape the death sentence, they told authorities they were pregnant. Read died in jail of fever; Bonny was granted amnesty.

Best Excursions

Big Ambergris Cay

South of South Caicos. Boats depart from Leeward Marina, Providenciales.

One of the joys of being in the Turks and Caicos is the ease of renting a boat—complete with captain—and exploring the uninhabited cays of the archipelago. **Long Bay Beach** at Big Ambergris Cay is nothing less than stunning—and completely deserted (unless others arrived before you). While away the hours sunning, swimming, snorkeling and fishing (if you brought your own pole) before you head back to the main islands.

Little Water Cay

East of Providenciales. 649-946-1723 (National Trust of Turks and Caicos). Boats depart from Leeward Marina, Providenciales.

The only inhabitants you'll see here are animals. Protected by the islands' National Trust, Little Water Cay is known for its endangered **rock iguanas** *(see sidebar, below)*. A boardwalk for day visitors provides added protection to these large lizards. You can take one of two trails through the native habitat, which is interpreted by panels along the way. Don't forget your swim suit: the deserted beaches of Little Water Cay are great spots to surf and sunbathe.

Iguanas Need Love, Too

And they're getting it in the Turks and Caicos. The islanders love their 2,000 endangered rock iguanas (*Cyclura carinata*). The shy, harmless creatures are found nowhere else in the world, so locals view them with pride. Once iguanas roamed nearly all of the isles in the archipelago, until man introduced domesticated animals, like dogs and cats, which found the large lizards quite munchable. Now the iguanas live the easy life in refuges on a few uninhabited cays protected by the islands' National

Trust. Once again they can fulfill their purpose in the ecosystem, feed on berries and leaves, and sleep in the shallow burrows they dig in loose sand. Mating begins in May when the female digs out a "nursery"—a side room in the burrow—where she lays her eggs. After she seals up the burrow, the heat of the sand incubates the eggs. Ninety days later the hatchlings instinctively dig their way out of the top of the chamber and into life in the sunlight.

Jamaica

Poster child of the Caribbean, **Jamaica**★★ is a land of striking geographical diversity: gorgeous waterfalls, majestic mountain peaks, rolling green countryside, misty forests and shady fern glades, not to mention white sandy beaches and clear ocean waters.

You'll find Jamaica tucked 90 miles south of the eastern end of Cuba. At about 146 miles long, the island is third in size after Cuba and Hispaniola. Called Xaymaca by the Arawaks, the first inhabitants here, Jamaica is the island birthplace of such celebrities as Harry Belafonte, Grace Jones and Chris Blackwell (founder of Island Records).

Meet-the-People Program

Sign up for an up-close-and-personal encounter with Jamaican volunteers eager to share common interests. You'll be paired, perhaps, with a fellow musician, nurse, gardener, artist, businessman or housewife for a true Jamaican take on the subject. You might hike, shop, tour the countryside or cook a traditional meal with the whole family. These experiences help you really get to know the islanders. *To find out the details, call 800-233-4582, or check online at www.visitjamaica.com.*

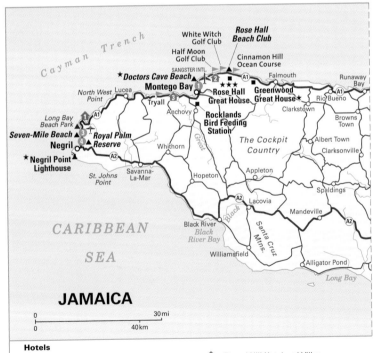

Hotels

1 Grand Lido Negril Resort & Spa
2 Half Moon Resort
3 Round Hill Hotel and Villas
4 Sandals Ocho Rios Resort & Golf Club

Jamaica's Famed Playgrounds

Kingston is the country's capital, historical center and cultural heart (home of the Bob Marley Museum and the National Gallery of Jamaica), but the city is also plagued by crime, to the extent that it's not so safe for tourists. Tourism really centers on the all-inclusive resorts, principally in Montego Bay, Ocho Rios and Negril. **Montego Bay** ("Mo Bay" to the locals) is tourism central: gorgeous beaches, premiere resort hotels, legendary plantation houses, championship golf courses and chic shops. Its neighbor, 67 miles east, **Ocho Rios** (nicknamed "Ochi") caters to cruise-ship passengers and tourists seeking activity rather than seclusion.

Once the hot spot for the 1940s Hollywood crowd, now-eclipsed **Port Antonio**★★, 60 miles southeast of Ochi, draws those in search of serenity. The "in" place for partying and pleasure seeking, **Negril**—some 50mi west of Montego Bay—was formerly an enclave for hippies attracted to bargain-basement room-and-board prices (remnants survive in Negril's West End). Plenty of vacationers still let their hair down, as well as their clothing, on the "au naturel" beaches of Negril's upscale East End.

Restaurants

1. Pork Pit
2. Almond Tree Restaurant
3. Cosmos Seafood Restaurant & Bar
4. Margaritaville, Negril

Must-See Beaches

Boston Bay Beach★★

7mi southeast of Port Antonio, off A4.

James Bond once owned this beautiful beach—well, actually, actor Roger Moore did. After Moore donated it to the government, the public beach became renowned for its "jerk shacks," where some of the best jerk *(see sidebar, below)* in the country can be found. After a swim, mosey up to a jerk shack to fill up on zesty jerk chicken or pork, washed down by a cold Red Stripe beer.

Jamaican What?

Centuries ago, Peruvian Quechua Indians sailed here and brought their way of preserving meat called *"charqui"* (pronounced *"jirk"* in Old English). Over time, *charqui* meshed with the earthen pit-style cooking of the Maroons, West Africans who escaped slavery by hiding in the mountains. In secrecy, the Maroons continued preparing meat the traditional way until the mid-1950s, when jerk pits popped up all over the island. The best jerk cooks concoct spicy rubs or marinades, and make only pimento- or guava-wood fires for slow cooking in steel drums or brick-lined pits.

James Bond Beach★★

In Oracabessa, 15mi east of Ocho Rios, off A3.
876-975-3663. www.jamesbondbeachjamaica.com.
Closed Dec 25. $5 entry fee.

Waverunner rides and fresh seafood at Moonraker Bar & Grill draw crowds to this spectacular beach, edged by gin-clear water. The privately owned beach prompts celebrity sightings (think P. Diddy, Kate Moss and Bono) and hosts international concerts.

Doctors Cave Beach★

Along Gloucester Ave., Montego Bay. 876-952-2566. www.doctorscavebathingclub.com.
$5 entry fee.

Looking for a beach party? This five-mile stretch of white sand attracts big crowds, given its backdrop of resort hotels. You'll find water sports and rentals, snack bars and changing rooms. Watch out for aggressive beach vendors.

> **Touring Tip:**
> **Savvy—and Safe**
>
> In public places, particularly on Jamaica's beaches, you may be approached by aggressive vendors and hustlers selling drugs or sex. Marijuana, called ganja locally, and other drugs are illegal in Jamaica. Be polite but firm in saying no.

Negril's Seven-Mile Beach
Along Norman Manley Blvd., Negril.

The sands of this impressive beach, edged with resort hotels and coconut palms, are pale and powdery. Protected by a reef, calm crystal-clear waters make for good swimming and snorkeling. To avoid surprises, look out for signs that designate nude beaches, where locals and tourists bare it all.

Ocho Rios Bay Beach and Fisherman's Beach
West of town center, Ocho Rios.

Looking for beach action? Water-sports lovers flock to the stretch of sand straddling the cruise ship pier off busy Main Street. Feel like a boat ride? Ask a fisherman at Fisherman's Beach for a tour. Agree on the price before you board.

Reggae Beach
4mi east of Ocho Rios, off A3.

Jamaicans call this length of soft sand a "tall" beach. You can catch the vibes and some rays at this popular site of reggae concerts. Graced with grand trees that cast cool shadows, the beach attracts volleyball players, Frisbee players and basketball shooters. Picnic tables set the stage for dominoes, and hammocks induce napping.

Rose Hall Beach Club
10mi east of downtown Montego Bay. $6.

Less crowded than other Mo Bay beaches, this half-mile expanse of brilliant white sand framing azure waters offers a lively family beach. Spend a lazy day in the hammocks here, washing down beach hotdogs with cold fruit daiquiris.

Reggae Music

Expect to see Rastas, with their hair twirled in dreadlocks, at Reggae Beach. Jamaica's Ras Tafari movement, born in the 1930s, spawned reggae, a simple island beat with lyrics about suffering, freedom and love. Thanks to the late Bob Marley, the "king of reggae," this musical phenomenon took the world by storm. His children, particularly his son Ziggy, carry on their father's music, as do Jamaicans Freddie McGregor, Dennis Brown and Gregory Isaacs. You'll hear the catchy beat of reggae everywhere, from beach bars and jerk shacks, to taxi cabs and fine restaurants.

Must-See Historic Sites

Rose Hall Great House★★★

10mi east of Montego Bay, off A1, across from Wyndham Rose Hall Resort. 876-953-2456. Open year-round daily 9am–6pm. $15.

Want to see where a witch supposedly lived? A popular attraction, Rose Hall (built in 1780) was the residence of Annie Mae Palmer, who was murdered in 1831. Tutored as a child in voodoo by her Haitian nanny, the mistress of this stately mansion was married three times. All of her husbands died mysteriously, rumored to have been murdered by Annie. You can read the whole story in H.G. de Lisser's novel *The White Witch of Rose Hall.*

Firefly★★

Port Maria, east of Ocho Rios. 876-725-0920 (Jamaican National Heritage Trust). Open year-round Mon–Sat 9am–5pm. $10.

Set on a hill overlooking Port Maria Bay, Firefly was the residence of the playwright who penned *Blithe Spirit* and *Private Lives.* Witty British songster **Noël Coward** (1899–1973) entertained the rich and famous in the 1950s at this sparsely furnished house, his home for the last 25 years of his life. You can visit Coward's grave, which is located on the grounds.

Greenwood Great House★

15mi east of Montego Bay, off A1 in the parish of St. James (5mi east of Rose Hall, above). 876-953-1077. Open year-round daily 9am–6pm. $12.

The center of a former sugarcane plantation, this hilltop mansion was built in 1790 by the family of English poet Elizabeth Barrett Browning. Born nearby, Barrett's father was a large landowner in the area. Today Greenwood is a house museum, showcasing antique furnishings, musical instruments and the Barrett family's books.

Negril Point Lighthouse★

South of Negril, off West End Rd. at the westernmost tip of Jamaica.

Shining 100ft above the sea, the light of this 66ft concrete structure has guided mariners since 1894. The beam, solarized in 1985, reaches 10 miles out into the ocean. To withstand earthquakes, the tower sits in a 14-feet-deep tank filled with water. Climb the 103 steps for a rewarding view of the Caribbean Sea, especially at sunset, but get permission from the light keeper first.

Must Shop

The Craft Market

Near Harbour St., in downtown Montego Bay.

Beautiful baskets of all sizes and shapes, straw hats made from the jipijapa plant, wood carvings, musical instruments and shell jewelry are just some of the fun finds at this small outdoor market. Before letting a vendor talk you into anything, be sure to browse around the entire market. When you're ready to buy, don't be shy about bargaining with the sellers.

Old Fort Craft Park

Howard Cooke Blvd., on site of Fort Montego, Montego Bay.

Some 180 vendors, each licensed by the Jamaica Tourist Board, sell island handicrafts of all kinds, from wall hangings and straw products to art-works and hair-braiding services. If a vendor becomes aggressive, keep walking until you find a vendor you can deal with comfortably.

Wassi Art

Great Pond, near Ocho Rios. www.exportjamaica.org/wassi.

It's worth a jostling cab ride down a winding, pothole-filled road to experience this pottery factory. Everything here is made the old-fashioned way—by hand. Founded in 1990 by amateur potter Theresa Lee, the "factory" employs 50 artisans who work with Blue Mountain clay and vibrant glazes in the bold colors that characterize Jamaican art. Tours *(15 minutes)* are free and include throwing a pot on a wheel.

Touring Tip: Take Precautions

Avoid being a crime victim in Jamaica by taking the following precautions:
- Never leave valuables in your room or rental car, or unattended on the beach. Keep passports in hotel safes.
- Carry little cash and few credit cards. Use a money belt or holder.
- Travel in small groups or in pairs. Stay close to the hotel after dark.
- Take only regulated taxi cabs, the ones bearing red license plates.

Jamaica

Musts for Outdoor Fun

Raft the Rio Grande River★★

Rafter's Rest, 5mi west of Port Antonio. 876-993-2778. $45.

For years rafts have transported bananas from inland plantations down the Rio Grande River to boats waiting in Port Antonio. Now you can hop aboard a bamboo raft, controlled by a raft guide, and drift for two to three hours down the gentle waters of this river past bamboo arches, plantation land, moss-covered Lovers' Rock and pristine riverbanks dressed in every imaginable shade of tropical green. Along the way, locals offer cold beer and crafts, such as hand-carved bamboo glasses. A driver takes you upriver where you begin the two- to three-hour ride.

Spend an Evening on the White River★★

The White River, Ocho Rios. Tues–Sun 7pm–9pm. Your hotel can make arrangements.

For one of the most exotic and romantic journeys in Jamaica, settle into a canoe for two and paddle in sync to the rhythms of a beating drum up the White River, set aglow with light from tiki torches burning along the banks. Upriver you'll be treated to a colorful folklore show, dinner and an open bar. A night to remember!

Ride Horseback on the Beach★

Hooves Riding Stables, 61 Windsor Rd., St. Ann's Bay. 876-972-0905.
www.hoovesjamaica.com. $55–$100 for 2hr–4hr rides.

Saddle up for a memorable ride on the beach. Your horse will walk on the sands and then head into the ocean, leg-deep in the waves. Or try the Bush Doctor Mountain ride, a glorious saunter through the lush mountainside. The Rainforest ride takes you trotting amid bamboo trees and other tropical flora of the forest. When you book these rides through your hotel, you'll be picked up and driven to the stables.

Blue Mountain Coffee

Jamaica's most famous mountains are the Blue Mountains, rising in the southeastern part of the island. Their beauty aside, they are known for the coffee grown there, raised by a handful of farmers below the 5,000-feet line. Coffee connoisseurs covet Jamaica's Blue Mountain Coffee, long ranked as one of the best in the world. A specially designed seal safeguards the authenticity of this expensive java. Top brands include Langford Brothers, Jablum, Wallenford Blue, Salada and Jamaica Standard. The island's famous coffee liqueur, Tia Maria, is made with Blue Mountain Coffee.

Golfing in Jamaica

Golfers have long known that Jamaica's fairways are a marriage of natural beauty, challenging greens, well-stocked pro shops and savvy caddies. That's what keeps them returning year after year to Jamaica's scenic courses.

Cinnamon Hill Ocean Course – *N. Coast Hwy., Montego Bay. 876-953-2650. www.wyndham-jamaica.com.* Watch out, you might miss your putt! The views of the sea and the Blue Mountains at the Wyndham Rose Hall Resort's fairways are mighty distracting. Laid out on the site of a sugar plantation, the 18-hole championship course is interspersed with stone walls, an aqueduct and other ruins. Hole 5, edged with a narrow beach, rates as the most beautiful of the course.

Half Moon Golf Club – *Rose Hall, 7mi east of Montego Bay. 876-953-3105. www.halfmoon-resort.com.* Get a good caddy to tackle this 18-hole championship course, highly regarded in the Caribbean. Designed by Robert Trent Jones, Half Moon's greens are graced with palm trees and lakes sitting at the foot of Montego Bay's verdant hills. Like the Cinnamon Hill course, half of the holes face into the trade winds, making this course tough as well as delightful.

White Witch Golf Club – *1 Ritz Carlton Dr., St. James, 7mi east of Montego Bay. 876-518-0174. www.ritzcarlton.com/resorts.* Despite the name's nod to the island's "witch" Annie Mae Palmer *(see p 48)*, there's nothing eerie about this 18-hole championship course at the Ritz Carlton Rose Hall Golf and Spa Resort. Frustrating, maybe, given the topography of ravines, gorges and jungle foliage filling Rose Hall's lush acres. The lovely views of Caribbean waters at 16 of the 18 holes should more than offset the testy terrain.

Tryall Golf, Tennis and Beach Club – *N. Coast Hwy., Sandy Bay, 12mi west of Montego Bay Airport. 876-956-5681. www.tryallclub.com.* Known for its entertaining caddies and holes that "kiss the shoreline," this celebrated course has hosted the Johnnie Walker World Championship, the Jamaica Classic, and Shell's Wonderful World of Golf. Signature holes like the 7th tee—shot through the pillars of a historic aquaduct—continue to make Tryall one of the best courses in all of the Caribbean.

Musts for Kids

Dunn's River Falls★★

About 1.5mi west of Ocho Rios, off A1. 876-974-2857. Open year-round daily 9am–5pm. www.dunnsriverja.com. $10 adults (ages 12 & up), $8 children (ages 2–11). Best to wear a swim suit, but there are changing rooms on-site. Aqua slippers can be rented.

Clasp a hand in the human chain of hikers *(note that rocks can be slippery)*, or tip a guide to get you to the top of Jamaica's famed waterfall. This broad, breath-taking cascade of water tumbles 600 feet over rocky ledges to the shores of the Caribbean Sea. Over the years, the limestone rock has been shaped by the water into tiers that hold small pools, perfect for sitting or dangling your feet in.

Dolphin Cove

West of Ocho Rios, adjacent to Dunn's River Falls. Open year-round daily 9am–5pm. 876-974-5335. www.dolphincovejamaica.com. $15 adults & children (encounters $35 & up). Reservations advised.

Spy on snakes, iguanas, parrots, turtles, eels and other exotic creatures when you walk the Jungle Trail through a tropical forest and along a lagoon. Then enjoy an encounter with a dolphin. Tots can touch the affectionate mammals in shallow water; older children can swim and play with them *(children under 13 years of age must be accompanied by an adult)*. A thrill, for sure.

Rocklands Bird Feeding Station

South of Montego Bay, near Anchovy. 876-952-2009. Open to the public year-round daily 2pm–5pm. $8 adults & children.

Kids love to sit on the veranda at this sanctuary and watch doves, nightingales, hummingbirds, finches or orioles eat from their hand. Get a feeding bottle filled with water and sugar; then point your finger out to make a perch and a bird will sit on it.

Royal Palm Reserve

3mi east of Negril. Take Sheffield Rd. to Springfield Rd.; turn left on Springfield Rd., then take the next left to the reserve. 876-364-7407. www.royalpalmreserve.com. Open year-round daily 9am–6pm. $10 adults & children. Reserve horse ride in advance.

Thumbs up, or should we say "palms" up, to this 300-acre reserve and its activi-ties. Learn about the wetlands at the museum. Ride a horse among royal palms, anchovy pear trees and crab-thatch ferns. Or walk the boardwalk with eyes peeled for the red-billed streamertail hummingbird, Jamaica's national bird. End your visit by catching tarpon or African perch in Cotton Tree Lake *(fishing pole rentals; fee for fish taken)*.

Best Excursion From Ocho Rios

Port Antonio★★

60mi east of Ocho Rios. Access by bus from Montego Bay (arrangements can be made by your hotel), or commuter plane from Donald Sangster Airport in Montego Bay to Ken Jones Aerodrome, 5mi west of Port Antonio; taxis are available from the Aerodrome.

Off-the-beaten path, Port Antonio boasts fine beaches, gorgeous twin ports, a slow-'n-easy attitude, and a backdrop of the misty **Blue Mountains** stretching to the sea. It's Jamaica's most overlooked destination, and one of its loveliest.

Once a thriving banana-boat town filled with the songs of tallymen (banana bunch counters), Port Antonio is said to be the inspiration for Harry Belafonte's Banana Boat Song. Bananas are still loaded on boats in the harbor here, but on a much smaller scale.

Scuba, snorkel or simply take a dip in the gleaming **Blue Lagoon**, fed by freshwater springs. Valley Hikes *(876-993-3881),* an award-winning eco-tour organization, offers excursions to the Maroon settlement of **Moore Town** nearby.

Port Antonio isn't a shopping mecca, but the vendors of the outdoor **Musgrave Market** downtown *(West St.)* offer great deals on spices, jerk, fruits and veggies. You can visit the ruins of 1729 **Fort George** *(Fort George St.),* and walk through the nine-chamber **Nonsuch Caves** at the Athenry Gardens in the village of Nonsuch *(3mi southeast of Port Antonio),* but the best reason to come here is simply to enjoy uncrowded peace and quiet.

Hollywood's Haunt

Port Antonio has long lured the rich and famous. Celebrities started coming here in the early 1900s with the opening of the Titchfield Hotel (one of the island's first). Rudyard Kipling came for the fishing. William Randolph Hearst, JP Morgan Jr., Bette Davis and Ginger Rogers came simply because they loved the place. But it was Hollywood heartthrob Errol Flynn who sailed in on his yacht, and stayed for the rest of his life. He bought the Titchfield Hotel, Navy Island, and some plantation land and grew coconuts and bananas. Flynn also livened up the place a bit—the bad boy of Hollywood became the bad boy of Port Antonio. Flynn's widow stayed on after his death in 1959.

Cayman Islands

Come to the Caymans and don your underwater gear—you just might meet a stingray, in person! You're on islands that are world-famous for below-the-sea enchantment. Tucked 150 miles beneath Cuba, the trio of small isles that make up the **Cayman Islands★★** are synonymous with exhilarating dive sites (the birding here is not bad either). A short flight from Miami, Florida, this British territory attracts a large number of visitors from the US.

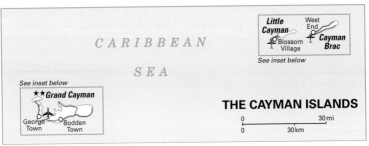

THE CAYMAN ISLANDS

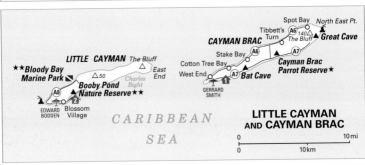

LITTLE CAYMAN AND CAYMAN BRAC

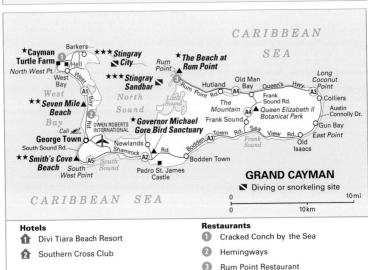

GRAND CAYMAN

◤ Diving or snorkeling site

Hotels

🏠 Divi Tiara Beach Resort

🏠 Southern Cross Club

Restaurants

1 Cracked Conch by the Sea

2 Hemingways

3 Rum Point Restaurant

A Cluster of Caymans

The largest and westernmost of the three islands, 22mi-long **Grand Cayman**★★ is the most developed. A port of call for cruise ships, the capital city of **George Town** mixes business and financial services with jewelry, souvenir and gem shops. Just north lies **Seven Mile Beach**★★, one of the Caribbean's best. Popular dive site **Stingray City**★★★ draws hoardes of tourists. Scattered along the west and east shores of the island, half a dozen shipwrecks, such as the Cali freighter wreck off George Town, lie beneath the waters.

To the northeast by 75 miles, **Little Cayman**, just 10 miles long and 2 miles wide, boasts **Bloody Bay**, a major draw for divers, and **Booby Pond Nature Reserve**★★, a bird lover's paradise. Bonefishing is also big here.

Five miles east, **Cayman Brac** is named for a 140-foot-high limestone bluff rising at the island's east end. The brac (Gaelic for "bluff") is pockmarked with caves, once hiding holes for pirates. **Bat Cave** and **Great Cave** provide haven for a colony of bats, while the **Cayman Brac Parrot Reserve**★ safeguards the island's endangered parrot.

Modern-Day Pirates?

The Caymans have always played a role in hiding loot. In the heyday of Caribbean piracy, Henry Morgan and Blackbeard hid their treasure here (locals continue to find pieces of eight). Today, with more than 600 international banks and 40,000 companies registered in the Caymans, the islands still provide a cache for riches—tax-free investment accounts, that is. There are no income taxes, capital gains taxes or estate taxes here. Bank secrecy laws in the Caymans are among the strictest in the world. Companies can form anonymously with a minimum of paperwork; trust-formation laws excel in flexibility, asset protection and privacy. Of course, not all of it is on the up and up. John Grisham's legal-thriller-turned-film-classic *The Firm* recounts a Tennessee law firm's money-laundering scheme played out on Grand Cayman.

Musts for Outdoor Fun

Stingray City and Stingray Sandbar★★★

In North Sound, about 2mi east of Barkers Head, Grand Cayman.

Think fear factor: you're surrounded by 50 scavenging stingrays in search of food. What do you do? Feed them, of course. Popular **Stingray City**, a spot in the 12-feet-deep waters of North Sound, is a magnet for rays. Some 20 years ago, fishermen cleaning their fish here noticed stingrays waiting for scraps tossed overboard. Soon a few dive masters took the plunge, getting into the water to hand-feed the critters. Divers feed the rays frozen squid these days, getting an adrenalin rush as the rays swarm, brushing the humans with their satiny bellies and spanned wings. Green moray eels may get into the picture, too—be careful with these guys, though; they have sharp teeth!

Non-swimmers, children and novice snorkelers can experience almost the same rush standing in chest-deep water on **Stingray Sandbar**, where the rays swim up to be hand fed. Have no fear; they have no teeth. Their only defense is their barbed, venomous tail, but if you treat them with respect, it's no problem. *(Your hotel can usually book a Stingray City tour for you. To find a diving tour yourself, see sidebar, below).*

Dive Shops

Several dive outfitters in the area mount diving expeditions to Stingray City. Here's a sampling:

Ambassador Divers – *George Town, Grand Cayman. 345-949-8839. www.ambassadordivers.com. $45/dive; $25/snorkel.*

Scuba divers and snorkelers fill the boat for this Stingray City dive. A dive master accompanies you below the water, and demonstrates how to handfeed frozen squid to the rays.

Cayman Diver Ltd. – *The Grand Caymanian Resort, near Seven Mile Beach. 345-925-4386. www.caymandiver.com. $30.*

Long known as one of the islands' best dive operations, this outfitter believes in small dive groups (no more than 16) under the guidance of excellent dive masters. Their snorkeling trip to Stingray Sandbar leaves early *(7:45am)* to beat the cruise-ship crowds. Then it's on to Barrier Reef to snorkel among coral, tropical fish and green moray eels.

Red Sail Sports. – *Seven Mile Beach, George Town, Grand Cayman. 345-945-5965. www.redsailcayman.com. Prices vary.*

One of the largest watersports outfits on Grand Cayman, Red Sail operates dive shops at several hotels, including the Hyatt, Marriott, Westin and Royal Palms. The company offers a range of dive and snorkeling packages, including trips to Stingray City.

Go Below the Sea with Atlantis Adventures★★

Departs from Atlantis Dock, George Town, Grand Cayman. 345-949-7700.
www.atlantisadventures.com. $84–$450. Advance reservations required.

If you're not into scuba diving, you can still experience an undersea adventure. Board the Atlantis XI submarine and descend to 100 feet for a 45-minute tour *($84; 90 minutes shore to shore)* of **Grand Cayman's Underwater Marine Park**. You're likely to see star corals, barrel sponges, colorful fish and perhaps a stingray or turtle. The 35-minute tour *($395; 75 minutes shore to shore)* aboard the Atlantis *Deep Explorer* reaches a depth of 800 feet. You'll see orange-rope, tube and barrel sponges, porcelain corals and black-basket starfish. Limited to two passengers, the 55-minute tour *($450; 90 minutes shore to shore)* aboard the Deep Explorer descends to a depth of 1,000 feet to show off—with the help of a powerful headlight—the famous shelf-like slope of the wall.

Scuba Dive at Bloody Bay Marine Park★★

Off the north shore of Little Cayman, between Spot Bay and Jackson Point.

One of the most spectacular dive spots in the world, this two-mile stretch of protected water encompasses shallow reefs that descend two vertical walls: the renowned **Bloody Bay Wall**—an ear-popping 12,000-foot plunge—as well as Jackson's Wall. Famous among the world diving community, the park boasts waters where the average visibility is 100 to 150 feet. This environment shelters a rich habitat for coral gorges, pinnacles, exotic fish, seahorses and other marine life. Since the show starts just 18 feet below the surface, the park also offers snorkelers unforgettable views.

> **Touring Tip**
>
> Bloody Bay Marine Park is a hot spot for underwater photographers, professional and novice. Please remember the Cayman Islands' marine conservation motto: Take only pictures; leave only bubbles.

Must-See Beaches

Seven Mile Beach★★

1mi north of George Town, Grand Cayman.

The focus of Grand Cayman's tourism, this popular white-sand beach actually stretches northward 5.5 miles, not 7 miles, along West Bay. Lined with condos and hotels that front a commercial strip of shops and eateries, the crowded beach is still a beauty, with its soft, silky sand and warm, gentle waters, which are great for swimming and snorkeling.

Crowds aside, the beach is free of hounding hawkers and litter. Water sports rentals are available.

Smith's Cove Beach★★

Off S. Church St. near South West Point, Grand Cayman.

A local favorite, this beautiful cove is a great spot for beginning snorkelers. Its super-clear waters are protected by a coral reef abounding with parrot fish, sponges, starfish and sea fans. Especially crowded on weekends, this stretch of heavenly white sand south of George Town is still less mobbed than Seven Mile Beach. Bring your snorkeling gear as well as your tanning lotion.

The Beach at Rum Point★

Rum Point, Grand Cayman.

Catch a ferry from the Hyatt Regency hotel to experience this somewhat secluded stretch of sand. Dotted with shady casuarinas trees strung with hammocks, the beach has picnic tables, changing rooms and a long dock extending into North Sound. The neon-blue waters off Rum Point are ideal for

swimming and snorkeling. Then watch the sunset while you sip a "mudslide" (vodka, Kahlua and Bailey's Irish Cream) at long-time watering hole, the **Wreck Bar & Grill**.

What Not to Wear

Modesty rules in the Caymans. Nude and topless sunbathing are illegal, so leave any skimpy attire at home. Islanders do not look kindly on anyone wearing beach attire—swim suits, tank tops, beach cover-ups—any place other than at the beach. Many shops have posted signs requesting customers to wear shoes. Shorts are tolerated during day-light hours, but it's best to dress up a bit (smart-casual wear, at least) when dining out.

Musts for Fun

Cayman Turtle Farm★

North West Point Rd., 8mi northwest of George Town, Grand Cayman. 345-949-3894. www.turtle.ky. Open year-round daily 8:30am–5pm. $6.

Come and be counted among the more than 30,000 annual visitors who oooh and ahhh at the sea of green sea turtles here. The 30-minute tour of this farm, the only commercial farm of its type in the world, gives you an overview of each stage of turtle development—from birth as an egg laid on a manmade beach to old age as a centenarian senior. The turtles, some 16,000 of them, range in size from tiny six-ouncers to gigantic 600 pounders. Accompanied by great community fanfare, a number of turtles are released into the sea each year during Pirates Week *(see sidebar, p 61)*; a much larger number wind up in turtle stew or turtle burgers.

Green Sea Turtles

These sea-going reptiles are so named because the green algae they eat causes their fat, as well as their body and shell, to turn green. Sea turtles are slow to reach sexual maturity, a stage that usually requires 25 to 50 years. Illegal poaching, pollution, loss of nesting sites and accidental drowning in commercial fishing nets have seriously depleted the numbers of this animal that, as fossilized evidence tells us, was around when the dinosaurs became extinct.

Touring Tip: Island Customs

When on the islands, do as the islanders do. The Caymans are a grand example of small-island culture, and you'll receive first-class treatment if you adopt local ways. Simple manners (the use of "please" and "thank you") and a "good day" go a long way—as does patience. Since island surnames are so similar, residents introduce themselves by first names, like "Mr. Joe" or "Miss Mary," the form to use when you address them. If you're asked to a local home for dinner, flowers are more appreciated than wine. Islanders take pride in their clean, litter-free lands, so help keep them that way (littering carries a fine in the Caymans).

Must-See Parks and Natural Sites

Booby Pond Nature Reserve★★

67 A8, near Blossom Village, Little Cayman. 345-949-0121 (National Trust Cayman Islands). www.nationaltrust.org.ky/info.

This is red-footed booby country! Little Cayman hosts the largest colony—5,000 of these birds—in all of the Western Hemisphere. Sitting on a saltwater lagoon rimmed with mangrove trees and old-growth forest, the 204-acre reserve provides habitat for many wetland and shore birds. The only breeding colony of Magnificent frigates in the Caymans nests here. Designed to show off traditional Caymanian architecture—which includes gingerbread trim—the **visitor center** features an observation deck. Go eyeball to lens with one of the telescopes on the veranda for a closer look at the reserve's feathered populations.

Cayman Brac Parrot Reserve★

Take Ashton Reid Rd. to Major Donald Dr., Cayman Brac. 345-949-0121 (National Trust Cayman Islands). www.nationaltrust.org.ky/info.

Look closely. You may just spot a wild parrot here in this 180-acre reserve, located among the woodlands crowning Cayman Brac's bluff. The reserve harbors about 400 endangered Cayman Brac parrots *(see sidebar, opposite)*, iridescent-green in color. Walk the one-mile loop **nature trail**, which crosses grass-covered former farmland, red-soil beds topped with mango trees, and assorted thickets and forests. Keep your ears open: the parrots make the most noise early in the morning and late in the afternoon.

Great Conservationists, Those Islanders

Caymanians consider themselves stewards of the beautiful sea that blesses them. They're avid conservationists who strictly enforce the islands' Marine Conservation Laws that outlaw the possession of spear guns, and the disturbance or removal of marine life while in scuba gear, or from marine parks. Islanders request the same freedom from harassment for the flora and fauna on land—from the succulent agave plant to the Grand Cayman blue iguana.

Governor Michael Gore Bird Sanctuary★

Spotts Newlands Rd., Grand Cayman, about 3mi east of George Town. Take Crewe Rd. to A2 east and turn left on Spotts Newlands Rd; take the first right and follow signs. 345-949-0121. www.nationaltrust.org.ky/info.

Ever seen a grassquit? You may just find one of these little yellow-faced birds at Gore Sanctuary. Situated on 1.84 acres of grassland, governor's pond, as it's locally known, preserves valuable habitat in an area that's rapidly being developed. Some 60 species of birds have been sighted here, including moorhens, herons, grebes, kingfishers, woodpeckers, flycatchers and warblers. Take the path to the observation blind to see how many different species you can spot.

Birds of a Feather

Cayman Islands' national bird, the Cayman Brac parrot *(Amazona leucocephala hesterna)*, is found nowhere else in the world. If you're lucky enough to spot one of these secretive creatures, you'll recognize it by its coloring: look for iridescent green feathers edged with black, a white patch on top of its head between its eyes, and red cheeks. When the birds stretch their wings, the underside flashes bright blue. The parrot's tail is blue, red and yellow-green, and you might be able to see a maroon-colored patch on its breast.

Must Shop

Bernard Passman Gallery

Cardinall Plaza Bldg., Cardinall Ave., George Town, Grand Cayman. 345-949-0123. www.passman.com.

Ditch the duty-free goods for something Cayman Island-special at this swank downtown gallery. Considered by many a "coral artiste extraordinaire," islander Bernard Passman began carving Caribbean black coral into sculptures and jewelry years ago. He opened his first gallery here in 1975. His exquisite coral creations (accented in diamonds and gold) are coveted by the rich and famous—Pope John-Paul II has a sculpture.

Pirates Week

For over 25 years, this national festival has celebrated the likes of Henry Morgan and Blackbeard, those rascally rogues who regularly dropped anchor in the Caymans. For 11 days every October, locals and tourists don colorful pirate-era costumes, and have a rollicking good time. *(see Calendar of Events).*

The Tortuga Rum Company

Three locations: The bakery on Rum Lane; a store in the heart of George Town (Tortuga Rum Lane, George Town); and a store just steps from the cruise-ship dock. 345-949-7701. www.torgugarumcakes.com.

What started 20 years ago as a local lady baking rum cakes in her home from a secret family recipe has turned into a world-wide hunger for the preservative-free and potently rummy Tortuga Rum Cake. From the moment Carlene Hamaty's cakes "went public" in a local restaurant, she could barely keep up with the demand. Her Tortuga Rum Cake keeps customers coming back.

What do you get when you mix Latin love of life with American efficiency? **Puerto Rico★★★**. The 110-mile-long island, 40 miles at its widest, lies east of Hispaniola. The long arm of American enterprise reached the island after it was ceded to the US in 1898 at the end of the Spanish-American War. Today Spain's legacy—evident in Old San Juan's ancient fortress, saucy Latin rhythms and religious festivals—coexists with American imports such as highways and fast-food chains. This island delights visitors with its 4,000-foot-high mountain peaks, dense rain forest, and golden beaches. Most of the island's 3.8 million residents live in or near the capital of San Juan, a busy port of call on the northeast shore.

Puerto Rico: A US Commonwealth

The islanders have been US citizens since 1917. They pay no federal income tax and cannot vote, but are afforded unrestricted migration to America. Puerto Ricans can vote for one representative in the House of Representatives, who is ineligible to vote, even on island-related issues.

Puerto Rico's Riches

Arriving as governor in 1508, Juan Ponce de Léon named the island Puerto Rico, Spanish for "rich port." Though the gold the Spanish mined is long gone, the island is not bereft of treasure: you'll find riches in the beauty of the landscape and the charm of the islanders. San Juan includes the 500-year-old walled town of **Old San Juan★★★**— a UNESCO World Heritage Site—as well as New San Juan, with its flashy hotels, casinos and glitzy nightlife, stretching eastward along the northern shore. Eastern Puerto Rico claims **El Yunque**, the largest rain forest in the US national forest system (*see sidebar below*), and off-the-beaten-path isles like Vieques and Culebra. The culture of the city of Ponce is a highlight of southern Puerto Rico, where a drier climate fosters open-air architecture. At the **Tibes Indigenous Ceremonial Center★** you can tour a site inhabited 1,000 years before Columbus' arrival (*Rte. 503, Ponce; 787-840-2255; open year-round Tue–Sun 9am–4pm; closed Mon; $2*). The Porta del Sol (the western shore), celebrated for breeding Paso Fino horses, lures sun-seekers and surfers to its award-winning beaches. Coffee plantations dot the island's central section, home to Puerto Rico's most revered craftsmen.

El Yunque—A Giant of a Rain Forest

Just 25 miles southeast of San Juan (*by Rtes. 3 east and 191 south*) lies the Caribbean National Forest (locally known as El Yunque), a 28,000-acre rain forest popular for its hiking trails, waterfalls and panoramas of the forest from several lookout towers. If you go, be prepared for heavy traffic en route, especially on weekends. Upon arrival, stop first at the El Portal Tropical Forest Center (*Rte. 191, Rio Grande; 787-888-1880; open year-round daily 9am–5pm; $3*) for an orientation to the forest.

Must-See Historic Sites

Fuerte San Felipe del Morro★★★ *(Fort San Felipe del Morro)*

Calle del Morro, off western end of Calle Norzagaray, Old San Juan. 787-729-6960. www.nps.gov/saju. Open year-round daily 10am–5pm. $3.

This impenetrable fortress, all six levels of it, has repelled enemy fire since 1595, when Sir Francis Drake gave it a shelling. Jutting 140 feet above San Juan Bay, El Morro—its nickname—is a funhouse of towers, tunnels, dungeons, vaults and ramparts. But the bastion wasn't much fun for soldiers on duty; just look at the reconstructed barracks. To learn El Morro's history, watch the video in the museum.

Old San Juan★★★

Bounded principally by Calle Norzagaray and Paseo de la Princesa.

You won't feel hemmed in when you stroll around this walled town, all seven square blocks of which stretch southeast from massive El Morro fortress. You'll be too busy admiring the pastel-painted Spanish buildings, cobblestone streets, grand plazas and monuments that showcase the town's colonial past.

Touring Tip

If you're not up to walking, take the free trolley, which departs from La Puntilla and the Marina. Wait at one of the clearly visible stopping points along the route, or hail a trolley, if you see one, and it will stop to pick you up.

Bacardi Rum Distillery★★

Rte. 165 at km 6.2, Cataño. 787-788-8400. www.bacardi.com. Open year-round Mon–Sat 8:30am–5:30pm, Sun 10am–5pm.

The $7 million Casa Bacardi Visitor Center spirits guests away into the heart of 150 years of rum making. Not since Castro seized the family business in 1959 has so much of the Bacardi legacy been under one roof: a replica of the first still; a stunning reproduction of the company's first head-quarters; antiques and mementos; and a dazzling re-creation of the Art Deco Executive Bar, the celebrity "in spot" of 1930s Havana.

La Fortaleza★★   *(The Fort)*

Calle Fortaleza, Old San Juan. 787-721-7000. Open year-round Mon–Fri 9am–4pm. Closed Sat & Sun.

La Fortaleza (Spanish for "stronghold") was com-pleted in 1540 to guard San Juan's harbor. Over the years, numerous reconstruc-tions and renovations have transformed the building into a palatial mansion, where the island's governors have resided for centuries. You'll be shown the dun-geon here, and a few rooms reserved for official ceremonies, but the governor's quarters are off-limits (in order to safeguard the family's privacy). Be sure to see the Moorish-style gardens.

Mundillo Lace

The highly prized bobbin-lace called *Mundillo* is a 500-year-old art unique to Puerto Rico and Spain. You can see artisans in action making this fine lace at the Folk Arts Center in Old San Juan (in the old Dominican Convent next to the San Jose church at Beneficencia and Cristo Sts.). You can't purchase the lace here, but ask for a list of shops that sell it locally.

Secret Gardens

As you stroll the streets of Old San Juan, peek at its many private gardens, secreted behind elaborate gates and wrought-iron fences. These Seville-style sanctuaries brim with bright frangipani, hibiscus and orchids, soothing waterfalls, airy bird cages and lovely statuary. Magenta-colored bougainvillea spills over balcony rails.

Puerto Rico

Fuerte San Cristóbal★★ *(Fort San Cristóbal)*

off Calle Norzagaray, Old San Juan. 787-729-6960. www.nps.gov/saju.
Open year-round daily 9am–5pm. $3.

This 27-acre fort is even bigger than El Morro. Begun in 1634 to guard the town's eastern land approach, San Cristóbal is awash in tunnels, moats, dungeons, casemates, batteries and *garitas* (round sentry towers). Be sure to see the scale model of the fort, and climb up to the *caballero*, the platform where the cannon sit, for a panorama of the city and the bay.

Catedral de San Juan *(San Juan Cathedral)*

Corner of Calle del Cristo & Calle San Juan, Old San Juan. 787-722-0861. Open year-round
Mon–Sat 8am–5pm (Sun until 2pm).

Explorer Ponce de Léon lies buried here; his sepulchre sits in the transept of this cruciform-shape church. Dating to 1540, the cathedral, modified over time, bears a Spanish Colonial facade and vaulted Gothic ceilings. The church's lovely stained-glass windows have survived hurricanes and vandalism.

Must-See Museums

Museo de Arte de Puerto Rico★★★

299 De Diego Ave., Santurce, southeast of Old San Juan. 787-977-6277. www.mapr.org. Open year-round Tue–Sat 10am–5pm (Wed until 8pm), Sun 11am–6pm. $5.

Here you'll see how talented Puerto Ricans are. The Puerto Rico Art Museum, showcases paintings, sculpture, ceramics, photography and other works. In the east wing, you can't miss the stained-glass window by artist Eric Tabales—it's five stories high. And check out the 400-seat theater's curtain: it's made of lace.

Museo de Arte de Ponce★

Ave. de las Américas, Ponce. From Plaza de Las Delicias, take Calle Concordia 1.5mi south. 787-848-0505. www.museoarteponce.org. Open year-round daily 10am–5pm. $4.

European and American art in a Caribbean setting. That's what you'll find in Ponce's art museum, designed by 20C architect Edward Durell Stone. Some 3,000 works trace 600 years of art, including Italian Baroque and the Spanish Golden Age. Be sure to see the contemporary works by Latin American artists.

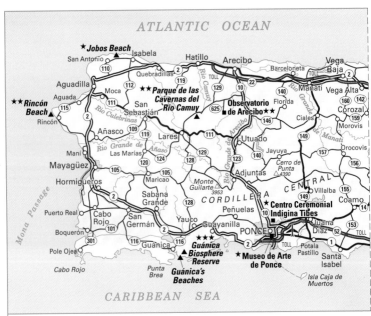

Hotels

1. Hyatt Dorado Beach Resort
2. Wyndham El Conquistador Resort

Must-See Gardens

Parque de las Cavernas del Río Camuy★★

Off Rte. 129, south of Arecibo (North Area). 787-898-3100. Open year-round Wed–Sun 8:30am–3:45pm. Closed Mon & Tue.

A great underground adventure awaits you at this 268-acre park. Explore subterranean caverns carved out by the Camuy River over a million years ago. Leave the sunshine behind as you hop aboard a trolley that descends 200 feet. Then walk with a guide through caves as tall as 150 feet, teeming with 1,000-year-old stalagmites and stalactites.

Jardin Botanico★

University of Puerto Rico campus, San Juan. Rtes.1 at Rte. 847. 787-250-0000. www.upr.clu.edu. Open year-round daily 9am–4pm.

"Flowers, flowers, everywhere" perfectly describes these gardens. Footpaths guide you through a lush, living laboratory blooming with more than 200 species of plants native to the island. Highlights include Egyptian papyrus, a bamboo promenade, a meditative lotus lagoon and an orchid garden.

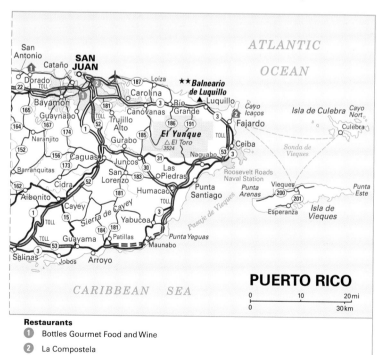

Restaurants

1. Bottles Gourmet Food and Wine
2. La Compostela

Musts for Kids

Observatorio de Arecibo★★ *(Arecibo Observatory)*

Rte. 129, Arecibo. Take Rte. 22 west from San Juan, then Rte. 129 south and follow signs.
787-878-2612. www.naic.edu. Open year-round Wed–Fri noon–4pm, weekends 9am–4pm.
Closed Mon & Tue, Jan 1, Jan 6 & Dec 25. $4.

Hold on to your eyeballs. You're about to see a
satellite dish bigger than 12 football fields! This
is the National Astronomy and Ionosphere
Center's cosmic listening post. Run by Cornell
University, the center houses the world's largest
radio telescope. Excellent science exhibits
explain the workings of the telescope, as well as
the cosmos. For even more fun, combine this trip with a visit to nearby Camuy
Caves Park, just 10 miles west of the observatory *(see Parks & Gardens)*.

Parque de las Ciencias Luis A. Ferre★

(Luis A. Ferre Science Park)

Rte. 167, in Bayamon. 787-740-6868. Open year-round Wed–Fri 9am–4pm, weekends &
holidays 10am–6pm. $5 adults, $3 children.

This 37-acre park offers thrills every minute. There's an aerospace museum with
NASA rockets, an archaeology museum displaying island artifacts, a transportation museum showcasing antique cars, an art museum filled with reproductions of
famous paintings, a natural-science museum for viewing mounted African animals,
a health pavilion devoted to the human body, a planetarium *($3 adults, $2 chil-*
dren), and a small zoo. Not enough? Pedal one of the paddleboats on the lake.

Museo del Niño *(Children's Museum)*

150 Calle Cristo (next to El Convento Hotel), Old San Juan. 787-722-3791.
www.museodelninopr.org. Open year-round Tue–Thu 9am–3:30pm, Fri 9am–5pm, Sat
12:30pm–5pm. Closed Sun & Mon.

Children have a blast at this interactive museum housed within a 300-year-old
villa. The exhibits encourage inquiring young minds to question how things
happen. They teach everything from the benefits of brushing teeth to the
reasons for recycling aluminum cans. There's a crafts area where a child's creativity can blossom. P.S.—Adults can relax while the kids explore.

Raspados (Snow Cones)

Loud horns and jingling bells announce the arrival of the snow-cone man, who navigates the streets with his brightly colored cart, weighted down by huge blocks of ice.
Rows of sweet syrups—some homemade, in fresh island pineapple, orange, strawber-
ry and mint flavors—line the cart. He shaves the ice into snow-like fluff, piles it into a
plastic cup and dowses it with syrup. For a true island treat, pay a little extra and ask
for condensed milk poured over the top. It's delicious—and wonderfully refreshing on
a sunny island day.

Must-See Beaches

Balneario de Luquillo★★

In Luquillo, 28mi east of San Juan.

This beach, a few blocks from Luquillos Plaza in the beach town of Luquillo, is touted as one of the most stunning in all of Puerto Rico: a mile-long stretch of pale, golden sand shaded by towering coconut palms. Reef-calmed waters, lifeguards, rest rooms and concession stands make Balneario Beach popular with families. At the east end, a "Sea without Barriers" facility offers trained staff and custom-designed equipment to provide travelers with disabilities easy access to the sea.

> **Touring Tip**
>
> All beaches in Puerto Rico are public. Some of them, called *balnearios*, are maintained by the government and are open all year-round Tuesday–Sunday 9am–5pm (they are closed Monday, unless the Monday happens to be a holiday).

Rincón Beach★★

In Rincón, 92mi west of San Juan.

Set smack dab in the midst of some of the world's best surfing waters, Rincón Beach may just be the crowning jewel of the island. Picture a backdrop of emerald hills, gin-clear waters, pale golden sands, and a mountain in the sea silhouetted by the setting sun. It's so famous with the surfer set that the Beach Boys wrote about Rincón in their hit tune, "Surfing Safari." In January and February, you can even spot humpback whales from the beach here.

Jobos Beach★

In Isabela, 72mi west of San Juan.

Isabela is a land of beaches, but world-famous Jobos Beach is the one that catches everyone's eye. It's a big, sandy beach where the water is only waist-high for the first 50 meters, making Jobos a perfect place for families with small children. In summer the water ranges from flat to choppy; in winter, the waves kick up, attracting droves of intermediate and advanced surfers. It's great fun to watch them ride the waves.

Guánica's Beaches

25mi west of Ponce by Rte. 2 west and Rte. 116 south. One of the most spectacular natural areas in Puerto Rico, **Guánica Biosphere Reserve★★★**, on the southwest coast, has been designated a World Biosphere Reserve by the United Nations. Within the reserve you'll find a shady beach and abandoned sugar-mill buildings, as well as 1,600-acre Guánica Forest. This uncommonly dry forest harbors 48 rare tree species and some 135 species of birds (it's internationally famous with bird-watchers).

Near the town of Guánica, touristy Copamarina Beach lures those seeking a day of sunbathing and snorkeling. Just past Balneario Caña Gorda, there's a dock where a ferry whisks you off to Gilligan's Island, favored by those in search of peace and quiet.

US Virgin Islands

A lively cruise port, Danish architecture and national parkland await those who venture here. Lying 13 miles east of Puerto Rico, the **US Virgin Islands**★★ (USVI) are an official territory of the United States; they neighbor their British counterparts in the northwest corner of the Caribbean Sea. Tourism—some 2 million visitors a year—centers on St. Thomas, St. John and St. Croix, the three largest of the 50 or so isles emerging from sapphire waters.

A Legendary Name

Arriving in 1493, Columbus named the Virgin Islands for the legend of St. Ursula, the daughter of a 4C British Christian king whose kingdom was threatened by the Huns. The pagan prince would spare the kingdom only if the beautiful princess married him. She consented on the condition that she first be allowed to gather 11,000 virgins and live with them for three years. Having no intention of marrying the Hun, Ursula trained the women to fight and took her army to Rome, where they pledged allegiance. The enraged prince and his army ambushed Ursula, killing her and all her female soldiers. Today Columbus' Virgin Islands are split between the US and the British Virgin Islands *(see p 80)*.

Three's the Charm

The three major islands of the US Virgin Islands are about as different from each other as they can be. Americanized **St. Thomas★,** the most visited isle, brims with fast-food chains and cruise-ship day-trippers who descend on

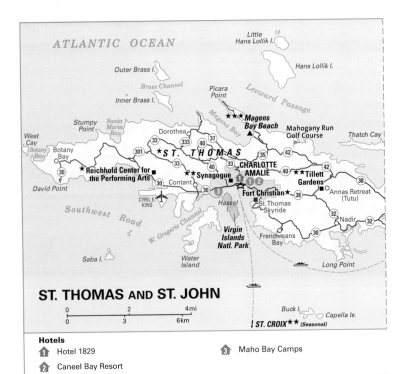

ST. THOMAS AND ST. JOHN

Hotels
1. Hotel 1829
2. Caneel Bay Resort
3. Maho Bay Camps

cosmopolitan **Charlotte Amalie** (ah-MAHL-ya) to shop the duty-free capital.
The popular St. Thomas Skyride *(340-774-9809; www.paradisepointtramway.com)*
is a great way to see the city's busy harbor from above. Much of stunning
St. John★★★ is a national park, boasting white-sand beaches, azure waters
and the world-class Caneel Bay resort. Sitting on its own 36 miles south of
St. Thomas, **St. Croix★★** is a tranquil, uncrowded place with a Danish-Caribbean
flair. Most of the faded yellow buildings in the capital city of **Christiansted** are
listed on the US National Registry of Historic Places. Dotted with windmills and
plantation ruins, St. Croix's countryside claims the grand vacation homes of the
rich and famous, from actress Maureen O'Hara to the Kennedys.

Restaurants

1 Fagioli Ristorante

2 Bumpa's

3 Craig and Sally's

4 The Palm Garden Café

Must Shop

Main Street and Back Street

One block north of St. Thomas Harbor, Charlotte Amalie, St. Thomas.

Shop 'til you drop in the swank stores and duty-free shops along these St. Thomas streets. Awash with brand names like Cartier, Gucci, Fendi and Mont Blanc, the stores specialize in gems, jewelry, cameras and perfumes. The charming alleys and side streets also hold unique boutiques and outdoor bars. A banana daiquiri may be in your future!

> **Touring Tip: Just Say "No"**
>
> In Charlotte Amalie, be prepared to face merchants who almost force you into their stores. Be firm with your "no, thank you" and stroll on. Don't let such aggressive behavior dampen your shopping.

S.O.S. Antiques

Royal Dane Mall, Charlotte Amalie, St. Thomas. 340-774-2074. www.lighthousemarinevi.com/sos.htm. Open year-round Mon–Sat 9am–5pm (open Sun afternoon if a cruise ship is in port).

Buzz Parlato, a commercial diver from Baltimore, came to St. Thomas as a charter boat captain, but switched to the salvage business. His inventory grew into an assemblage of nautical antiques, which he sells at this store. S.O.S. Antiques is filled with the likes of rare bronze thunder mugs, lighthouse lanterns, and a Spanish Armada chest from the 1600s used in the film *Pirates of the Caribbean*; there's a piratical parrot, named Taco Bell, on the premises.

Tillett Gardens – *See p 74. 4126 Anna's Retreat, St. Thomas.*

The shops at these gardens sell raku pottery, jewelry and other local crafts, and there's an art gallery showcasing water colors and oil paintings by local artists.

A Great Buy

In 1672, the Danish took control of the islands, establishing Charlotte Amalie in the name of their queen. By 1680 sugar estates dotted St. Thomas island. Centuries later, after the sugar industry faltered, Denmark put its islands up for sale. Concerned about potential enemy bases in the Caribbean during World War I, the US purchased the islands for $25 million in gold in 1917.

Must Be Pampered: Spas

The Self Centre at Caneel Bay

Caneel Bay Resort, Caneel Bay, St. John. 888-767-3966. www.caneelbay.com.

Take a slow, soothing dip into total relaxation. The Self Centre's devotion to nurturing guests' mental, physical and spiritual well-being is evident in its unique menu of mind/body therapies. Masters in healing arts offer sessions in such treatments as Thai yoga therapy, sound healing therapy, Jing Energy Flow Therapy, breathwalks, and for children, island drumming classes. The "Rhythm of Relationships" course brings couples closer through playful practices designed to awaken the senses.

The Ritz-Carlton Spa

6900 Great Bay, St. Thomas. 340-775-3333. www.ritzcarlton.com/resorts/st_thomas/spa.

Get that "spa-induced glow" at this intimate boutique spa, accented with a Mediterranean flair. An extensive spa menu offers massages that range from hot stone to modified Shiatsu. Try the spa's signature therapy: the Le Renovateur body treatment (a secret sunflower-based mixture brings a stimulating luster to the body). Choose to be pampered either in a serene treatment room or under an open-air cabana. End your visit by relaxing on the outdoor terrace, cooled by sea breezes.

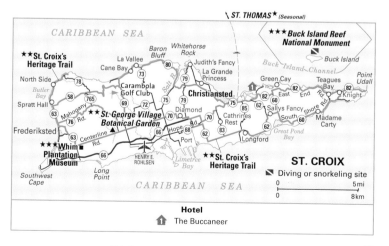

Must Go: Performing Arts

Caribbean Dance Company★★

Based in St. Croix. 340-778-8824.

To spark your island spirit, seek out this dance troupe, founded in 1977 to preserve the rich heritage of West Indian folk dance. Lively beats, haunting music, colorful costumes and stilt-dancing **mocko jumbies** *(see sidebar, below)* make for a dazzling performance you'll never forget. The company is based in St. Croix, but they often perform at the Reichhold Center for the Performing Arts *(opposite)* in St. Thomas. They have received international acclaim for their performances in the Americas (including Spoleto USA Festival in Charleston, South Carolina), Europe and throughout the Caribbean.

Tillett Gardens★★

4126 Anna's Retreat, St. Thomas. 340-775-1929. www.tillettgardens.com.

In 1959 British artist Jim Tillett arrived on St. Thomas and fell in love with an old Danish farm, which he described as "a peaceful sanctuary of creativity and wonderment." Over the years, he transformed the farm into a center dedicated to the visual and performing arts. Today Tillett Gardens encompasses two stages for theatrical productions and concerts, a music school, resident-artist studios, a marketplace for local arts and crafts *(see Must Shop)* and a restaurant surrounded by gardens.

Mocko Jumbies

Part of island culture for more than 200 years, the brightly costumed, stilt-dancing mocko jumbies trace their origin to 13C West Africa. Depending on the African language, the word "mock" usually means "healer" or "protector." The towering 10-feet- to 20-feet-high stilts traditionally worn by a mocko jumby gave him power to see approaching enemies or evil spirits in time to warn fellow villagers. A goat skin mask decorated in cowry shells kept his identity secret and inspired fear in the villagers, especially children.

When West African slaves landed in the Virgin Islands, colonists prohibited this ancient African art form. In the 1940s John Farrell and Fritz Sealy reintroduced the mocko jumby to the isles. In 1959, Alli Paul began a lifelong fascination with the practice. He introduced acrobatics to his stilt dance and toured the world, the first mocko jumby to do so. Today men, women, and children of all nationalities dress up and dance on stilts as mocko jumbies.

Reichhold Center for the Performing Arts★

Rte. 30, Brewer's Bay, St. Thomas. On the campus of the University of the Virgin Islands. 340-693-1550. www.reichholdcenter.com.

Such luminaries as concert violinist Itzhak Perlman and revered poet Maya Angelou have wowed audiences under the stars on the stage of this 1,200-seat outdoor amphitheater. Live theater and local folk-dancing performances are also winners in this peaceful venue that's cooled by sea breezes.

What's Quelbe?

It's the authentic rhythms of the Virgin Islands that date to the days of the African slave trade. Slaves were forbidden by colonists to perform their own dances or music. But the self-taught musicians, who made instruments from animal skins and discarded materials, learned to camouflage their *bamboula* rhythms and *cariso* melodies within traditional European jigs and military tunes. The resulting musical style became an integral part of their work, worship and celebration. In 1969 the local Cruzan (St. Croix) band "Stanley and the Ten Sleepless Knights" resurrected Quelbe. Today you can hear its lively beat in festivals throughout the islands.

Must Be Seen: Nightlife

Duffy's Love Shack

Downtown Cruz Bay, St. John. 340-776-6065. www.duffysloveshack.com.

You'll drink and dance under a thatched roof at this fun nightspot in Cruz Bay (where the ferry docks). Order potent drinks with names like Jaws or Baracuda Bomber to go with your Jamaican jerk nachos.

Epernay Bistro

24-A Honduras, Frenchtown, St. Thomas. 340-774-5348.

In the wine bar of this intimate bistro, you can order champagne by the glass with appetizers like caviar or brie with crostini. Then head to Epernay's roomy dance floor to do the calypso along with local islanders.

Greenhouse Bar and Restaurant

Waterfront Hwy., Charlotte Amalie, St. Thomas. 340-774-7998.

Well after the dinner hour is over, this large, popular burger joint converts to a dance venue, where patrons move to the reggae rhythms of a live band. Join in.

Iggies Beach Bar & Grill

Bolongo Bay Beach Club, Rte. 30, St. Thomas. 340-775-1800. www.bolongobay.com.

This rollicking beach bar packs 'em in for karaoke *(Thu & Sat)*, live music and dancing in the sand. Not enough diversion? Watch a game of night volleyball.

Musts for Outdoor Fun

Snorkeling Buck Island Reef National Monument★★★

2mi off the northeast shore of St. Croix.

Bright parrotfish, lavender sea fans, delicate angelfish, towering staghorn coral. Those are just a few of the things you'll see on this spectacular 19,015-acre nature preserve, which fills 176 acres on uninhabited Buck Island and 18,839 surrounding acres of clear water. Snorkeling trips to the spectacular coral reef off Buck Island's shores are among the best in the Caribbean; there's an easy, marked trail for novice snorkelers, yet the reef satisfies experienced divers. On the island itself, you'll find picnic tables, a gorgeous white-sand beach and a walking trail. Stay clear of the sticks of the manchineel tree *(see sidebar, below)*.

Driving St. Croix's Heritage Trail★★

St. Croix Landmarks Society, 52 Estate Whim, Frederiksted. 340-772-0598. www.stcroixheritagetrail.com.

The best way to become intimate with St. Croix is by renting a car and driving the 72-mile-long, self-guided tour that circles the island, linking the historic seaport of Frederiksted with Point Udall, the easternmost point of the US in the Western Hemisphere. One of 50 national Millennium Legacy Trails, the trail showcases the island's architecture, culture, history and natural sites. If you're lucky, you may have an opportunity to meet the locals and learn about their oral traditions, food and music. Trail brochures and maps are available from the St. Croix Landmarks Society.

Beware the Manchineel Tree

Found throughout the Caribbean, the native manchineel tree—a small tree with long, leathery leaves and yellow apples—is poisonous. *Never* touch a manchineel tree, or even stand under it when it rains (in case the sap should drip on you). Its sap, fruit, and even the smoke from its burning wood are highly toxic! Painful blisters result from contact—and possible blindness, if the smoke or sap gets in your eyes. Islanders often paint a skull and crossbones on the trunk to warn visitors.

Hiking Virgin Islands National Park★

*1300 Cruz Bay Creek, St. John. 340-776-6201. www.nps.gov/viis. Cruz Bay Visitor Center
open year-round daily 8am–4:30pm; closed Dec 25.*

Thank Laurance Rockefeller for placing three-fifths of St. John's 20 square miles
of emerald-green hills, white sandy beaches and plantation-era ruins into the
protective custody of the National Park Service. Explore this vast park on 22
easy-to-difficult hiking trails, or take a guided hike with a national park ranger.
Start with these two outstanding trails:

Annaberg Historic Trail★★ – This marked trail leads to the **Annaberg Sugar
Mill ruins**, a popular attraction on St. John. Your trek will be rewarded with the
c.1733 ruins of the mill, slave quarters and a sugar factory—and stunning views of
the azure sea and the British Virgin Islands. Oftentimes artisans demonstrate
island crafts or play music on old-time instruments. To extend your hike, continue on the unmarked trail to **Leinster Bay** over former sugar-plantation land.

Reef Bay Trail★ – The 2.5-mile path begins on Centerline Road, descends
through a shady forest and passes several sugar plantations. The ancient rock
carvings, or petroglyphs, made by the Taino Indians are the highlight. The trail
ends at Reef Bay sugar mill near Genti Bay.

Play a Round of Golf

The 18-hole championship course at **Mahogany Run** on
the north side of St. Thomas *(340-777-6006; www.
mahoganyrungolf.com)* is not only scenic, it's challenging. If you play here, you'll discover why its
signature trio—the 13th, 14th and 15th holes—is
named The Devil's Triangle. Golf great Robert Trent
Jones designed the 18-hole course at **Carambola
Golf Club** *(Davis Bay; 340-778-5638)*, set in a valley
along the north shore of St. Croix. Carambola's lush
fairways, accented with bright bougainvillea and
towering palms, roll past shimmering lakes.

Must-See Beaches

Magens Bay Beach★★★

On the north shore, St. Thomas. $3.

Islanders hail this mile-long stretch of powdery white sand as one of the best beaches on St. Thomas. Its shallow waters make great wading for kids. Water sports, a snack bar and a trail through a coconut grove are added amenities.

Salomon Bay Beach★★★

Near Cruz Bay, St. John.

For would-be beach bums, take the easy .7-mile Lind Point Trail from Cruz Bay to this off-the-beaten-path spot. Illegal nude sunbathing is no longer overlooked here: park rangers patrol the beach and issue tickets for baring it all.

Sapphire Beach★★

East end of St. Thomas, behind the Sapphire Beach Resort.

This wide expanse of snow-white sand lures sun worshippers; the water and wind draw windsurfers. If you want to try the latter, you can rent windsurfing equipment here, along with kayaks, jet skis and snorkel gear.

Trunk Bay Beach★★

Virgin Islands National Park, St. John. Open year-round daily 8am–4pm. $4.

This gorgeous beach fronting calm turquoise waters is world renowned for its talcum-powder-white sand and its 650-foot underwater trail. Expect monstrous crowds when cruise ships are in port on St. Thomas, though.

Touring Tip: No Shelling Allowed

Virgin Islands' law makes it illegal to collect shells from the beaches; if you do so, US customs officials will confiscate your finds. Keep receipts for store-bought seashells.

Must-See Historic Sites

Whim Plantation Museum★★★

Rte. 70, Estate Whim, southeast of Frederiksted, St. Croix. 340-772-0598.
www.stcroixlandmarks.com.Open year-round Mon, Wed, Fri & Sat. 10am–3pm. $6.

One of the best-preserved plantation estates in the whole Caribbean, Whim Plantation showcases a mid-18C manor, a cookhouse, a windmill and other buildings, ruins of a sugar factory and gardens where sugar cane is still grown. You can watch the cane being processed and listen as guides interpret life on an 18C sugar plantation.

Beracha Veshalom Vegmiluth Hasidim Synagogue★★

15 Crystal Gade, Charlotte Amalie, St. Thomas.

The current synagogue opened in 1833, replacing one of the oldest synagogues under the American flag, built in 1796. At the entrance, you'll see pillars formed of round bricks. Inside, the sand floor is said to symbolize the desert the ancient Hebrews wandered in for 40 years after their exodus from Egypt.

Fort Christian★

Waterfront Hwy., Charlotte Amalie, St. Thomas. 340-776-4566. Open year-round
Mon–Fri 8:30am–4:30pm. Closed weekends.

Fort Christian has guarded St. Thomas Harbor since 1672. The brick-red structure was built during Danish occupation, and has served as the first government house, a church and in other capacities. Today the National Historic Landmark is home to the **Virgin Islands Museum**, which displays island memorabilia. Climb to the top of the fort for a panoramic view of the harbor.

Must-See Gardens

St. George Village Botanical Garden★★

127 Estate St. George (off Centerline Rd.), St. Croix. 340-692-2874. www.sgvbg.org.
Open year-round daily 9am–5pm. $6.

Some 1,500 varieties of exotic and native plants—including palm trees, orchids, bromeliads and cactus—grace this former sugar plantation. Walk through the rain forest among heliconias and butterfly ginger.

British Virgin Islands

Ahoy, mateys! Drop anchor in the protected waters around the 60 islands and cays of the **British Virgin Islands**★★★ (BVIs to those in the know)—truly a boaters' heaven. Stretching 35 miles along Sir Francis Drake Channel, the sailing capital of the Caribbean lies 2 miles northeast of the US Virgin Islands. Whether you go by water or air, the BVIs are a relaxing place. The favorite pastime of the super-friendly locals is "liming," Caribbean slang for hanging out, and tuning in to the glorious sensations of the moment. So step ashore and prepare to de-stress.

BVI Lineup

Yachts and sailboats dot the bays of mountainous **Tortola**★★, the largest of the BVIs. Nearby **Beef Island** is home to the airport. Once the haunt of the Rockefellers, **Virgin Gorda**★★★ boasts posh hotels and **The Baths**★★★. Picturesque **Jost** (Yost) **Van Dyke**★ is world-famous for its beach bars and local characters. Tiny, roadless **Cooper Island** attracts charter boats. Privately owned **Peter Island**★ hosts an ultraluxurious resort. Virgin Airways' owner Richard Branson created a fantasy escape for the rich on his private **Necker Island**. Snorkelers love the underwater caves of unpopulated **Norman Island**. Off-the-beaten-path **Anegada** offers solitary beaches, bright-pink flamingoes and superb lobster.

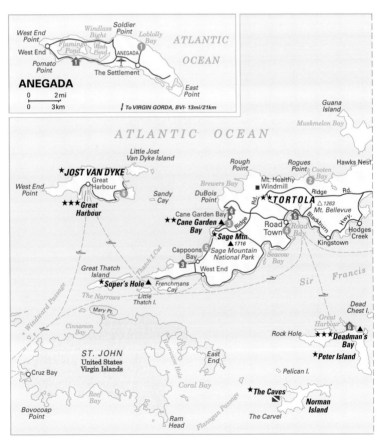

Musts For Outdoor Fun

Island Hopping

Ban the thought of staying landlocked! If you don't fancy being a skipper, ferries run regularly between Jost Van Dyke, Tortola, Peter Island and Virgin Gorda. Otherwise, charter a sailboat for a week or rent a power boat and zip off on your own. Turn the page for some of BVIs' best anchorages.

A Notorious Watering Hole

Sitting atop tiny Bellamy Cay in Trellis Bay on Beef Island, **The Last Resort** fills up with sailors ready for a cold one, while they listen to the bawdy ballads and "yachtie" jokes of Englishman comedian/owner Tony Snell. His rollicking, cabaret-style one-man show has been entertaining audiences for decades.

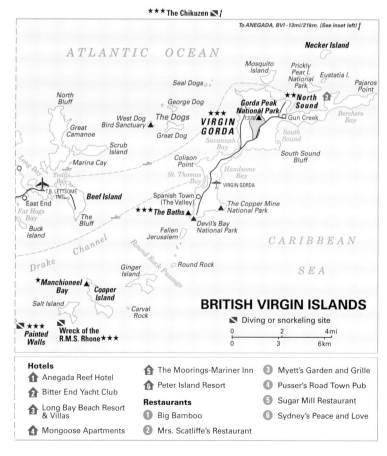

★★★ The Chikuzen ◪ /

To ANEGADA, BVI -13mi/21km. (See inset left) ↑

ATLANTIC OCEAN

Necker Island

Mosquito Island
Seal Dogs
Prickly Pear I. National Park
Eustatia I.
Pajaros Point

North Bluff

George Dog
West Dog The Dogs
Bird Sanctuary
Gorda Peak National Park
★★ **North Sound**
Gun Creek
Berchers Bay

Great Camanoe
Great Dog
★★★ **VIRGIN GORDA**
1370

Scrub Island
Savannah Bay
South Sound

Marina Cay
Colison Point
South Sound Bluff

Long Bay
Trellis Bay
St. Thomas Bay

T.B. LETTSOME INTL.
Beef Island
Handsome Bay
VIRGIN GORDA

East End
Fat Hogs Bay
The Bluff
Spanish Town (The Valley)
★★★ **The Baths**
The Copper Mine National Park

Buck Island
Fallen Jerusalem
Devil's Bay National Park

Drake Channel
Round Rock Passage
Ginger Island
Round Rock
CARIBBEAN

★ **Manchioneel Bay**
Cooper Island
SEA

Salt Island
Carval Rock

BRITISH VIRGIN ISLANDS

◪ ★★★ **Painted Walls**
◪ **Wreck of the R.M.S. Rhone** ★★★

◪ Diving or snorkeling site

0 — 2 — 4mi
0 — 3 — 6km

Hotels
🏠 Anegada Reef Hotel
🏠 Bitter End Yacht Club
🏠 Long Bay Beach Resort & Villas
🏠 Mongoose Apartments
🏠 The Moorings-Mariner Inn
🏠 Peter Island Resort

Restaurants
① Big Bamboo
② Mrs. Scatliffe's Restaurant
③ Myett's Garden and Grille
④ Pusser's Road Town Pub
⑤ Sugar Mill Restaurant
⑥ Sydney's Peace and Love

Deadman's Bay★★★

On the eastern tip of Peter Island.

Part of the posh, private-island resort that welcomes nonguests, this palm-lined, white-sand beach always ranks among the world's 10 most romantic beaches. It's an uncrowded paradise, with little noise and few children. Take a dip and discover great snorkeling at each end. A wonderful restaurant/bar overlooking Dead Chest, a small island with pirate ties, offers beach barbecues, live music and dancing in the sand.

Chartering a Boat

The following charter companies operate out of the BVIs. Rates vary according to boat, season and provisioning package; ask about special deals. Think twice before signing up for full provisioning (all the food you can eat in a week); you'll find good on-the-water restaurants along the way. Below are a few of the more well-known charter companies. For additional information, check online at: *www.b-v-i.com/charter*.

The Moorings – *Wickhams Cay II in Road Town, Tortola.* 888-952-8420. *www.moorings.com*. This company offers catamarans and monohulls ranging from 32-footers (perfect for a couple) to 61-footers with five cabins. Choose bareboat, captained or fully crewed. Get acquainted with your boat through The Friendly Skipper program: an experienced skipper takes you out for the first afternoon.

BVI Yacht Charters Ltd. – *Inner Harbour Marina, Road Town, Tortola.* 888-615-4006. Here you can rent 32- to 65-footers, mainly Dufours and Beneteaus for bareboat, captained, fully crewed, or all-inclusive charters.

Horizon Yacht Charters – *Nanny Cay Marina, Road Town, Tortola. www.horizonyacht charters.com*. Horizon's fleet of Beneteau Oceanis range from 44 to 57 footers, which come with a free first-day check-out skipper, if you need to brush up on your skills.

Virgin Traders Motor Yacht Charters – *Nanny Cay Marina, Road Town, Tortola.* 888-684-6486. *www.virgintraders.com*. If you want speed, this company offers a Horizon 82, Virgin Traders 44 and smaller Powercats.

Great Harbour★★★

South central Jost Van Dyke.

This pretty little harbor might just be *the* most popular one in the Caribbean—mainly because of Foxy Callwood and his open-air, hammock-strewn **Tamarind Bar**. To everyone's delight, he strums his guitar and sings calypso tunes. Foxy's Friday and Saturday barbecues are great, and his New Year's Eve parties, with entertainers like The Beach Boys, are world-famous *(see Calendar of Events)*.

Cane Garden Bay★★

North shore of Tortola.

Jimmy Buffet sings about this beautiful harbor, where tire swings hang from coconut palms and beach bars line the sand. Delve into water sports or take a stroll to discover Cane Garden Bay village.

North Sound★★

Eastern tip of Virgin Gorda.

This high-spirited hub of marine activity is accessible only by water. The gorgeous harbor is an off-the-beaten-path destination, brimming with adventures like sailing, diving, windsurfing, sea kayaking, parasailing and ultralight flying.

Manchioneel Bay★

Northwest shore of Cooper Island.

This laid-back "liming bay" has a popular beach bar that serves up delicious conch fritters and tasty lunches; it's a perfect spot for toasting the sunsets. Only one small resort, one local family and loads of goats inhabit the island.

Soper's Hole★

West End of Tortola.

Sail or drive to this spot to shop, sip rum at **Pusser's Landing** *(Frenchman's Cay)* and ogle the yachts.

Take a Dive

Get your scuba gear ready. The BVIs boast some prime **dive sites.** Here's a sampling:

The Chikuzen★★★ – *6mi north of Beef Island.* Touted as one of the BVIs' great dive sites, the 246-foot Japanese refrigeration ship, *The Chikuzen,* which sank in 1981, sits at a depth of 75 feet and teems with stingrays, horse-eye jacks and barracudas. The eerie site offers a great photo op for snapping octopi, giant rays and Goliath grouper.

The Painted Walls★★★ – *Off the southern point of Dead Chest Island.* The most photographed BVI dive site, these walls explode with color and spill down into three canyons, papered in neon-bright sponges and cup corals. An added bonus: peeks at flame scallops and Christmas-tree worms.

Wreck of the R.M.S. Rhone★★★ – *Salt Island, just upwind from Deadman's Bay, Peter Island.* In 1867 a hurricane ran the *Rhone*, the pride of the Royal Mail Steam Packet Company, into Salt Island, where it broke in two and sank. Now a marine park, the well-preserved wreck lies on a sandy bottom, home to tropical fish and corals. It's a great two-tank dive, and a good snorkel spot, too.

The Caves★ – *Tip of the peninsula between The Bight and Privateer Bay, Norman Island.* Curious snorkelers find these caves perfect for snorkeling. Extending 80 feet under the island, one cave offers adventure for night divers, even when the sun is shining. Nearby Angelfish Reef possesses remarkably clear waters and visibility at 90 feet, perfect for eyeing eagle rays and schools of angelfish.

The Caribbean Spiny Lobster

There's nothing better than munching on grilled spiny lobsters and washing them down with a fresh mango daiquiri. The lobster-bearing reefs surrounding Anegada have long supplied the tasty crustaceans to many Caribbean islands. For the freshest around, make a date with an outdoor grill on one of Anegada's famous bays.

Must-See Parks and Natural Sites

The Baths★★★

Lee Rd., along the southwestern shore of Virgin Gorda.

The star attraction of the BVIs, these house-sized boulders, toppled on each other and strewn along several coves, evoke a prehistoric setting. If you want to clamber, be careful—the rocks are slippery, but the rewards are many: secret niches lit by shafts of sunlight, clear tidal pools and cathedral-styled grottos. A top cruise-ship excursion, the spot gets really crowded, so go in the early morning or late afternoon.

Sage Mountain★

West-central Tortola.

The highest point in the Virgin Islands rises 1,716 feet above sea level within a 92-acre national park. Hikers have a field day listening for the sounds of Bo-peep frogs, spotting soldier crabs and watching hummingbirds hover around tropical flowers. Seven hiking trails through moist and dry forests, where the plants and trees are labeled, offer fabulous vistas—and solitude.

Gorda Peak National Park

North Sound Rd., Central section, Virgin Gorda.

Signs mark the two paths that lead to the peak, the highest on the isle at 1,370 feet. The first path ascends the mountain in a strenuous, 45-minute climb; the second path, a little farther down North Sound Road, offers a somewhat difficult 15-minute trek to the summit through heavy bush and woods. At the top, stand on the small observation deck to take in the stunning panorama of all of the islands, both US and British.

Must Shop

Sunny Caribbee

119 Main St., Road Town, Tortola. 284-494-2178. www.sunnycaribbee.com.

Housed in a bright little West-Indian structure, this shop overflows with tropical products concocted by the owners. Some 30 years ago, they started experimenting and came up with winners like coconut shampoo, mango tea, Caribee vinegars and their famous hot sauces—from Jerk Delight to XXX Calypso Hot. Stop next door to see paintings and hand-painted furniture from all over the Caribbean at the **Sunny Caribbee Art Gallery**.

The Lesser Antilles

With administrative ties to France, the Netherlands and the United Kingdom, the insular little worlds of the Lesser Antilles offer a wide range of landscapes, nuances of climate and diverse cultures. Ancient volcanoes, rugged coasts, arid deserts and white-sand beaches backdrop an equally diverse mix of West African, Dutch, French, Creole and British architecture, cuisine, and traditions. Strung out like a strand of pearls, this arc of more than 35 large and small islands stretches 750 miles from the Anegada Passage in the north to the waters off Venezuela, bordered by the Atlantic Ocean on the east and the Caribbean Sea on the west.

The Greater and the Lesser

The islands known as the **Greater Antilles** occupy the Western Caribbean (Cuba, Cayman Islands, Jamaica, Dominican Republic, Puerto Rico and the Virgin Islands). The **Lesser Antilles** make up the Eastern Caribbean, and consist of the French Antilles (Guadeloupe, Martinique, Saint-Barthélemy, Saint-Martin); the Netherlands Antilles (Aruba, Bonaire, Curaçao, Saba, Sint Eustatius, Sint Maarten); the United Kingdom's Anguilla and Montserrat; and the independent countries of Antigua and Barbuda, Barbados, the Federation of St. Kitts and Nevis, Dominica, Grenada, St.Lucia, St. Vincent and the Grenadines, Trinidad and Tobago. This chapter highlights selected islands in the Lesser Antilles *(other islands will be described under their own headings)*.

THE LESSER ANTILLES

The Valley
Anguilla (UK)
St-Martin/Sint Maarten ★★ (France/Neth.)
ATLANTIC
OCEAN
Gustavia ○ St-Barthélemy ★★ (France)
The Bottom
○ Saba ★ (Neth.)
Sint Eustatius (Neth.)
★ Barbuda
★★ St. Kitts Basseterre
ANTIGUA & BARBUDA
★★ Nevis
St. John's ○
0   50mi
0   50km
★ Antigua

What's in a Name?

In the Middle Ages, the term "Antila" was used to describe a legendary island in the middle of the Atlantic Ocean. After Columbus' voyages, the Spanish preferred "Indies" for their newly discovered continent of America *(see History)*. The Lesser Antilles themselves were sometimes called "The Cannibal Islands" due to mispronunciation of the word "Caribbean." During the 17C and 18C, the term "Antilles" was still seldom used; the archipelago was normally described as the "West Indies" or "American Isles." It was not until the French Revolution in 1789 in France that the term Antilles came into common use.

Anguilla

Shaped like an eel (*anguille* in French), this coral island (19 miles long and 3 miles at its widest) is famous for its beaches, its crystalline waters and its undersea world. With some 45 white-sand beaches lining its quiet bays and inlets, Anguilla may well be the beautiful beach capital of the Caribbean.

Must-See Beaches

Rendezvous Bay★★★

West Shore.

Intertwined with salt marshes, this bay—and its mile-long strip of white sand—is one of the dreamy, away-from-it-all beaches for which Anguilla is justly famous. To the southwest lies **Maunday's Bay★**, a splendid half-moon cove, a veritable Eden of clear waters and sparkling sand. Farther north, **Meads Bay★** beach is caressed by the gentle waves.

> **Touring Tip**
>
> Topless and nude sunbathing are illegal on Anguillan beaches; the law is strictly enforced. Show respect by covering up before venturing into the shops and restaurants from the beach.

Shoal Bay East★★

North Shore.

This beach is renowned for its fine-grained quartz sand. Turquoise waters add to its beauty, but day-trippers, live music and beer joints diminish its appeal for those seeking solitude.

Stoney Bay Marine Park

In 1986 a local fisherman swam upon the remains of *El Buen Consejo*, a 960-ton Spanish galleon that was shipwrecked off the southeastern shores of the island in 1772. Today the site has been designated an Underwater Archeological Preserve *(http://spanishgalleon.ai)* by the government of Anguilla. Littered with cannon, anchors and devotional medals (the ship was carrying 50 friars), the intact wreck makes the dive of a lifetime. Shoal Bay Scuba & Watersports offers diving expeditions for this preserve *(www.shoalbayscuba.ai)*.

Must Be Seen: Nightlife

The Dune Preserve

Rendezvous Bay. Turn at the road between Anguilla Great House and Sonesta resort. 264-497-2660. www.dunepreserve.com.

This famous beach bar was built from old boats, driftwood and other flotsam and jetsam by Bankie Banx. The Anguilla native is a renowned reggae artist, who often jams here. Music lovers from around the globe show up for his yearly Moonsplash—three days of partying to live music under the full moon *(Mar)*.

Sandy Ground Village

Located between North Hill and South Hill, Sandy Ground is the island's hotspot for local nightlife. Here's a sampling of its lively clubs:

Johnno's Beach Shop – *264-497-2728.* Johnno's is considered the best "jump up" on the island (a Caribbean tradition where you just jump up and dance). You'll find yourself jivin' in the sand or on the piers jutting out over the water.

> **Mayoumba Folkloric Theatre**
>
> This is the troupe that keeps Anguilla's pre-20C music, dance, storytelling and costumes alive. Elaborate productions are staged year-round, but you can catch their show at La Sirena Hotel in Meads Bay *(Thu 9pm; 264-497-6827; www.la-sirena.com).*

The Pumphouse – *264-497-5154.* This place rocks nightly after the restaurant shuts down at 10pm, but on Saturdays, when the live local band Reggae Groovers plays, the roof nearly blows off!

Must Shop

Anguilla Arts and Crafts Center

Next to the library in The Valley. 264-497-2200. Open year-round Mon–Fri 9am–4pm. Closed weekends.

The building with gingerbread trim sitting to the right of the library is *the* place to find locally made souvenirs such as hot sauces, jams, ceramics, needlework and gifts crafted from shells. Check out the unusual homemade flower wines.

Cheddie's Carving Studio

The Cove. On the main road west at the Cove Rd. intersection. 264-497-6027. www.cheddieonline.com. Open year-round Mon–Sat 10am–6pm. Closed Sun.

Anguilla-born Cheddie Richardson scours local beaches for limestone and other natural materials. He carves them into sculptures of birds and other island wildlife. One of his sleek dolphins carved from driftwood was presented on behalf of the Anguillan people to Queen Elizabeth when she visited the island.

Saint-Martin★★/Sint Maarten★★

One island, two personalities: French and Dutch. Lying 5 miles south of Anguilla, this 35-square-mile island is the world's smallest island divided into two sovereign states. Here the French and the Dutch coexist so peacefully that there is no border crossing. The French zone, with its capital in **Marigot**, occupies the northern part of the island. Sint Maarten, with its capital based in **Philipsburg**, forms the southern part. In the last 30 years, the island has become a top destination for international travelers in search of duty-free shops, Las Vegas-style casinos, authentic French restaurants and white-sand beaches.

The Tipsy Dutchman

According to folklore, instead of fighting to establish the border, the early Dutch and French settlers each sent one of their own citizens to walk the perimeter of the island. The point where their paths crossed would be the border. Armed with a flask of gin, the Dutch representative headed south; carrying a carafe of wine, the French designee headed north. The Frenchman walked faster, gaining 21 square miles to the Dutchman's 16 square miles. Some say the gin got the better of the Dutchman.

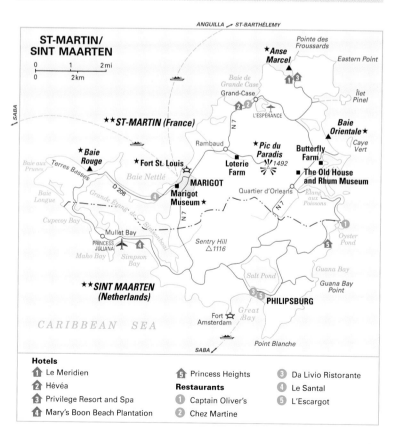

Hotels

1. Le Meridien
2. Hévéa
3. Privilege Resort and Spa
4. Mary's Boon Beach Plantation
9. Princess Heights

Restaurants

1. Captain Oliver's
2. Chez Martine
3. Da Livio Ristorante
4. Le Santal
5. L'Escargot

Must-See Beaches

Anse Marcel★ *(Marcel Cove)*

Northwest Grande Terre, Saint-Martin. After passing L'Esperance Airport, take the road on your left; drive 1 mi and turn left.

This beautiful cove and its golden sand were wilderness only 10 years ago. Today the beach hosts a marina and a vast hotel complex, Le Méridien. The beach lies within the hotel perimeter, but you can access the sands here even if you're not staying at the hotel *(see the warden at the estate entrance).* The gentle waves are ideal for youngsters.

Baie Orientale★ *(Orient Bay)*

Northeast Grande Terre, Saint-Martin. About a half-mile before the Quartier d'Orléans, Saint-Martin.

Probably the best-known beach on the island, this mile-long stretch of fine sand attracts a lot of tourists. Rent some beach chairs and an umbrella and take in the scene. The seashore is lined with hotels, restaurants, bars, fashion boutiques and water-sports pavilions (windsurfing, surfing, diving, jet-skiing, water-skiing). You won't need a swimsuit at the nearby Club Orient Naturist Resort.

Baie Rouge★ *(Red Bay)*

Grande Terre, Saint-Martin. Just west of Baie Nettlé, make an abrupt turn and take the dirt road.

Powerful waves batter the golden sands of this vast beach, which enjoys a beautiful location. There's no shade here, but you can rent beach umbrellas to shield you from the sun.

A Real Crab Race

Ready your bets! Come high season, high-spirited crowds throng Orient Bay Beach to cheer on hermit crabs in the annual crab race. A circle is etched in the sand, the entrants paint their name or a number on the back of their hermit crabs' shell, and place the crabs at the "starting gate." The first three crabs to cross the circle and step over the finish line win!

Must-See Historic Sites

Fort Saint-Louis★

North of Marigot village, Saint-Martin.

Climb to the summit of the hill to visit the ruins of this fort, the largest historical landmark in Saint-Martin. Built by the French in 1767 to ward off invaders, it was briefly occupied by the Dutch during the French Revolution.

Loterie Farm

Rte. de Pic du Paradis, Saint-Martin.
590-87-86-16. www.loteriefarm.com.
Open year-round daily dawn to dusk. $5.

Located at the base of 1,492-foot **Pic du Paradis★** (Paradise Peak), this farm was converted into a 150-acre nature preserve by an ex-Californian. As you hike its forested trails, you'll see mango, guavaberry and mammy (apricot) trees, as well as waterfalls and birds. The renovated main house dates to 1721.

> **The Hope Estate**
>
> Archaeologists are constantly digging up history on Hope Estate plateau. Artifacts discovered here date to 1800 BC and include the oldest remains of the Ciboney, who arrived in 800 BC. Excavations at this site have uncovered a village, ceramics and costumes of the first people to bring pottery and horticulture to the plateau. If you want a closer look at some of the artifacts, visit the **Marigot Museum★** *(Rte. de Baie Nettlé, Saint-Martin; 590-29-22-84; open Mon–Sat 9am–1pm & 3pm–6pm; closed Sun).*

Must-See Museums

The Butterfly Farm

Le Galion Beach Rd., Quartier d'Orléans, Saint-Martin. 590-87-31-21.
www.thebutterflyfarm.com. Open year-round daily 9am–3pm. $10.

Watch caterpillars transform into butterflies at this living museum. Then wander through tropical gardens and waterfalls (covered by large mesh enclosures) populated with colorful, exotic butterflies from many parts of the globe.

The Old House and Rhum Museum

On the road between Orléans and Orient Bay, Saint-Martin. 590-87-32-67.
Open year-round daily 9am–4pm.

See how the richer half lived in this 18C Creole-style house, once occupied by the master of a sugar plantation belonging to the island's Beauperthuy family. Descendents of the family have opened it to the public to showcase original family antiques and other remnants of Saint-Martin's heyday. Next door stands the **Rhum Museum**, where old bottles, labels and a recipe of rum made in years gone by are on display. Sign the "gold book" in the wake of Queen Juliana of Holland and other notables.

Must Shop

Greenwith Galleries

33 Front St., Philipsburg, Sint Maarten. 599-542-3842. Open year-round Mon–Sat 10am–6pm.

Opened in 1985, Greenwith Galleries specializes in Caribbean art. The works of some 35 island artists are on hand in the form of paintings, pottery and prints.

Guavaberry Shop

8-10 Front St., Philipsburg, Sint Maarten. 599-542-2965. www.guavaberry.com.

This colorful Creole house, once the governor's residence, serves as the headquarters of the Guavaberry Company, which makes its namesake liqueur from rum, sugar and guavaberries on the premises. The emporium sells fanciful bottles of the liqueur, rum and condiments. Bring home a jar of banana jam or mango chutney for your foodie friends.

Nanette Bearden Fine Arts Gallery

Maho District, Simpson Bay, Sint Maarten. 599-543-1540.

The wife of renowned 20C American artist Romare Bearden, dancer-choreographer Nanette Rohan-Bearden, owns this art gallery. Relocated from Philipsburg in 2004, the gallery specializes, of course, in the paintings of Romare Bearden, who spent 17 years on the island. Many of his works on view here depict life on Sint Maarten.

Roland Richardson's Gallery

6 Rue de la République, Marigot, Saint-Martin. 590-87-32-24. www.rolandrichardson.com.

When you walk into this gallery, you may find local artist Roland Richardson putting the finishing touches on a still life in his studio at the back. His colorful canvases capture the beauty of Saint-Martin's meadows, flowers and dwellings. If you like what you see, you can purchase his oils, watercolors, pastels here.

Must Be Seen: Nightlife

Take a Gamble

Most island casinos are on the Dutch side—13 of them, in fact. A few are open for day play, but the action gets into high gear at night. Here's a sampling:

> ### Touring Tip: Spanish 21
>
> If you're an experienced player and want to gamble on something new, try "Spanish 21," a challenging combination of blackjack and poker played only in Sint Maarten, at the Port de Plaisance Resort in Cole Bay.

Atlantis – *Cupecoy Beach, Rhine Rd. 106, Sint Maarten. 599-545-4601. www.atlantis world.com.html.atlantis.* Place your bets amid an ancient mariner theme à la the Lost Continent of Atlantis. This casino is nothing if not lively—with flashing lights and the clink of coins dropping from slots. High rollers head to the private gaming rooms to bet their fortunes on baccarat, French roulette and seven-card-stud poker.

Casino Royale – *Maho Beach Resort, Maho Bay, Sint Maarten 599-545-2115. www.mahobeach.com.* The table limits at this huge hotel are $2,000 for blackjack and $500 for craps. In high season, the hotel hosts Las Vegas-style shows from Latin reviews to circus acts.

Coliseum Casino – *74 Front St., Philipsburg, Sint Maarten. 599-543-2101.* The decor of this three-floor casino is patterned on ancient Rome. The Coliseum has it all—from slot and poker machines to private rooms with serious betting on Caribbean stud poker and other high-stakes games.

Diamond Casino – *Front St., Philipsburg, Sint Maarten 599-543-2583. www.diamond casinosxm.com.* Park yourself in front of the bank of 250 slot machines at lively Diamond Casino. The betting gets exciting at tables that offer everything from roulette to blackjack.

Local Bands

When you're in Sint Maarten, make a point to hear these local entertainers: **King Beau-Beau**, Sint Maarten's equivalent of Elvis Presley; **Neville York**, a steel-band virtuoso; and **Tanny and the Boys**, who pound out Latino and African rhythms on handmade instruments.

Wanna Dance?

Here are a few of the island's hippest spots for dancing to a pulsing beat, be it DJ tunes, live music or spicy Latin rhythms:
- **Bliss** – *Caravanserai Beach Resort, Beacon Hill #2, Maho District (near the airport), Sint Maarten. 877-796-1002.*
- **Cheri's Café** – *45 Cinnamon Grove Shopping Centre, Maho District, Sint Maarten. 599-545-3361.*
- **L'Atmo Village** – *Marina Royale, Marigot, Saint-Martin. 590-87-98-41.*

Saba★

Don't expect beaches or posh hotels on this five-square-mile extinct volcano, the smallest island of the Netherlands Antilles. Sitting just 28 miles southwest of Saint-Martin/Sint Maarten, Saba (SAY-bah) is the place for beautiful landscapes, hiking trails and the warm welcome of its 1,500 residents. The island's official language is Dutch, but everyone speaks English.

On the Fly

Located on Flat Point—a tongue of land jutting into the sea—Saba's **Juancho E. Yrausquin Airport** features what may be the world's shortest runway—only 1,312 feet long. Flying in to Saba is one of its thrills; there's a reason that shops on the island sell T-shirts proclaiming: "I survived the Saba landing." In the shed used as a terminal, a showcase presents the types of airplane that can land on this tiny airstrip.

Musts for Outdoor Fun

Take a Scenic Drive

Hire a taxi (at the airport) to take you along **The Road** (the island's main road), with its 15 hairpin curves. In the small village of **Hell's Gate**, you'll see stone or picket fences, small country gardens and typical Saban cottages: white houses with green trim and red-tiled roofs. In **Windwardside**, stop at the former home of a sea captain, now the **Henry L. Johnson Museum**, which displays antiques and furniture. Then continue to the hillside village of **St. John's**. Before beginning your descent, look down from the road's edge to see what is believed to be the main crater of Saba's volcano. Continue to **The Bottom**, the tiny, sleepy capital with several official buildings, nestled in a valley. Turn south on the road—watch out for sheep or iguanas—that runs through a gorge. The 800-foot descent leads to **Fort Bay**, the base of dive operations for **Saba Marine Park**, which encircles the island.

> **Touring Tip**
>
> Take this scenic drive on Sunday afternoons, when you can either watch or play croquet—an island tradition. Be sure to wear white, the attire of choice for croquet (and be careful not to spill your Mimosas!).

Take a Hike

Saba's many marked trails (Boiling House, Booby Hill, Mary's Point and Mt. Scenery, to name a few) vary in difficulty, but all have rest stops. Pick up a brochure and find a guide *(all-day hike $50)* at the Saba Conservation Foundation's **Trail Shop** *(599-416-2630)*, located behind the tourist office in Windwardside.

Sint Eustatius

Like Saba, Sint Eustatius is a small, volcanic island in the Netherlands Antilles. Nearly 12 square miles in size, the island lies 33 miles south of Sint Maarten. The official language of "Statia" (its nickname) is Dutch, but everyone speaks English. In **Oranjestad**, the capital, planters pass by on donkeys and houses sport gingerbread trim.

Days of Glory

In 1780 Sint Eustatius was a bustling port; it was common for 200 ships to be waiting in the harbor to unload legal—or smuggled—cargo. In fact Statia smuggled arms and supplies to the Americans during the Revolutionary War. You can see blue-glass beads used as trading money and other artifacts from the island's heyday in the **Sint Eustatius Historical Foundation Museum** *(Upper Town, Oranjestad; 599-318-2288)*.

Musts for Outdoor Fun

Dig up the Past

Take part in an ongoing dig. Wanna-be archaeologists can work at island sites such as Pleasure Estate, an active sugar plantation from 1742 to 1977, or a pre-historic Amerindian site. Sign up online with the Sint Eustatius Center for Archaeological Research at www.secar.org.

Scuba Dive in Statia Marine Park

West side of the island, near Lowertown.

Looking for a thrill? You'll find it when you spy bits of an antique plate or maybe a clay pipe below the waters of this national park, where, two centuries ago, some 200 ships sank. A number of the shipwrecks are popular dive sites. Don your gear to see the barracuda, spotted moray eels, schools of snapper, eagle rays and black-tip sharks that swab the decks now.

Dive Partners

These dive companies are authorized to operate within Statia Marine Park waters:
• **Caribbean Explorer** *(800-322-3577; www.caribexplorer.com)*
• **Dive Statia** *(599-318-2435; www.divestatia.com)*
• **Golden Rock Dive Center** *(599-318-2964; www.goldenrockdive.com)*
• **Scubaqua** *(599-318- 2345; www.scubaqua.com)*

Walk into a Volcanic Crater

Attention hikers! Take the most popular trail on the island: a 2000-foot ascent to the dormant volcano called **The Quill**. Stop for a breather and then hike down 900 feet into the crater, where a lush rain forest shelters rare orchids, bromeliads, raspberry bushes, giant elephant-ear plants and other flora.

Saint-Barthélemy★★

The Paris of the Caribbean, tiny **Saint-Barthélemy** packs a wallop of *la bonne vie*: sophisticated, upscale (read expensive) and very French. The 5-mile-long island sits 19 miles southwest of Sint-Maarten. For centuries, its sparse, mostly white popula-tion—largely from Brittany and Normandy—lived in relative isolation. But thanks to Old-World charm, beautiful beaches and duty-free shopping, St-Barts—as it's affectionately called—is now a thriving tourist mecca and playground for the well-heeled. The hot spot is **Saint-Jean**, a north shore enclave of posh hotels, boutiques and places to be seen. Dotted with red-roofed houses, the capital, **Gustavia**, was named for a Swedish king when that country controlled the island (1784 to 1878). Hope you've brushed up on your French—they don't speak much English here!

Touring Tip: Parlez-Vous Française?

Attempt a little French during your visit; it will go a long way with the locals.

Hello – Bonjour. . . *boh(n) zhoor*
Goodbye – Au revoir. . . *oh ruh-vwahr*
How are you? – Ça va?. . . *sah-vah*
Excuse me – Pardon. . . *pahrdoh(n)*
How much, please? – Combien, s'il vous plaît. . . *koh(m)byeh(n), seel voo pleh*
The check, please – L'addition, s'il vous plaît. . . *lah-dee-ssyohn, seel voo pleh*
Thank you very much – Merci beaucoup. . . *mehr-see boh-koo*
Where's the beach? – Où est la plage?. . . *oo eh lah plahzh*
Your island is very pretty – Votre île est très jolie. . . *vohtruh eel eh treh jōh-lee*

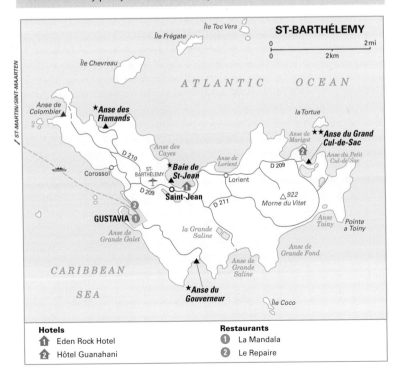

Hotels

🏨 Eden Rock Hotel
🏨 Hôtel Guanahani

Restaurants

❶ La Mandala
❷ Le Repaire

Must Shop

Boutique Paradoxe

Rue du General de Gaulle, Gustavia and Villa Creole, St-Jean. 590-27-84-98.

Ladies' shoes to die for! Need we say more?

Iléna

Villa Creole, St-Jean. 590-29-84-05.

This wild and wonderful boutique is filled
with the softest and sexiest French lingerie
you can imagine, as well as French swim-
wear that's sure to make heads turn on any
beach. Add a spritz of French perfume
and—*ooh la la.*

Ligne de St. Barth

Rte. de Saline, L'Orient. 590-27-82-63. Rue de Bord de Mer, Gustavia. 590-52-48-29.
www.lignestbarth.com.

You don't have to go to the world's best spas to experience this coveted line
of skin-care products; you can buy them on St. Barts. These much-in-demand
lotions and suntan oils are made on the island from plants, fruits and flowers
native to the Caribbean. Fresh papaya, for example, is whipped into a fragrant
moisturizer, and the seeds of the native *roucou* (a fruit tree bearing red pods)
are pulverized into sunscreen lotion.

Lolita Jaca

Le Carré d'Or, Gustavia. 590-27-59-98. www.lolitajaca.com.

The door opens to a feast of colorful fabrics and the heavenly scent of in-
cense. This tiny boutique specializes in hand-designed clothes with a classy,
Middle-Eastern flair. Tunics, kimonos, Moroccan djellabas (a long, hooded
garment with full sleeves) and other women's wear come in one-size-fits-all.
Don't overlook the satiny slippers.

Made in St-Barth

La Villa Creole, St-Jean. 590-27-56-57.

The women of the fishing village of Corossol, about one mile north of Gustavia, are known for the quality handicrafts they weave from the fibers of the
red latan palm tree. You can purchase their hats, handbags and baskets at this
store, as well as local works of art.

Touring Tip: Sale Days

If you're on St-Barts in June, you're in luck: everything goes on sale in the stores this
month! Designer brands like Polovich are marked down 50% to 70%. Most shops
close for lunch *(from noon to 2pm)*, but stay open until 7pm.

The Lesser Antilles

Must-See Beaches

Anse du Grand Cul-de-Sac★★ *(Grand Cul-de-Sac Cove)*

Northeast shore, off Rte. D 209.

This beach is breathtaking. A sand bar encloses the bay, creating a separate body of water the color of a Polynesian lagoon. Waves break gently on coral reefs offshore, making the calm waters here ideal for children. The coconut grove of the Guanahani Hotel *(see Must Stay)* shades the northwest section of the beach, and intermittent high winds attract windsurfers and kite boarders *(see sidebar, opposite)*.

Kite Boarding

This hot new water sport is hugely popular on St-Barts, especially off the shores of the Guanahani Hotel. Sip champagne at La Paillote *(open daily 8am–7pm)*, the hotel's beach bar, and watch the kite boarders in action. Harnessed to an elevated sail, they plant their feet on a short board as they alternately skim the surf and ride the winds.

Anse des Flamands★ *(Flemish Cove)*

Northwest shore, off Rte. D 210.

Beckoning sunbathers with finely grained sand, this beach is lined with coconut trees, private houses and a hotel. If you're an inexperienced swimmer, be careful—the waves can be strong at times. Around the point separating Anse des Flamands and Petite Anse, the seabed is worth exploring—so take your diving gear.

Leave That Bikini Top at Home

Topless sunbathing, in the French tradition, is legal on St-Barts' beaches. So ladies have the option to bare their chest. Nudity, however, is against the law on the island.

Anse du Gouverneur★ *(Governor's Cove)*

South-central coast. Accessible through a dead-end road south of Gustavia, beyond the Carl Gustav hotel.

This lovely place shows off white sand and red latan palms. Its sunbathers show off as well, since nudity is common, though not legal *(see sidebar, above)*, on the secluded beach. Not all eyes are on those well-tanned bodies—views of neighboring Saba and Sint Eustatius command a steady gaze.

Baie de Saint-Jean★ *(Saint John Bay)*

Saint-Jean, Rte. D 209.

The postcard-perfect white sand and half-moon curve of shoreline here would be ideal—if it weren't for their proximity to the airstrip. Some people like to bask in the sun while watching the aerobatics of planes landing on the island. Baie de Saint-Jean's waves and a windsurfing club attract thrill seekers who come to challenge the surf.

St. Kitts★★ and Nevis★★

Twice the fun. Just a ferry hop apart, the islands of St. Kitts and Nevis (NEE-vis) offer two-for-one adventure. Part of the British Commonwealth, the dynamic duo makes up an independent federation ruled by a governor general appointed by the Queen. British influence can be seen, for example, in the Nevisian passion for cricket, and in **Basseterre's**—St. Kitts' capital—traffic roundabout, patterned on London's famed Piccadilly Circus. Called the Maui of the Caribbean, Nevis is nurtured by lush rain forests that hug the velvety-green slopes of Nevis Peak; the island's liveliest hub is **Charlestown**, the capital. St. Kitts is a little busier (but not much), with more shopping venues, and a casino at the base of Mt. Liamuiga (Lee-a-MWEE-gah), a dormant volcano.

Touring Tip: Outdoor Markets

If you want to get to know the locals, go to Saturday market *(Bay Rd. in St. Kitts; downtown Charlestown in Nevis; open year-round Mon–Sat)*, a place of lively chatter, with as many as three generations of women manning one stall. Don't insult them by trying to bargain, though.

Hotels

1 Golden Lemon Inn & Villas
2 The Hermitage
3 Montpelier Plantation Inn
4 Ocean Terrace Inn
5 Ottley's Plantation Inn

Restaurants

1 Ballahoo
2 Bayembi Café
3 Café des Arts
4 The Dining Room at The Four Seasons
5 Miss June's Cuisine
6 Sunshine's Beach Bar & Grill

Musts For Outdoor Fun

Dr. Kennedy Simmonds Highway★★

Leave Basseterre, St. Kitts, by Pond Rd., heading south to Frigate Bay, where the highway begins.

Rent a car to experience this scenic drive along St. Kitts' peninsula—the narrow strip of land at the island's southern end. Mostly deserted, the wide paved road runs six miles from Frigate Bay to Majors Bay through the wildest landscape on the island. You'll be treated to vistas of hills covered with dry grass anchored by brackish ponds, and virgin beaches nestled in picturesque bays, dominated by the pyramidal mass of Nevis Peak. Stop at the small parking area on Sir Timothy's Hill for a stunning view of the peninsula and its beaches. Below, in the foreground, you'll notice the stagnant waters of the Salt Ponds. *Return to the crossroads and turn left.* The road ends at the low point of **Majors Bay**, a cove with a creek.

Nevis Peak★★

Center of the island, Nevis.

This mountain has the feel of sacred ground—a silent, godlike presence that pervades the whole island. An ascent up this dramatic 3,232-foot peak is a challenging hike that lands you at the crater of a dormant volcano. If you're not up to it, there are easier hikes through the mountain's rain forests, with guides. Our favorite guides are Jim Johnson *(869-469-9080)*, with three science degrees, and walking-encyclopedia Nevisian Lynell Liburd *(869-469-2758)*.

Nevis Turf and Jockey Club★

Indian Castle Race Track, Gingerland, Nevis. One Sunday a month, usually on a holiday, at 2pm. For more information, contact The Hermitage Plantation Inn: 869-469-3477.

Horse racing is second only to cricket in popularity here, so arrive early and place your $2 bet on a minimum of five races. Then cheer for your pick of the island's thoroughbreds as they race this sandy oceanside track, where a goat or donkey occasionally slips into the pack.

> #### Touring Tip
> After the races, stay on at the Nevis Turf and Jockey Club for the barbecue, cold Caribbean beer and dancing that lasts into the night—it's a tradition.

Carriage Rides

Carriages depart from The Hermitage Inn, Gingerland, Nevis. 869-469-3477. $60.

Succumb to the clippety-clop of Belgian horses pulling an authentic adaptation of a mid-19C Creole carriage, made of West Indian mahogany. This relaxing carriage ride will take you back to a bygone era, as you travel the island's countryside and take in grand views of local villages, Nevis Peak and the sea.

Four Seasons Resort Nevis Golf Course

Pinney's Beach, Nevis. 869-469-1111. www.fourseasons.com/nevis/vacations.

This 18-hole championship golf course, designed by Robert Trent Jones Jr., is touted as one of the most beautiful in the Caribbean, with exceptional views throughout. The course coils up the slope of Nevis Peak to its signature hole 15, an awe-inspiring 450 feet above the sea; then it rolls downhill to the beach. A putting green, chipping area and driving range are located close to the pro shop.

Must-See Gardens

Botanical Garden of Nevis★★★

Cole Hill, south of Charlestown, Nevis. From the main road, turn right towards Montpelier Plantation Inn and follow the signs. 869-469-3509. Open Nov–Mar Mon–Sat 9am–4:30pm. Closed Sun. Rest of the year Mon–Sat 10am–4pm. Closed Sun. $9.

The sound of flowing water makes the ideal background for a leisurely stroll through these eight acres, planted with bamboo, cacti, ficus trees and fruit trees. Mosey along paths framed by orchid terraces, linger at ponds where water lilies bloom around bronze sculptures of dolphins and mermaids, and be wowed by a collection of palms gathered from all parts of the globe. The Mayan-themed Rain Forest Conservatory showcases Caribbean ecosystems. Have lunch or afternoon tea on the veranda of the Tea House.

Home and Garden Tour

Each February a handful of residents open up their homes and private gardens to the public for a peek into Nevisian-style living. The gardens abound in bougainvillea, gingers, allamandas, crotons and other tropicals as well as mango, papaya and cashew trees. *For schedules, contact the Nevis Historical and Conservation Society; 869-469-5786.*

Must-See Beaches

Sand Bank Bay Beach★★

Southeast peninsula, St. Kitts.

This secluded, half-moon-shaped beach is touted as the island's best place to take a walk or a swim. Even though the beach lies on the Atlantic side, its shallow coves make it ideal for families.

Pinney's Beach★

1mi north of Charlestown, Nevis.

Perhaps St. Kitts' most famous beach, Pinney's is the occasional haunt of movie stars and other celebrities. Order a tropical drink from Sunshine's Beach Bar & Grill *(869-469-5817)* and lounge beneath a palm-topped hut.

South Friar's Bay Beach★

On the peninsula, southwest side of St. Kitts.

A few coconut trees lean gently on the golden sands of this lovely beach. Its smooth waters make for good swimming.

North Friar's Bay Beach

On the peninsula, southeast side of St. Kitts.

A wide and elongated sandbank beaten by waves, North Friar's Bay holds a beautiful and often empty beach.

Musts for Kids

Ride the Sugar Train★★

Departs from Needsmust Station at the airport, St. Kitts. 869-465-7263. www.stkittsscenic railway.com. Jun–Sept Mon 1pm & Wed 9:30am. Rest of the year, call for departure times. $89 adults, $44.50 children ages 3-11.

All aboard! The 30-mile **St. Kitts Scenic Railway** chugs down tracks built in 1912 to carry sugarcane from the plantations to the mill in Basseterre. Hop aboard the double-decker coach cars for a four-hour scenic ride along the coastline. You'll see such sights as Brimstone Hill *(opposite)*, Thomas Jefferson's great grandfather's grave and the rain forest of Mt. Liamuiga.

Snorkel with an Expert

Oualie Beach Hotel, Tamarind Bay, Nevis. 869-469-1291. www.undertheseanevis.com. $50 ages 12 and over, $35 ages 5-11 (fee includes snorkeling gear).

Sign up for a Touch and Go Snorkel Trip with marine biologist Barbara Whitman at her **Under the Sea Sealife Education Centre**. You'll learn about the behavior of sea critters, have a hands-on encounter with live sea animals and cruise to a great snorkel spot to put your new knowledge to the test.

Must-See Historic Sites

Brimstone Hill Fortress National Park★★

10mi northwest of Basseterre, St. Kitts. Turn right before Charles Fort. 869-465-2609. www.brimstonehillfortress.org. Open year-round daily 9:30am–5:30pm. Closed Good Friday & Dec 25. $8.

In a grown-up version of the childhood game "capture the flag," this military construction went from British to French to British hands in just two years. Completed by the English in the 18C, the fort was captured by the French in 1782. A year later, the Treaty of Versailles returned it to the British crown. Today the fortress and the national park rank as a UNESCO World Heritage Site.

Watch a video on fort history in the welcome center. Then dawdle among the buildings, which include the bastion, the hospital and the ammunition warehouses. The main structure, Fort George Citadel, houses a museum *($5)*, several rooms of which are dedicated to the British and the short-lived French occupations.

Perched on Brimstone Hill, the site makes a great scenic point for views of the sugarcane fields and the island of St. Eustatius offshore; if visibility is good, you can see the outlines of Saba and St. Barthélemy.

Outnumbered

The citadel's fame stems from the tale of 1,000 British soldiers who hunkered down in the fort as 8,000 French soldiers steadfastly bored holes through the massive walls. The Brits finally surrendered.

Must Be Pampered: Spas

The Spa at Four Seasons Resort

Pinney's Beach, Charlestown, Nevis. 869-469-1111. www.fourseasons.com/nevis.

Come to this award-winning spa for total relaxation. Disguised as treatment rooms, pretty little West Indian "cottages" are scattered along a cobblestone path that winds through a garden of tropical trees and flowers. While away the day, before and after your treatment, in this serene setting, hanging out in hot whirlpools with waterfalls, taking quick dips in the cold pool, enjoying a spa lunch and contemplating Nevis Peak. Heavenly treatments include the Ginger Soak Body Wrap, the Mango Sea Salt Glow and the Papaya Hot Stone Massage.

Antigua★ and Barbuda★

Looking to party? Then come to Antigua for Sailing Week *(see Calendar of Events)*. Antigua's protected harbors and clear waters draw the pleasure-yacht crowd, while nature lovers head to sparsely populated Barbuda. Due east of Nevis 43 miles, Antigua (an-TEE-gah) is known for pretty beaches, cricket *(see sidebar, p105)* and historic sites. Its capital is bustling **St. John's**. Barbuda, 26 miles north, boasts pink-sand beaches,

shipwrecks and **Codrington Lagoon**, a haven for frigatebirds. Former British colonies, Barbuda, Antigua and the small island of Redonda, 30 miles southwest of Antigua, have shared independent statehood status since 1981.

Hotels		Restaurants	
🏨	The Admiral's Inn	①	Abracadabra
🏨	Curtain Bluff	②	Catherine's Café
🏨	Hawksbill Beach Resort	③	Chez Pascal

Must-See Historic Sites

Nelson's Dockyard★★

English Harbour, south coast, Antigua. 268-460-1379. Open year-round daily 9am–4:30pm. $5.

Walk in the footsteps of England's most famous naval officer at this historic dockyard, protected inside the deep bay of **English Harbour**. Built in 1743, the naval base served as headquarters of the British navy for the West India Islands. From 1784 until 1787, Admiral **Horatio Nelson** was its commander. Explore restored Georgian buildings, which include the naval officer's house and a pitch-and-tar store—now the Admiral's Inn *(see Must Stay)*. Then enjoy dinner at a neighboring restaurant and browse the gift shops for a souvenir or two.

Betty's Hope

Southeast of St. John's, near the village of Pares, Antigua. 268-462-1469. Open year-round Mon–Sat 9am–4pm. Closed Sun. $2.

A dirt road leads to this former sugar plantation, begun in the mid-17C. Here you'll find a restored windmill, reputedly the only one in the Caribbean that still works. Peek into the small museum to see old prints and a model of the plantation.

Caribbean Cricket

A holdover from Britain's colonial days, cricket is wildly popular on several Caribbean islands, including Antigua, which produced legendary Viv Richards. Once reserved for British officers and wealthy planters, the game was considerably enlivened when slaves "pitched" for privileged batters on days of oppressive heat. A West Indies team soon rose to prominence, dominating the game internationally from the mid-1970s to mid-80s. To see a match while you're in Antigua, contact the Antigua Cricket Association *(60 Newgate St., St. John's; 268-462-9089)*. In 2007 the Cricket World Cup will be held in the Caribbean for the first time, on various islands, including Antigua *(for information, go online to www.worldcupweb.com)*.

Must-See Beaches

Southern Beach★★

South end of Barbuda, between the Martello Tower and Coco Point.

This uncrowded, five-mile-long beach shimmers with pink sand. Its protected waters are ideal for swimming and snorkeling. The luxurious K-Club and Coco Point Lodge occupy the eastern shore, but the entire beach is open to the public.

Dickenson Bay Beach★

Northwest Antigua, 3.5mi north of St. John's.

A great place for families with young children, this beach is awash with tranquil waters and soft sand. A host of shoreline lodgings sets the scene for snorkeling and other water-related activities, as well as après-beach relaxation at their hotel bars.

Half Moon Bay Beach★

Southeastern shore of Antigua, 1.5 mi from Freetown.

Considered among in-the-know beach-goers as the best beach on Antigua, this long curve of sheltered shore lining Half Moon Bay is one of the island's most scenic beaches. Trade winds and agitated Atlantic waters lure windsurfers to challenge their skills, but the rough sea is not great for swimming.

Touring Tip

Topless or nude sunbathing on Antigua's public beaches is prohibited by law.

Bring Your Snorkeling Gear

Most of Barbuda's coast is lined with coral reefs and dotted with shipwrecks. Conditions for snorkeling are excellent: little or no current, warm waters (average 80°F) and visibility of up to 140 feet.

Must-See Parks and Natural Sites

Bird Sanctuary★

North end of Codrington Lagoon, Barbuda. Arrange a boat tour in advance with your hotel or at the pier with a local fisherman in the settlement of Codrington. $50.

Codrington Lagoon hosts the largest colony of frigate birds in the West Indies. These fork-tailed seabirds, with wingspans of more than 6 feet, have made huge nests in the mangrove swamps here. Because their feathers aren't waterproof, they can't dive and so must catch their prey on the water's surface or steal it from another bird. The boat stops only a few yards from the nests. On the way back, the guide offers to stop on **Low Bay** beach, a dreamy strip of sand.

Devil's Bridge

On the east coast, east of the village of Willikies, Antigua.

This natural formation is called a blowhole: the water plunges with a crash into a marine cavity and then shoots into the air like a geyser.

Guadeloupe★★★

France with a Caribbean twist—that's what the large islands of Guadeloupe and Martinique *(see p113)* bring to the table. Here you'll feast on spicy Creole cuisine washed down with French wine. Colorful Creole headdresses and brightly painted fishing boats sidle up to croissant-packed patisseries and boutiques with French fashions. Within the Lesser Antilles group, these French territories and the nearby islands of **Marie-Galante** and **Les Saintes★★★**, along with Saint-Barthélemy *(p96)* and Saint-Martin *(p89)*, make up the French Antilles, otherwise known as the French West Indies. French is the official language *(French phrases p96)*, and many residents also speak Creole, a pidginized version of French.

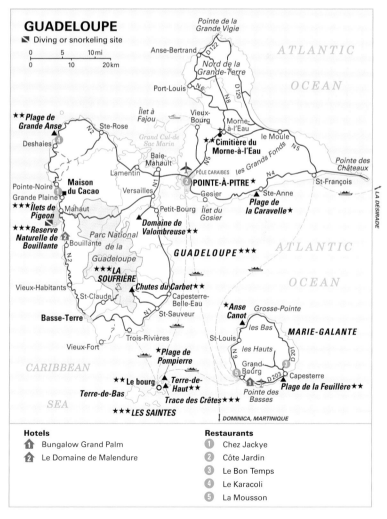

Hotels
1. Bungalow Grand Palm
2. Le Domaine de Malendure

Restaurants
1. Chez Jackye
2. Côte Jardin
3. Le Bon Temps
4. Le Karacoli
5. La Mousson

Les Belles Isles

Sitting 38 miles south of Antigua, Guadeloupe's two islands of Basse-Terre and Grande-Terre, each resembling a butterfly's wing, are connected by a bridge. Basse-Terre is home to the administrative capital of **Basse-Terre** and **la Soufrière★★★**, an active volcano at an elevation of 4,815 feet. Grande-Terre's economic hub is populous **Pointe-à-Pitre★**, an active port and shopping mecca. Sidekick island **Marie-Galante** lies 16 miles to the southeast, peaceful and largely undeveloped. About 6 miles off Guadeloupe's southwest shore, two islands (**Terre-de-Bas** and **Terre-de-Haut★★**) and seven islets make up the archipelago of **Les Saintes★★★**, a nature-lover's paradise.

Must Shop

Marché Saint-Antoine★   (St. Anthony Market)

Downtown Pointe-a-Pitre, Grande-Terre, Guadeloupe. Open year-round daily 8am–2pm.

This indoor market—a number of booths housed inside a metal building—spills outside, where umbrellas shade folding tables piled with produce. Female vendors dressed in madras show off wares of spices, fruits, vegetables, teas and secret preparations said to have magical powers. The vast array of spices for sale includes cloves, saffron, fenugreek, ginger, coriander, nutmeg, pepper, chili pepper and cinnamon. Check out the items crafted of dried gourds, and the hats, baskets and brooms woven from banana, coconut or red latan trees. But watch out, sometimes live crabs are moving on the ground.

Marché Basse-Terre   (Basse-Terre Market)

Rue de la République and Général-de-Gaulle Blvd, Basse-Terre, Guadeloupe. Open year-round daily 8am–2pm.

Saturday morning is the best time to come here, when the scents and colors of a whole range of tropical products animate the market. Good buys are cocoa sticks (for grating; *see sidebar, below*), fruit punches, spices like bija, bay leaves and fenugreek, bananas, iced *chadec* (a kind of grapefruit) and hats made from coconut trees. If you're looking for madras fabrics, the selection is better along Cours-Nolivos Street.

The Humble Cocoa Bean

Did you know that cocoa beans were used as currency in pre-Columbian times? Before sugarcane was widely used, the colonial economy relied on cocoa and tobacco. Today, cocoa production is limited; the beans are used mostly by the families who grow them. If you want to know more—and taste a sample—visit the **Maison du Cacao** (**Cocoa House**), where wooden panels trace the history of the cocoa pod (*in Grande Plaine, south of Pointe-Noire, Guadeloupe; 590-98-25-23; open year-round Mon–Sat 9am–5pm; closed Sun & Jan 1, May 1, May 29 & Dec 25; $5*).

Must-See Beaches

Plage de la Feuillère★★ *(Feuillère Beach)*

South of Capesterre, Marie-Galante.

Coconut and sea-grape trees provide the ideal shade to laze around on this beach of golden sand. The force of the waves is broken by the coral reef.

Plage de Grande Anse★★ *(Grand Cove Beach)*

1.25mi north of Deshaies, Basse-Terre, Guadeloupe.

This is certainly the most beautiful beach on Basse-Terre. The waves pounding the shore don't seem to bother beachgoers enjoying this strip of caramel sand.

Anse Canot★ *(Canot Cove)*

Northwest Marie-Galante.

Be careful as you walk down the steep slopes to this beach. You'll reach a small, shaded stretch of white sand topped with tables and gazebos.

> **Touring Tip**
>
> If you want to get an all-over tan (a-hem), nudity is legal at Anse Crawen beach, on the west coast of Terre-de-Haut—although you'll notice that very little is worn on *any* of les Saintes' beaches.

Plage de la Caravelle★ *(Caravelle Beach)*

Off Rte. N 4 near Ste-Anne, Grande-Terre, Guadeloupe.

Shaded by small coconut trees, this narrow beach belongs to Club Med, but it's open to non-guests, who must pass through a turnstile.

Plage de Pompierre★ *(Pompierre Beach)*

Northern part of Terre-de-Haut, Les Saintes.

This lovely crescent beach, backdropped by palms, is nearly enclosed by rocky islets. As you approach it, you might see iguanas nestled in the fields. A line of parked scooters confirms that you've come to the right spot.

Musts for Outdoor Fun

Réserve naturelle de Bouillante ★★★
(Bouillante Nature Reserve)

West shore of Basse-Terre, off the coast of the town of Bouillante, Guadeloupe.

Created to protect the marine environment and limit fishing around Malendure and the Pigeon Islets, this 990-acre underwater sanctuary is also called
the Cousteau Reserve. Undersea legend Jacques-Yves Cousteau (1910-97) is said
to have shot film scenes here. Follow in his flippers at this divers' paradise.

Dive Shops

Several dive outfitters service sites off Basse-Terre's
west coast. Here's a sampling:

Les Heures Saines– *Malendure Beach, Bouillante.*
590-98-86-63. www.heures-saines.gp. $45 and up. An
attentive team of instructors is ready to help divers
at all levels of experience. Three expeditions daily.

Plaisir Plongée Caraibes – *Malendure Beach.*
opposite the tourist office, Bouillante. 590-98-82-43.
www.plaisir-plongée-caraibes.com. $45. Dive expeditions for groups of 15 and 35 div-
ers, accompanied by certified instructors.

UCPA (Union Nationale de Centre Pleine Aire) – *Pigeon, on the road to l'Anse à Sable.*
590-98-89-78. www.ucpa.com. $45. Dives possible on a space-available basis with
trainees in getting certification. Reduced dive rates.

Îlets de Pigeon Dive Site★★★

West shore of Basse-Terre, off the coast near the town of Mahaut, Guadeloupe.

The best way to explore this underwater site within Cousteau Reserve is to
scuba dive. Les Heures Saines *(see sidebar, above)* offers a beginner's package
that takes divers underwater for only five minutes—long enough to be awe-
struck. You'll see sponges, colorful fish, brain coral, mushroom coral and mad-
repores, also called flower coral or star coral. If you don't want to get wet,
take a glass-bottom boat ride from Malendure Beach *(contact Bateau à Fond
de Verre; 590-98-89-08).*

Trace des Crêtes★★★   *(Trail of the Cretes)*

*Trail starts at the eastern end of Pompierre Beach, Terre-de-Haut, Les Saintes. Wear good
shoes, bring drinking water and avoid the midday heat.*

This marked trail will take you about an hour to reach Grande-Anse Beach.
Along the way, you'll enjoy bewitching views of the northern and central parts
of the island, and meet goats, chickens and cows as well. Lined with bushes,
the dirt path climbs quickly to 330 feet, where you'll be treated to an expansive view of Pompierre Beach to your right, the Grand Souffleur cliffs mid-
point, and lovely Grande Anse Beach on your left.

Chutes du Carbet★★ *(Carbet Waterfalls)*

From Rte. N 1 at Saint-Sauveur, Basse-Terre, Guadeloupe. Take Rte. D 4 towards Chutes du Carbet; be cautious when passing the many buses on this narrow road. Wear nonskid shoes; the footwalk sways slightly. Bring drinking water. About 1-hour round trip.

From the parking lot, you'll have a splendid view of the first and second waterfalls. When the sky is clear, you can see, from left to right, the peaks of Citerne (3,789 feet), Echelle (4,583 feet), Soufrière (4,815 feet) and Carmichaël (4,639 feet). The hiking path leads to the bottom of the **second waterfalls★★**, which are impressive—from a height of 361 feet, the water thunders into a basin. Swimming is permitted, so bring your swimsuit.

On the way back from the second falls, take the path that climbs to the left; after 10 minutes turn left again. *(hiking shoes necessary; don't take this hike after a rainfall; allow 3 hours round trip).* You'll find much less foot traffic on this path that leads to the highest of the falls. After crossing Longueteau ravine, turn right at the junction. The trail goes down to the Carbet Valley and follows the river to the bottom of the **first waterfall★** (377 feet).

Cimetière du Morne-à-l'Eau★★ *(Cemetery of Morne-à-l'Eau)*

Off Rte. N 5, Morne-à-l'Eau, north central Grande-Terre.

Don't miss seeing this unusual cemetery. It's an impressive ensemble of above-ground tombs and funerary chapels covered with black and white checked ceramic tiles. Nowhere else in Guadeloupe or Martinique does anything like this exist. The graveyard is a veritable "city" of the dead.

Terre-de-Haut★★

Terre-de-Haut, Les Saintes.

The best way to explore this island is on foot. Stroll the main village of **Le bourg★★**—pretty much just one long street—built on the shores of a splendid bay. Tiny multicolored houses covered with red metal roofs add to the charm. On the pier plaza, friendly women and young girls sell homemade pies made with coconut jam, a specialty of the Saintes archipelago. The church used to mark the boundary between the community leaders' residences on one side and the Fond Curé fishermen's community on the other. Fishermen's cottages, simple wooden structures with colored facades and sometimes a porch with gingerbread trim, sit half-hidden by hibiscus trees.

Must-See Gardens

Domaine de Valombreuse★★
(Guadeloupe Botanical Gardens)

Off Rte. N 1, east Basse-Terre. Before Petit-Bourg, turn right after the Lézarde River bridge, then drive 3mi and follow the sign "Parc floral." 590-95-50-50. Open year-round daily 9am–5pm. $9.

Lose yourself in this setting of lush vegetation. The botanical garden contains more than 300 species of tropical and subtropical flowers, bushes and trees. Here you'll walk along the paths and see blue ferns, begonias and gingers, and crotons and philodendrons that grow to tree height. Near greenhouses filled with orchids, you'll discover spices and condiments used in the local cuisine: nutmeg, cayenne pepper and star anise to name a few; recipes explain how to prepare *poudre de Colombo* (Caribbean curry spice), and other delights. Not far away, there's a collection of palm trees: red latan, sago palm, oil palm, royal palm and triangular palm, among others. In the huge aviary, multicolored birds fly in all directions or hide behind thick foliage. Outside the wire mesh, dozens of hummingbirds, showing no sign of shyness, love to pose for a photo.

> **Touring Tip**
>
> At the end of the route, a flower shop sells candies and souvenirs. You can purchase flowers like heliconias, porcelain roses and anthuriums at the park reception desk. Take your flowers with you, or ask to have them delivered to your hotel.

Martinique★★★

Legally French. Brassy, beautiful Martinique brandishes her savoir faire to secure top-class status among the Caribbean islands. An 81-mile jump south over Dominica from Guadeloupe, Martinique is a French-speaking island where nature competes with the skyscrapers of its capital, **Fort-de-France★**. The island's imposing 4,577-foot **Montagne Pelée★★** is an active volcano that was responsible for 30,000 deaths when it erupted in 1902.

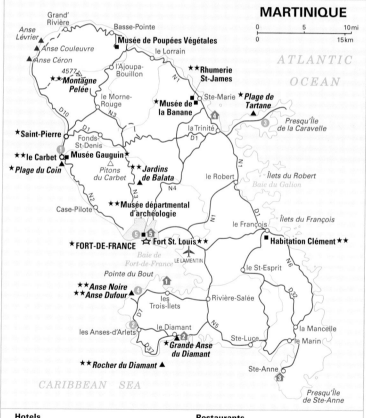

MARTINIQUE

| 0 | 5 | 10mi |
| 0 | | 15km |

Grand' Rivière
Anse Lévrier
▲ Anse Couleuvre
▲ Anse Céron
Basse-Pointe
■ **Musée de Poupées Végétales**
le Lorrain
l'Ajoupa-Bouillon
4577△
★★**Montagne Pelée**
★★**Rhumerie St-James**
le Morne-Rouge
N1
★ **Plage de Tartane**
■ **Musée de la Banane** Ste-Marie
D10
★**Saint-Pierre** Fonds St-Denis
la Trinité
Presqu'Île de la Caravelle
★★**le Carbet** ■ **Musée Gauguin**★
★ **Plage du Coin** Pitons du Carbet
★★ **Jardins de Balata**
le Robert
Îlets du Robert
Baie du Galion
N4
Case-Pilote
★★**Musée départemental d'archéologie**
le François
Îlets du François
★ **FORT-DE-FRANCE** ☆ **Fort St. Louis**★★
■ **Habitation Clément**★★
Baie de Fort-de-France
LE LAMENTIN
le St-Esprit
Pointe du Bout
★★**Anse Noire**
★★**Anse Dufour** ▲ les Trois-Îlets
Rivière-Salée
les Anses-d'Arlets
le Diamant
Ste-Luce
la Mancelle
le Marin
★ **Grande Anse du Diamant**
★★ **Rocher du Diamant** ▲
Ste-Anne
CARIBBEAN SEA
Presqu'Île de Ste-Anne

ATLANTIC OCEAN

Hotels
1 Bakoua Sofitel
2 Hôtel Diamant-les-Bains
3 Manoir de Beauregard
4 Saint Aubin Hôtel
5 Squash Hotel

Restaurants
1 Chez de Pêcheurs
2 Fatzo
3 La Caravelle
4 L'Anse Noire
5 Le Marie-Sainte

French Isles

Must-See Beaches

Anse Dufour★★ *(Dufour Cove)*

Southwest coast, across the bay from Fort-de-France. Watch for signs on the right side of the road. After the crossroads, drive 1.6mi; park your car in the small lot at the end of the road.

Come early: this beach is jammed by 10am. Anse Dufour lies below the parking lot. Gum and sea-grape trees border the broad, white-sand beach. The deep waters of the cove provide a safe mooring for the colorful boats of local fishermen. Their huts and the tranquility of the Caribbean Sea enhance this picturesque place, very different from the crowded, resort-lined beaches on Pointe du Bout to the east.

Anse Noire★★ *(Black Cove)*

Southwest coast, next to Anse Dufour; park in the same lot.

At the end of the parking lot, steps lead down to the beach at Anse Noire— and to a geological surprise: just a few dozen yards from the white sands of Anse Dufour appears an ash-colored beach, shaded by coconut trees. To really enjoy this peaceful paradise, arrive mid-morning and, after swimming, have lunch in L'Anse Noire, the small restaurant set under the trees *(596-68-62-82; lunch only, year-round Tue–Sun, closed Mon).*

Grande Anse du Diamant★ *(Diamond Cove)*

South coast, off Rte. D 37 and west of the village of le Diamant.

Crowned by coconut and sea-grape trees, this white-sand beach stretches some two miles. Bring a lunch to enjoy at one of the many wooden picnic tables. In spite of strong waves and dangerous currents, the beach attracts large crowds on weekends. It's a great spot for a superb view of **Diamond Rock★★**, anchored a mile offshore.

Sands of Many Colors

In Martinique and Guadeloupe, beaches can be divided in two categories according to the color of the sand. Strips of white or golden sand line limestone plateaus or face fringing reefs; the sand is composed of fragments of seashells and coral. Strips of gray or black sand lie at the bottom of volcanic depressions; a high concentration of heavy metals found in lava (amphibole, iron, titanium, for instance) explains their color.

Plage du Coin★ *(Corner Beach)*

Northwest coast, Off Rte. N 2.

Come here if you're looking for relaxation on an empty beach. This long, wide strip of gray sand sees few visitors. Idle fishing boats beached under coconut, palm and sea-grape trees brighten the shoreline with their vivid colors. Coin Beach continues toward the town of **Saint-Pierre★**, where its name changes to **Grande Anse**.

Plage de Tartane★ *(Tartane Beach)*

Northeast shore, off Presqu'ile de la Caravelle (Caravelle peninsula).

Turquoise waters, gentle surf, a long strip of white sand bordered by coconut trees—and few people. This is a very pleasant beach, indeed. But beware: the waters of the Atlantic here can be rough. Waves break in the distance on a coral reef, which you can explore with flippers, mask and a snorkel. Traps, nets and boats lying on the sand are proof that traditional fishing still survives in Tartane. Late in the morning, fishermen selling spiny lobsters stand near the road, scaling congers, boxfish and snappers on a few wooden tables.

The Common Octopus

Frequently in Martinique you'll see fishermen on shore with their catch of octopus. These 8-armed mollusks come in 50 varieties, but the most common in the Caribbean is octopus *briareus*, a chewy (if eaten raw) and much-appreciated delicacy offered in restaurants throughout the island.

Must-See Gardens

Jardins de Balata★★ *(Balata Gardens)*

Off Rte. N 3, 6.25mi north of Fort-de-France. 596-64-48-73. Open year-round daily 9am–5:30pm. Closed Mon–Thu in Sept. $9. Photos authorized for personal use only.

Thriving on the lower slopes of the peaks of Carbet, this botanical garden sits in the midst of a tropical forest that receives lots of rain (13 feet a year). Opened in 1986, the garden was created around a small, wooden Creole house, which serves as the ticket office and bookstore. The free map *(distributed at the entrance)* will help you identify about 200 species. You'll see orchids, heliconias, porcelain roses, alpinias and other flowers, decorative or fruit shrubs and trees such as palm and banana, as well as bamboo. The grove of epiphytes is especially spectacular: these plants die after blooming, but regenerate themselves through lateral sprouts. Take the path leading to a lookout for great views of Fort-de-France Bay.

Must-See Museums

Musée départemental d'archéologie et de préhistoire de la Martinique★★
(Martinique Museum of Archaeology and Prehistory)

9 Rue de la Liberté (near the post office), Fort-de-France. 596-71-57-05. Open year-round Mon–Fri 8am–5pm (Mon 1pm), Sat 9am–noon. Closed Sun. $4.

This museum contains more than 1,000 artifacts unearthed during archaeological digs. They span 2,000 years of Martinique's pre-Columbian history. Maps, tools, ceramics and costumes evoke the daily life of the Arawak and Carib peoples. On the second floor, you'll notice the *adornos*, human and animal faces commonly found on pottery handles. Sketches, models and exhibits on legends round out the museum's collections.

Musée de la Banane★ (Banana Museum)

Habitation Limbé. Off D 24, west of Ste-Marie. Watch for signs. 596-69-45-52. Open Dec–Mar daily 9am–5pm. Rest of the year Mon–Sat 9am–5pm, Sun 9am–1pm. Closed Jan 1. $7.50.

Did you know there are about 300 species of bananas in the world? Some 50 species can be found on Martinique. You'll learn all about bananas, Martinique's chief export, as you stroll around this working estate. An on-site boutique stocks banana perfumes, soaps, jams, cakes, cocktails and more.

Musée Gauguin★ (Gauguin Museum)

Anse-Turin, Carbet. Take the path under the road bridge. 596-78-22-66. Open year-round daily 9:30am–5:30pm. $6.50.

Famed painter Paul Gauguin spent five months on the island in 1887 *(see sidebar, below)*. During that time, he is said to have produced several canvases, replicas of which are on exhibit in this museum, situated not far from where he lived. His letters and memorabilia are also on view.

An Inspired Tourist

Hoping to escape the "disease of civilization," Paul Gauguin came to Martinique with fellow painter Charles Laval in 1887, where he lived in **Carbet★★** from June to November. Gauguin claimed that he produced about 10 works while in Carbet. Today, those paintings belong to private and public collections: *La Mare* (Neue Pinakothek, Munich), *Végétation tropicale* (National Gallery of Scotland, Edinburgh), *Au bord de l'étang* and *Aux mangos* (Rijkmuseum Van Gogh, Amsterdam), to name a few. Gauguin believed that the future belonged to the artists depicting the unknown tropics. He considered setting up a studio in Martinique, but illness forced him to return to France. In 1891 Gauguin sailed for Tahiti, where he painted some of his most famous works.

Musée de Poupées Végétales *(Doll Museum)*

Leyritz Plantation, northeastern tip of the island. If approaching from the south, turn left before the town of Basse-Pointe. 596-78-53-92. Open year-round daily 10am–5pm. $3. (price includes visit of the estate house & gardens).

This former sugar plantation, now an inn, is the secluded setting for showcasing some 50 dolls from the collection of resident-artist Will Fenton. The talented artist creates the figures using some 600 types of plant materials found on the island, including fibers, fronds and leaves. You'll be amused by his doll-size miniatures of famous women such as Madam Pompadour and Josephine Baker.

Must-See Historic Sites

Fort Saint-Louis★★

Entrance on Boul. Chevalier-de-Sainte-Marthe, Fort-de-France. Open year-round Mon–Sat 9am–3pm. $5.

Come here to "relive" some Martinique history. After defeating the Dutch, Louis XIV ordered the construction of a stronger fort; successive governor generals gave the site its current appearance. Still used by the military today, the fort houses the local headquarters of the French Navy. Take the guided tour, interspersed with historical tidbits. It retraces the colonization of the island and leads to the Grand Cavalier. From there you'll enjoy an excellent view of Flamands and Carénage bays and Pointe du Bout on the sea side; landward, you can see the contour of the peaks of Carbet.

Habitation Clément★★ *(Clement Estate)*

South of the town of François off Rte. N 6. 596-54-62-07. www.rhum-clement.com. Open year-round daily 9am–6pm. Closed Sept. $7.

See how the wealthy plantation society lived at the 40-acre Clément property, a protected historic site, where rum is still produced. Carefully restored, the surviving house, now a museum, dates back to 1820. It will give you an idea of architecture characteristic of the 18C plantation style common to the islands. Constructed mostly of wood, the manor features eight spacious rooms on the first floor furnished with pieces in the style of the Dutch West and East India companies. Try a free sample of aged rum from the bar.

Breaking Bread

Presidents François Mitterand, George H.W. Bush and other high-profile political figures have eaten a meal at the impressive mahogany table in the manor house at Habitation Clément.

Rhumerie Saint-James★★ *(St. James Rum Distillery)*

Off Rte. N 1, just north of the town of Ste-Marie. 596-69-30-02. Museum open year-round daily 9am–5pm. Guided tours of the distillery Mar–Jun daily 9am–5pm; $6.

Located in the heart of a sugarcane region, this 740-acre estate grows its own crop and also buys the production of other farmers. The house serves as a ticket counter and shop where you can sample *(free)* and buy rum. Behind the house stands the red and green metallic building housing the distillery, which is in operation when the cane is harvested. Tubs, milling rolls and a steam machine are exhibited on the grounds. The **museum** displays posters, tools and other objects relating to the favorite drink of the Caribbean islands.

A Word about Rum

Sugarcane gave birth to rum. Considered among the best in the world, the rum produced on Martinique has been awarded the prestigious French label "appellation d'origine controlee" (controlled label of origin) or AOC, previously reserved only for French wines and cheeses. AOC is the French system for indicating and controlling the geography and quality of alcoholic and food products. Martinique is definitely *the* place to buy fine, aged rum.

Must Be Seen: Nightlife

Cotton Club

The beach at Anse Mitan, Trois Îlets.

This club is *the* spot for drinking amid a friendly crowd of locals who come for nightly live jazz and zouk *(see sidebar, at right).*

Casino de la Bateliere Plazza

Rue des Alizes, north of Fort-de-France. 596-61-7323.

Place your bets in the most popular casino on the island. American roulette reigns, along with blackjack and poker. Or simply settle in and try your luck with the 140 "one-armed bandits" (read: slot machines) on site.

Casino Trois-Îlets

Kalenda Resort, Pointe du Bout. 596-66-0000.

Roulette and blackjack are favored at this small casino, but many people come simply to dance the night away at the hotel's lively disco.

Zouk

A fun word that once meant "to go out and party," *zouk* now refers to Martinique's hottest dance music with Creole lyrics and a seductive beat. A dozen clubs in Fort-de-France feature it. To take the rhythm home, buy a CD of zouk bands like Kassav, Malavoi, Joelle Ursull and Zouk Machine in a local music store.

Must Shop

Grand marché   *(Great market)*

At the corner of Blénac and Isambert Sts., Fort-de-France. Open year-round daily 6am–3pm.

Here's your opportunity to discover the secrets of Caribbean nature cures. This covered market offers more than just a colorful, fragrant display of pineapples and bananas. In exchange for a modest purchase—or even a smile—the *doudous* (female vendors dressed in madras) love

> **Touring Tip**
> While strolling through the market, taste some ginger cookies or the delicious candy *cannelle de coco*, made of caramelized coconut pulp.

to give long explanations about their concoctions. At these stalls you can find bay rum recommended for skin care and *sirop de cresson* (watercress syrup) for stomachaches. And don't forget *citrocol*, used for an after-bath rubdown and *huile de roucou (*annatto oil), a sun lotion that helps tanning.

The large metallic building is also the place to buy all the additional ingredients for real Creole cooking, like almond or banana syrup for pastry, or *crème de piment (*chili pepper) for pasta.

Marché de la rivière Madame *(Madam River Market)*

Near José-Marti Square, Fort-de-France. Open year-round daily 6am–3pm.

This rather informal market, where women sell their produce directly on the ground, has a lively, colorful atmosphere. You'll see a whole range of spices (cinnamon, saffron, *colombo*, nutmeg), vegetables (sweet potatoes, breadfruits, yams, christophines), ingredients for various homemade remedies, and flowers, mostly anthuriums, of superb quality.

Marché aux poissons   *(Fish Market)*

At the end of the Général-de-Gaulle Blvd., along the Madame River, Fort-de-France. Open year-round daily 6am–3pm.

Want some local color? This market is very busy, especially on Saturday mornings, a great place to see islanders interact. The tiled stands overflow with snapper, mackerel and big-eyed scad. Outside, women sell their goods in large basins, and scale the fish while chattering away under umbrellas. Early birds can watch the multicolored boats unloading their catch on the Madame River.

Nature as it was intended—the Old Caribbean, undeveloped and unspoiled—that's **Dominica★**. Emerging from the ocean between Martinique and Guadeloupe, this island is the most mountainous of the Lesser Antilles. Early navigators could see its 3,000-foot peaks from a long way off. Today, with only a few beaches of gray sand to offer, Dominica fosters ecotourism, especially hiking. Creole and English are the languages spoken here. Avid conservationists, Dominicans talk openly of their love of country.

Musts for Outdoor Fun

Hiking rules on Dominica. Trails thread the island's mountainous sections, offering glimpses of waterfalls, hot springs, the island's flora and fauna and the coast. Here are two of the island's many trails, one difficult, one easy.

Boiling Lake★

From Roseau, head east on King George V St. Turn left three times to reach the village of Laudat, the starting point for this 7-hour round-trip hike on slopes made slippery by frequent showers. A guide is strongly recommended: contact Ken's Hinterland Adventure Tours (767-448-4850; www.kenshinterlandtours.com; $160/4 people). Take food and drink, warm clothing and a windbreaker.

For experienced hikers only, this excursion into the heart of Morne Trois Pitons National Park is a beautiful one. The path leads to the boiling lake of a volcano crater. The scenic, uneven path traverses tropical forest, crosses streams, and ascends hills before running into the eerie **Valley of Desolation**, where the vegetation, burnt by sulfuric gases, has been reduced to lichens and transformed into mountainous savanna. After you cross several brooks, Boiling Lake—the second-largest hot-springs lake in the world—appears through a cloud of hot sulfur steam. The warm air is rewarding after such a long, damp march.

Carib Territory

Off the coastal route north of Castle Bruce.
Since 1903 about 3,000 descendants of the Caribbean Indians have lived on the 3,706-acre **Carib Indian Reservation★★**, situated between Castle Bruce and Pagua Bay on the Atlantic coast. The population is concentrated in three villages that bear very characteristic Caribbean names: Bataka, Salybia and Sineku. They live in self-made cabins, often built on stilts, that serve mainly as bedrooms, since most activities take place outdoors. The Carib have contempt for private property; they don't own much except for their huts. You can buy their handcrafted baskets and wood carvings at stalls along the coastal road.

Trafalgar Falls

Begins 2.5mi west of Laudat, turn left toward Trafalgar.

This short, easy trail to the Trafalgar Falls takes only 10 minutes on the path starting one mile beyond the outskirts of Trafalgar. You'll reach a vantage point where you can enjoy a spectacular view of the falls, which are 197 feet high. Hope you've brought your swimsuit—one of the pools makes a good swimming hole.

Touring Tip

If you'd rather not hike, take the **Rain Forest Aerial Tram** for views of Dominica's rain forest from the air. The tram boards near the village of Laudat and takes 90 minutes round-trip *(reservations required; 767-448-8775; www.rainforesttram.com; $70)*.

End-to-End Trail

The Waitikubuli (Dominica) Ecological Foundation has proposed the development of the **Waitikubuli National Trail**, which would traverse the island from north to south, passing some 700 villages. It's estimated that when the trail is completed, it will take 13 days to hike the entire route.

St. Lucia

Twin Peaks could be St. Lucia's alias. The lush natural pyramids called the **Pitons**★★ are the island's identity badge. Located 22 miles south of Martinique, **St. Lucia**★★ is a land of volcanic mountains blanketed in tropical rain forests. Natural harbors carve its coasts, sheltering dreamy, uncrowded beaches, especially near **Castries**, the capital. Day-trippers arrive to hike the lunar landscape of **Soufrière**, a semi-active volcano. Others come for soft adventures like whale-watching, bay-hopping and just relaxing at a world-renowned resort. Saint Lucia belongs to the British Commonwealth, but has been an independent state since 1979.

Heritage Tourism

A community-based program puts you in the midst of the rich culture of the St. Lucians. Your best bets:

- **Fond Latisab Creole Park** for tropical fruit, river crayfish and a chak chak band.
- **Toraille Waterfall** for a paradise of island flowers.
- **Fond Doux Estate** for a cup of cocoa tea at a working cacao plantation. *Contact Heritage Tours: 758-451-6058; www.heritagetours-stlucia.com.*

Hotels

1. Anse Chastanet
2. LeSPORT
3. Ti Kaye Village
4. Windjammer Landing Resort

Restaurants

1. The Coal Pot
2. The Great House
3. The Still

Must-See Beaches

Marigot Bay Beach★★

Central west coast, near Anse La Raye.

This bewitching bay was used as the setting for *Doctor Doolittle*, a film (1967) starring Rex Harrison. Clear waters, majestic coconut trees and a bower of steep hills call to mind a veritable Garden of Eden. From the small strip of sand, you can wade into the protected waters of the bay for a swim.

Choc Beach

Northwest coast, north of Castries.

You'll find easy access from the coastal road to this agreeable stretch of sand and palms. Calm waters make the beach ideal for families with little ones.

Pigeon Island National Landmark

A military base during Franco-British rivalry for St. Lucia, Fort Rodney (1778), now reduced to stone ruins, includes an interpretation center museum filled with artifacts; the original mess hall serves as a restaurant. Bring your bathing suit: there are two beaches at Pigeon Point, within this national landmark *(St. Lucia National Trust; 758-452-5005; www.slunatrust.org; open year-round daily; $2).*

Musts for Fun

Anse La Raye Fish Fry

7mi south of Castries.

Every Friday evening, the streets of the little fishing village of Anse La Raye are closed to vehicles so locals can set up their popular fish fry in the village square. Vendors cook up homemade fish cakes, fried or stewed fish and whole Caribbean lobster. The toe-tapping music from a live band gets people dancing in the streets. Here's a great opportunity for you to meet and chat with locals.

Traditional Bread

In Anse La Raye and elsewhere, islanders make the traditional bread of the island by shaping the flour of the cassava (a woody shrub grown for its edible root) into thick patties and baking them on a banana leaf on an old-fashioned griddle. Tasty and filling, cassava bread is perfect for taking on hikes or cycling trips.

Musts for Outdoor Fun

The Pitons★★

Anse des Pitons, southwest part of the island.

For daring hikers only! The island's most popular hike is the ascent of Gros Piton (2,619 feet) on a steep but safe trail. Or you can scramble up Petit Piton (2,460 feet), but the last half of the hike requires rock climbing, and safety equipment is not provided. To hike either peak, you must get permission from the Forest and Lands Department *(758-450-2231)* and hire a competent local guide to lead the way *(see sidebar, below)*.

Touring Tip

Early morning hikes to the Pitons are best. Arrange the hike with your hotel concierge, or call Gros Piton Guides Association *(758-459-9748)* or SunLink Tours *(758-456-9100; www.sunlinktours.com)*.

Biking

Sign up for a bike ride through 12 incredible miles of private trails within the jungle of **Anse Mamin**, a former sugar plantation. Designed for novice and experienced bikers, single-track loops weave uphill alongside the 18C ruins of a sugar mill and a church. Watch for wild orchids and a host of mango, banana and other tropical trees. Then cool off the old-fashioned way—in a natural swimming hole. *For information, contact Bike St. Lucia, Anse Chastanet. 758-451 2453. www.bikestlucia.com. Prices range from $60–$100 per person.*

Deep-Sea Fishing

If thoughts of challenging white marlin wet your appetite for ocean fishing, the waters off St. Lucia are the right place to do it. The mighty marlin makes its home here, along with sailfish, kingfish, king mackerel, mackerel and barracuda. For half-day *($400 & up)* or all-day *($750 & up)* excursions on fully equipped 31-foot Bertram boats, contact Hackshaws Boat Charters & Sportfishing *(in Castries; 758-453-0553)* or Captain Mike's Sportfishing Cruises *(in Castries; 758-452-7044)*. *Access both companies online at www.worldwidefishing.com/stlucia/salt.htm.*

Desbarras Turtle Watch

Grande Anse, northeast coast.

Self-taught naturalist Jim Sparks *(758-452-9829)* leads volunteers to monitor the nests of leatherback turtles who lumber ashore to lay eggs from March to July. Call him when you land and ask to tag along. You'll nap in tents and rotate duty throughout the night. When a leatherback weighing up to 1,500 pounds lays her eggs, everyone wakes up to witness this miracle of nature.

Mineral Baths

Southwest section of the island. Take the road on the right about 2mi before Soufrière. 758-459-7565. Open year-round Mon–Sat 10am–5pm, Sun & holidays 10am–3pm (Dec 25 til 2pm). $15.

Wear your swimsuit and ask your guide which springs to soak in at St. Lucia's **Sulphur Springs★**. This is an active volcanic area, with sulfur fumes, steaming brooks, bubbling blackish mounds (temperatures higher than 300°F)—a fascinating, but potentially unfriendly landscape.

You can soak in the mineral baths at **Diamond Botanical Gardens** *(drive 1.2mi on Soufrière River Rd., and turn right),* that site's main attraction. The baths were built in 1785 at the request of French king Louis XVI, who, having learned the virtues of the waters, wanted his soldiers stationed on the island to benefit from them.

Must Be Pampered: Spas

Jalousie Hilton Resort & Spa

Bay St., Soufrière. 758-456-8000. www.hilton.com.

Resting between the famous Pitons, this world-famous spa is known for its use of St. Lucia's indigenous plants and natural ingredients taken from the island's rain forests. You'll be treated to honeysuckle body scrubs, sea botanical aromatic wraps and, the most sought after treatment, sulfur mud baths with mud made from local volcanic soil.

Kai Belté Spa

Anse Chastanet Resort, near Soufrière. 758-459-7000. www.ansechastanet.com.

Romance reigns here, so treatments are geared to couples, including a simultaneous in-room massage. Ask for the Wosh Cho, local patois for a heavenly massage combo of hot stones and shiatsu. Natural Treats products of local flowers, fruits and vegetables are used in the spa's soothing facials and sunburn therapy. If you stay at the resort, a complimentary treatment is yours upon arrival. Does it get any better?

Oasis Spa

LeSPORT, Cariblue Beach, Cap Estate (northern tip of the island). 758-457-7800. www.thebodyholiday.com.

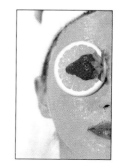

Set on a hillside with views of Cariblue Beach, this retreat is known for its massage menu, which ranges from Swedish and Thai to heavenly Ayurvedic Abhyanga, a hypnotic synchronized treatment where two therapists massage your body simultaneously! A meditation temple adds to the serenity. If you're not a hotel guest, you can phone in a reservation for a spa treatment once you're on the island.

Barbados

ring your sunglasses. **Barbados**★ positively radiates color—from the bright wooden houses and church-goers' multihued dresses to the yellow-and-blue buses on the coastal roads. Located 125 miles east of the arc formed by the Lesser Antilles, Barbados boasts magnificent beaches, stately plantation houses and swank resorts. Three centuries of British rule have left their mark: high tea and cricket are commonplace, and the capital, **Bridgetown,** has its version of London's Trafalgar Square. Music is part of island life: bus passengers clap their hands to reggae rhythms; musicians accompany a religious procession. Prepare to be happy!

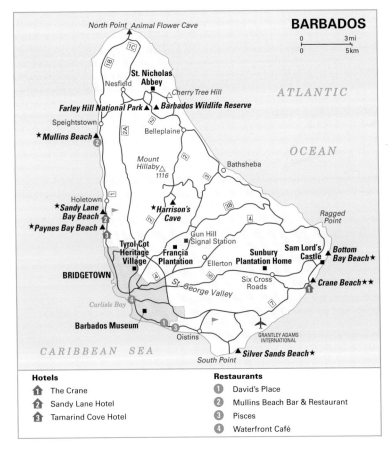

BARBADOS

| 0 | | 3mi |
| 0 | | 5km |

North Point · Animal Flower Cave

St. Nicholas Abbey

Nesfield · Cherry Tree Hill

Farley Hill National Park ▲ ▲ **Barbados Wildlife Reserve**

ATLANTIC

Speightstown

Belleplaine

★ **Mullins Beach** ▲

Mount Hillaby △ 1116

Bathsheba

OCEAN

Holetown
★ **Sandy Lane Bay Beach**
★ **Paynes Bay Beach** ▲

★ **Harrison's Cave**

Ragged Point

Tyrol Cot Heritage Village

Gun Hill Signal Station

Francia Plantation · Ellerton

Sunbury Plantation Home

Sam Lord's Castle ▲ **Bottom Bay Beach**★

BRIDGETOWN

St. George Valley

Six Cross Roads

▲ **Crane Beach**★★

Carlisle Bay

Barbados Museum

Oistins

GRANTLEY ADAMS INTERNATIONAL

CARIBBEAN SEA

South Point

▲ **Silver Sands Beach**★

Hotels		**Restaurants**	
🏨	The Crane	①	David's Place
🏨	Sandy Lane Hotel	②	Mullins Beach Bar & Restaurant
🏨	Tamarind Cove Hotel	③	Pisces
		④	Waterfront Café

Must-See Beaches

Crane Beach★★

Southeast shore. Access through a small path north of The Crane hotel (see Must Stay).

Two strips of white sand with a pink hue and clear turquoise waters describe this beach, one of the most beautiful on the Atlantic coast. Because of a bank of reefs not far offshore, only a few waves caress the sand.

Bottom Bay Beach★

East of Crane Beach, past Sam Lord's Castle.

Take the large staircase hugging the cliff to reach this golden-sand beach, dotted with tall palm trees and flanked by large coral cliffs. It's best to simply sunbathe here, rather than swim—the waves can be quite forceful.

Mullins Beach★

On the west coast, about 3.5mi north of Holetown. Parking along the coastal route.

This beautiful shaded beach abounds in white sand and turquoise waters. It's a great place for snorkeling and swimming. Take a break at the popular Mullins Beach Bar, which serves drinks and food.

Paynes Bay and Sandy Lane Bay Beaches★

Just south of Holetown (across from Coach House Restaurant and Sandy Lane Hotel).

These two lovely beaches deserve a stop. You'll love their calm, clear waters and white sand. Try your skill at snorkeling and other nautical activities.

Silver Sands Beach★

At the southern tip of the island, south of the airport.

Named for its sparkling silver-white sand, Silver Sands Beach makes a good spot for windsurfing—but not swimming. Frequent high winds whip up some awesome waves here.

> **Touring Tip**
>
> All of Barbados' beaches are public. The majority can be accessed by public road; only a few require entrance via hotel properties.

Must-See Historic Sites

Farley Hill National Park

Off Rte. 2 in north-central Barbados, opposite Barbados Wildlife Reserve, in the parish of St. Andrew. Open year-round daily 9am–5pm. Parking $1.75.

Imagine living in a mansion. In the heart of this 17-acre park lie the ruins of a once-magnificent 19C mansion. Walls, columns and arched hallways are all that remain after a fire swept the former plantation in 1965. At the height of its glory, the manor house served as the location, in 1956, for scenes in the film *Island in the Sun*. To preserve this remnant of plantation life, the site was inaugurated by Queen Elizabeth II as a national park in 1996.

Francia Plantation

Gun Hill, in the parish of St. George, northeast of Bridgetown. 246-429-0474. Open year-round Mon–Fri 10am–4pm. Closed weekends. $10.

This elegant house was built of coral stone by a French planter in 1913. Double-sash inclined shutters on the *demerera* windows prevent rainwater from entering the house, yet let air through. Look behind the greenhouse to see how rainwater was filtered through cones made of coral stone for drinking water. Inside the spacious house, wood is used lavishly—in parquet floors, for example. Outside, look out on the Saint George Valley from the three-stepped terrace.

A Bit of History

You might actually enjoy learning the island's history—and in a former military prison, to boot. Ameridian civilization, colonization and other topics come to life in the re-created colonial interiors at the **Barbados Museum** *(The Garrison, Bridgetown; 246-427-0201; open year-round Mon–Sat 9am–5pm, Sun 2pm–6pm; closed Dec 24–27; $3)*. The prison's cells are devoted to exhibits on military history.

Touring Tip: Open House

On Wednesdays *(2:30 pm–5:30 pm, mid-Jan to mid-Apr; $7.50)*, historic buildings and private homes throughout the island are open to the public. A bus tour *($18.75)* includes transportation from hotels and entrance to the houses. In addition to Francia, other attractions on the tour include **St. Nicholas Abbey** (1650) in St. Peter, **Sam Lord's Castle** and **Sunbury Plantation Home** in St. Philip, and **Tyrol Cot Heritage Village** in St. Michael. For reservations, contact the Barbados National Trust *(246-426-2421)*.

Must-See Parks and Natural Sites

Harrison's Cave★

Off Rte. 2, south of the town of Welchman Hall, in the parish of St. Thomas. 246-438-6640. http://harrisoncave.com. Open year-round daily 9am–6pm. $16.

Put on a hard hat and prepare for a mile-long ride on a small train through this eerie, mammoth cave, sitting in the heart of Barbados. Part of the network of caverns carved into the limestone by subterranean rivers, Harrison's Cave is the most popular attraction on the island. Its stalactites and stalagmites will dazzle you. Tours begin with a video on the geology of Barbados.

Hiking Groups

Join a group and go hiking. Highland Adventure Center offers a two-hour excursion for both children and adults every Sunday morning from January through March. Call the center for details and reservations *(246-431-8928; www.barbados.org/tours/highland).*

Barbados Wildlife Reserve

Opposite Farley Hill National Park in the parish of St. Andrew. 246-422-8826. Open year-round daily 10am–5pm. Closed Jan 1 & Dec 25. $12.

Watch out: you might find yourself walking with an agouti (looks like a large rabbit). The amazing thing about this sanctuary is that, apart from the reptiles (read pythons!) and birds, the animals here are free to roam. Covered in a mahogany forest, the reserve is home to animal species native to Barbados, the other Caribbean isles and else-where. Keep your eyes peeled for green monkeys, parrots, turtles, iguanas, flamingos and other creatures as well as lovely plants like flowering cactus.

Saint Vincent and the Grenadines

Dreaming of a Robinson Crusoe-style escape? Come to these 33 islands and cays to find the perfect hideaway. Sitting 26 miles south of St. Lucia, **Saint Vincent★**, the largest island (18 miles by 11 miles) of this independent nation, holds the capital of **Kingstown**, an active port. North of Kingstown lie the volcanic island's black-sand beaches, like **Wallilabou Beach★**. St. Vincent serves as the gateway to the **Grenadines★★** —**Bequia★**, **Mustique★** and other small islands, begging to be hopped. They arc the waters of the Caribbean Sea and the Atlantic in a southerly direction to the picturesque **Tobago Cays★★**.

Teasers

Bequia, Mustique and the Tobago Cays aside *(see Excursions)*, other Grenadines are worth exploring. Sun on Mahault Bay's secluded beach, or hike the white-cedar forests of Mount Royal on **Canouan** (CAN-oh-wan), where Donald Trump is constructing a hotel. Stroll to Salt Whistle Bay on the northern tip of **Mayreau★**, and swim at Salt Whistle Bay Resort's beach. On private **Petit St. Vincent,** the cottages at the resort of the same name have no AC, TV or phones; guests raise a yellow flag outside to get the staff's attention.

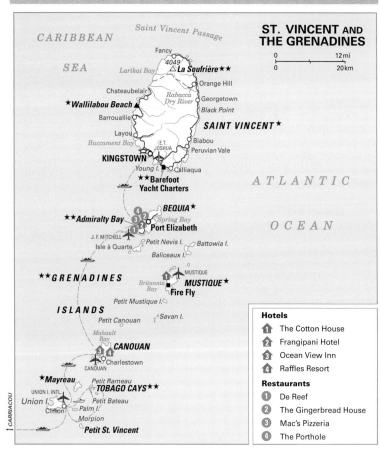

ST. VINCENT AND THE GRENADINES

CARIBBEAN SEA

Saint Vincent Passage

Fancy
4049
△ La Soufrière★★
Orange Hill
Larikai Bay
Chateaubelair
Rabacca Dry River
Georgetown
★Wallilabou Beach
Black Point
Barrouallie
Layou
SAINT VINCENT★
Buccament Bay
(E.T. JOSHUA)
Biabou
Peruvian Vale
KINGSTOWN
Young I.
Calliaqua
★★Barefoot Yacht Charters

ATLANTIC

★★Admiralty Bay
BEQUIA★
Spring Bay
Port Elizabeth
J. F. MITCHELL
Isle à Quarte
Petit Nevis I.
Battowia I.
Baliceaux I.

OCEAN

★★GRENADINES
Britannia Bay
MUSTIQUE
MUSTIQUE★
Fire Fly
Petit Mustique I.

ISLANDS
Petit Canouan
Savan I.
Mahault Bay
CANOUAN
Charlestown
CANOUAN
★Mayreau
Petit Rameau
TOBAGO CAYS★★
UNION I. INTL
Petit Bateau
Clifton
Palm I.
Morpion
Petit St. Vincent
↑ CARRIACOU
Union I.

Hotels
1 The Cotton House
2 Frangipani Hotel
3 Ocean View Inn
4 Raffles Resort

Restaurants
1 De Reef
2 The Gingerbread House
3 Mac's Pizzeria
4 The Porthole

0 ——— 12 mi
0 ——— 20 km

Musts for Outdoor Fun

Barefoot Yacht Charters★★

Blue Lagoon, St. Vincent, east of the airport. 784-456-9526. www.barefootyachts.com. $1,199 (for 6 days & nights, including breakfast & lunch).

Want to learn to sail? This may be the best sailing school in the Caribbean; it's especially good for beginners, and for more advanced sailors who want to get their bareboat certification. For six days and nights you live onboard a 40-foot (or larger) yacht, learning the basics of sailing, coastal navigation and safety drills. Swimming, snorkeling. and dining on a different island each night round out the fun.

La Soufrière★★

Northwest end of St. Vincent. After Rabacca Dry River, take the road on the left. The trail to the top begins 2.5mi farther.

Hire a guide *(see sidebar, below)* and leave early for the four-hour, round-trip hike to the rim of this imposing volcano. More than 4,000 feet high, the active volcano has made headlines since the beginning of the 19C; it last erupted in 1979. Despite the smell of sulfur dioxide, you'll be rewarded with an emotional high and spectacular landscapes: bamboo groves, cultivated fields, waterfalls, an immense tropical forest, rocky terrain carpeted with lichens and a panorama of the island.

Expert Companions

Sign up for an ecotour with HazECO Tours *(Kingstown, St. Vincent; 784-457-8634; www.hazecotours.com).* The friendly staff will personalize an itinerary and transport you by luxury van or Land Rover jeep, powerboat or catamaran. The company specializes in off-the-beaten-path hikes.

Best Excursions

Tobago Cays★★

Captain Yannis Day Charter catamaran cruises depart from Union Island year-round. 784-458-8513. www.captainyannis.com. $50.

For an unforgettable experience, laze the day away aboard a 60-foot catamaran in the translucent blue-green waters surrounding the Tobago Cays (Tah-BAY-go KEYS). These four islets, sitting 4.5 miles north of Union Island, are widely considered the most beautiful, not only of the Grenadines, but of all the Lesser Antilles. First you'll stop at 100-acre Palm Island for a swim in the warm waters offshore; the private island is home to the all-inclusive Palm Island Resort, with two restaurants. Then you'll sail northeast to the Tobago Cays, where the captain anchors between Petit Rameau and Petit Bateau. After a generous buffet lunch, snooze on the white-sand beach surrounding Petit Bateau, or don a mask and snorkel and explore the closest coral reef. On the return voyage, you'll detour to treeless Morpion, a minuscule cay of sand topped, surprisingly, by one palm-thatched beach umbrella. The boat trip ends back at Union Island late in the afternoon, but your memories will last forever.

Touring Tip: Moveable Feasts and More

There are no services and no restaurants in the Tobago Cays, a protected national park. Yet traders from Union Island pull up in their boats to offer everything from jewelry and T-shirts to lobsters and fresh bread—some may even cook you up a meal of conch and lobster on the spot.

Bequia★

Access by ferry from Kingstown, St. Vincent. One-way crossing 1 hour. $11 round-trip.

Come experience this peaceful haven, a verdant island in the midst of the ocean. The largest (7 square miles) and the most populous (5,000 inhabitants) of the Grenadines, Bequia *(BECK-wee)* attracts an artsy crowd, lots of yachtsmen and Europeans. You'll come ashore by way of **Admiralty Bay★★**, one of the most striking bays of the West Indies, jam-packed with magnificent sailboats and impressive cruise ships at the mooring. The biggest town on the island, **Port Elizabeth**, shows off smart wooden houses scattered on the slopes bordering the bay. The town's nonchalance, the beauty of its flower-bedecked homes shaded by almond trees, and the cheerful welcome of its residents will surely seduce you. Take the walkway along the piers and the hotels close to the shore.

Touring Tip: Island Taxis

Hire one of the numerous taxis to discover the island of Bequia. These wide-open vehicles allow a good view of the landscape. And water taxis with fun names like "No 'fraid Dat" or "Why Worry" crisscross the harbor for easy bar-hopping and shopping.

Mustique★

No scheduled service by boat. Flights from St. Vincent or Bequia offered by Mustique Airways 784-458-4380; www.mustique.com.

A paradise for billionaires, this small island, just 3 miles long, is known the world over as a remote hideaway for public figures. Sumptuous residences, such as **Fire Fly** *(Britannia Bay; 784-456-3414; www.mustiquefirefly.com/firefly/main.htm)*, can be rented, but few can afford the price tag of as much as $30,000 a week for these privately owned villas *(reserve with The Mustique Co., Ltd.; 784-458-4621; www.mustique-island.com)*. With some luck, especially if you frequent **Basil's Bar** *(Britannia Bay; 784-458-4621)*, you may bump into Mick Jagger, David Bowie or other celebrities who frequent Mustique. This restaurant-bar, a cafe, a grocery store and a few shops are the island's only amenities. Sign up with the Mustique Equestrian Center for a trail ride ending with a gallop on the beach *(784-458-4316; $60)*.

Day-Trip Charters

The *S/Y Pelangi*, a 44-foot sailing yacht with two guest cabins, is available through the Frangipani Hotel *(784-458-3255; see Must Stay)* in Bequia for day trips *($200 per day for 4 people)* to Mustique and Tobago Cays. Skipper Cyril "Bamo" Stowe has a wealth of sailing experience; in the 1980s he crewed for Bob Dylan aboard the singer's Bequia-built schooner.

Grenada

Sugar and spice and every-thing nice—but mostly spice. Known as the Isle of Spice, **Grenada★** (Gren-AY-dah) pro-duces more spices per square mile than anywhere else on earth; the 21-mile-long island supplies one-third of the world's nutmeg, and grows clove, ginger, cinnamon and tumeric as well. You'll find these spices at the **market square★** in **Saint George's**, the capital of this

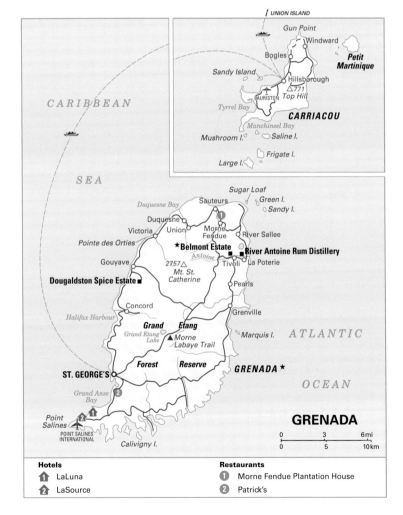

Hotels		Restaurants	
🏠	LaLuna	❶	Morne Fendue Plantation House
🏠	LaSource	❷	Patrick's

three-island nation, of which Grenada is the largest. Though geographically part of the Grenadines, **Carriacou** (CAR-ee-ah-coo), 17 miles to the north, and **Petit Martinique**, 2.5 miles farther northeast, are politically joined with Grenada. Both make pleasant day excursions.

Must-See Historic Sites

Belmont Estate★

Belmont, in the Parish of St. Patrick. 473-442-9524. www.belmontestate.net. Open year-round daily Sun–Fri. Closed Sat. $1.50.

You a chocoholic? At this 300 year-old plantation, you'll see how cocoa beans are transformed into the rich, dark substance in hot chocolate and candy bars. The estate, which first produced sugar, then coffee, then cotton, and now cocoa, includes sugar-mill ruins and a museum of mid-20C household items.

Dougaldston Spice Estate

14mi north of St. George's. Take the road to the right just before the Gouyave River bridge. Open year-round Mon–Fri 9am–4pm.

Ever wonder about nutmeg? Come to this estate to get the inside scoop. Converted to a museum, this former spice factory features a wooden building, where nutmeg, gathered by the local villagers, dries out front on large platforms mounted on rails. The platforms can be moved under the building to keep the nutmeg dry in case of rain.

> **Touring Tip**
>
> Buy a necklace crafted of spices at Dougaldston Spice Estate for a mere $1; it will add fragrance to your kitchen back home. Or take home a small sack of spices for just $2.

River Antoine Rum Distillery

River Antoine Estate, St. Patrick's. 473-442-4537. Open year-round daily 9am–4pm. $2.

Step back, way back, to 1785, at this, the oldest functioning water-propelled distillery in the Caribbean. The original methods of making rum are still used here, from crushing the sugarcane to the distillation. You'll have an opportunity to sample the over-proof rum: with an alcohol content of 75%, it might just bowl you over!

Must-See Parks and Natural Sites

Grand Etang Forest Reserve

8mi northeast of St. George's. Take the main road in the island's interior.

There's a short trail in this national park, the Morne Labaye Trail, with steps so you can climb to a watchtower. From there, a panorama stretches out along the east coast south to the town of Grenville.

Trinidad and Tobago

Trinidad★ is the party; **Tobago**★★ is the place to sleep it off. After Trinidad's world-famous Carnival *(see sidebar, below)*, the residents of this two-island nation head for Tobago's beaches to chill out. Lying 86 miles south of Grenada, Trinidad, 50 miles long and 37 miles wide, hugs the coast of fellow oil-exporter Venezuela. Anchoring the Gulf of Paria, Trinidad's capital of **Port of Spain** is an industrialized city, heavy with traffic and fast-food eateries. Rain forests cover much of the island, harboring tropical plants and animals, especially birds. Sleepy Tobago, 22 miles northeast, is devoid (for now) of modern development. It's the quintessential Caribbean island, with friendly people, quaint villages and secluded beaches. Bring your party clothes *and* a swimsuit.

Carnival★★★

Get ready to par-teeee! Carnival was born in Trinidad in the late 18C when Catholic settlers from France feasted and held masquerades before Lent. The internationally known two-day celebration begins the Monday before Ash Wednesday with "J'ouvert", the wild and extravagant opening ceremony. Then the blitz continues with bizarre costumes, calypso and steel-pan music, street dancing, and consuming corn soup and aloo (potato) pies washed down with plenty of Trinidad rum or coconut water.

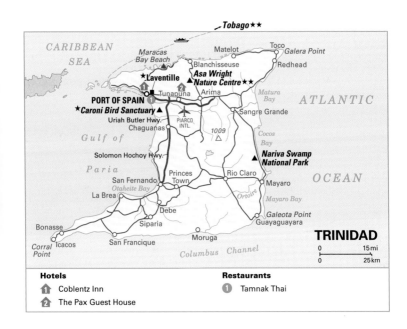

Hotels		Restaurants	
🏠 1	Coblentz Inn	⬤ 1	Tamnak Thai
🏠 2	The Pax Guest House		

Must-See Beaches

Bloody Bay Beach★★

Northwest coast of Tobago (last beach access before heading into the rain forest).

Said to be named for a supposed naval battle here in 1666, in which the British defeated combined Dutch and French fleets, this beach is a glorious place to catch rays or swim in the clear blue waters. Save for a fisherman or two, you'll probably be the only one on these golden sands.

Castara Beach★★

West central coast, Tobago.

Encompassing two gold-sand beaches, Castara is a great place for families. Spend the day on the Big Bay side, which is the focus of Castara village. You'll be able to pitch in and help the fishermen "pull seine" (pull in their nets). Stay long enough to watch the sunset and have a beachside dinner at Cascreole Restaurant *(Castara Beach Rd., Castara; 868-639-5291)* at the end of the beach.

Pirates Bay Beach★

20-minute walk northwest of Charlotteville, Tobago. Access is via an old cocoa plantation and 170 steps down to the beach.

Worth going the extra mile, this beach is named for the dastardly buccaneers who camped out here over three centuries ago. Filmed extensively for the original 1952 movie *Robinson Crusoe*, Pirates Bay is the epitome of a dream beach. Friendly vendors sell fruit and coconut water to quench your thirst.

Store Bay Beach★

South of Pigeon Point, southwest coast, Tobago.

Because this is the most popular public beach on the island, it gets crowded (by Tobago standards). You'll find changing rooms here, and lifeguards are on duty. Best of all, vendors here sell crab-n-dumplings, the signature Tobagan dish. If you need a beach break, hotels, motels, shops and restaurants line the sand.

Must-See Parks and Natural Sites

Asa Wright Nature Centre★★

*Off Blanchisseuse Rd., north-central Trinidad. 868-667-4655. www.asawright.org.
Open year-round daily 9am–5pm. $6.*

This former cocoa and coffee plantation in Arima Valley is now a privately run reserve that attracts thousands of nature lovers a year, including those who overnight in the center's 24-room lodge. At the 250-acre estate, guests and nonguests can take guided hikes *(reservations advised)* or just sit on the lodge's veranda to see toucans, hummingbirds, bats, butterflies, agouti (large rabbit-like animals), armadillos and other wildlife, as well as vibrant flowering plants *(best viewing Jan–May & Oct)*.

Caroni Bird Sanctuary★

Off Uriah Butler Hwy., 7 mi south of Port of Spain, Trinidad. 868-645-1305.

To see mangrove trees full of scarlet ibis (the national bird), stunning in their rich red plumage *(best viewed at dusk)*, is worth the visit to this sanctuary. Protected within 15,000-acre Caroni Swamp National Park, the 337-acre wetlands attract some 130 species of birds, from pelicans to roseate spoonbills and the rare red-capped cardinal. *Reserve a boat tour in advance with Winston Nanan (38 Bamboo Grove Settlement #1; 868-645-1305; 3hrs; $10).*

Nariva Swamp National Park

East-central coast of Trinidad, off Cocos Bay. Bring binoculars & insect repellant.

This 3,840-acre wetland, including forested Bush Bush Island, nurtures manatees, turtles, red howler monkeys, Amazon parrots, macaws and other creatures. But beware of anacondas, 30-foot-long snakes that constrict their prey. Best to go with a guide! *For entry permit and tour operators, contact the Forestry Division: Long Circular Rd., Port-of-Spain; 868-622-4521.*

Tobago Forest Reserve

*Eastern interior of Tobago. From Speyside, head south on Windward Rd. to Roxborough.
Take Roxborough-Parlatuvier Rd. to the reserve.*

Hike just over a mile *(2.5hrs)* through the lush rain forest of this 14,000-acre reserve with expert guide David Rooks. A self-taught ornithologist, he consulted with famed bird authority Sir David Attenborough on the documentary series *Trials of Life*, filmed on **Little Tobago** (one mile off Tobago's northeast coast). *Make advance reservations with David Rooks Nature Tours, Scarborough (868-756-8594; www.rookstobago.com; $50; bring your lunch).*

Musts for Fun

Laventille★

East of Port of Spain, Trinidad. Take Wrightson Rd. east to S. Quay Rd., which becomes Eastern Main Rd., into Laventille.

Don't go alone to this rather rough neighborhood; take a taxi and a friend to *the* place to hear steel-pan (steel-drum) bands. This suburb of Port of Spain is home to the widely known Desperados Panyard. A month or so before Carnival *(see sidebar, p136)*, it and other panyard bands are in high gear practicing for island competitions, which begin the Friday before Lent.

Buccoo

Southwest coast of Tobago.

A tradition since 1925, Sunday-afternoon goat racing in this village is a serious matter. Long-legged goats are put through their paces as jockeys run alongside (rather than ride), holding the animals on leashes. With great ceremony, the goats are assigned lanes and paraded before the crowds. Then, to the roar of the onlookers, hooves fly until the winner crosses the finish line.

Kariwak Village Holistic Haven

Kariwak Village Holistic Haven & Hotel, Store Bay, Local Rd., Crown Point, Tobago. 868-639-8442. www.kariwak.com.

Sign up for a session *($7)* of Tai Chi, Hatha yoga or Buddhist meditation at this South Pacific-style getaway. Holistic activities, including stretching exercises and relaxation classes, take place within a tranquil garden of tropical shrubs and flowering trees. After your session, enjoy vegetarian dishes like stuffed butternut pumpkin in Kariwak's Village Restaurant; herbs and vegetables grown on the premises are incorporated into the cuisine.

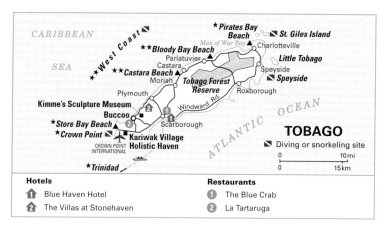

Hotels

1. Blue Haven Hotel
2. The Villas at Stonehaven

Restaurants

1. The Blue Crab
2. La Tartaruga

Musts for Outdoor Fun
Scuba Diving in Tobago

Scuba diving is a huge draw in Tobago, where coastal waters offer a diversity of sea life comparable to Australia's Great Barrier Reef. Thank the Guyana current for this diversity; it flows up South America's eastern shore, bathing Tobago's southern and eastern coasts with warm water rich enough in nutrients to sustain an incredible array of marine animals. Pristine canyons, tunnels, caves and sheer walls teem with manta rays, whale sharks *(June–July)*, tarpon and dolphin, as well as a host of coral. Here are the crème de la crème of Tobagan diving sites:

West Coast★★
West coast of Tobago.

Reefs offer great sites along Tobago's west side. Spectacular sites within Columbus' Passage include Diver's Dream, Flying Reef and Cove Reef. If you dive Mount Irvine Wall, especially at night, you'll glimpse octopi, lobsters, batfish and orange-ball anemones. Arnos Vale Reef hosts stingrays and moray eels.

Crown Point★
Southwest tip of Tobago.

Explore The Shallows, a 50-foot to 100-foot dive along a submarine plateau favored by turtles, dolphins, angel fish, and nurse and tiger sharks. Flying Reef is a quick drift with great viewing of rays and moray eels.

Speyside
Atlantic side, northeast Tobago.

Batteaux Bay lures Atlantic manta rays *(Nov–Jun)*—elusive creatures comfortable with divers around, but keep your distance so these flying fish have room to maneuver. Named for its mountainous formation, The Alps is an advanced dives because of strong currents that deposit you at Tarpon Bowl, a photo op with silvery tarpons. Hard and soft corals highlight the Japanese Gardens.

St. Giles Island
Off the northeast coast of Tobago.

It's worth the short boat trip (seas can sometimes be rough) from Charlotteville to see bridges of rock called London Bridge, Fishbowl and Marble Island.

Dive Shops

Here are a couple of dive outfitters who specialize in Tobago's underwater sites:

AquaMarine Dive Ltd. – *Blue Waters Inn, Batteaux Bay, Speyside. 868-660-5445. www.aquamarinedive.com.* This shop offers some 20 different dives.

Man Friday Diving – *Man-O-War Bay, Charlotteville. 868-660-4676. www.manfridaydiving.com.* Eco-tours and expert instruction for all levels.

Must-See Museums

National Museum and Art Gallery★

117 Frederick St. at Keate St., Port of Spain, Trinidad. 868-623-5941. Open year-round Tue–Sat 10am–6pm, Sun 2pm–6pm.

The highlight here is the exhibit of costumes and head-dresses from past Carnivals—exquisite, colorful creations with feathers, sequins, beads, lace and other adornments. Be sure to see the gallery showcasing artists from Trinidad, including 19C painter Jean Michel Cazabon.

Kimme's Sculpture Museum

Overlooking the Mt. Irvine Golf Course in Mt. Irvine, Tobago, due west of Scarborough. 868-639-0257. www.luisekimme.com. Open year-round Sun 2pm–4pm and by appointment.

Make the trip to Luise Kimme's self-designated white castle on the side of a hill overlooking Mount Irvine Bay. This German sculptor's two-story residence serves as a museum showcasing her larger-than-life sculptures. Made of oak or cedar tree trunks, her tall, slim figures depict dancers, bathers and other Tobago islanders. A resident of Tobago since 1979, she sells her work in Europe as well as locally.

Must-See Gardens

Queen's Park Savannah★★

Off Queen's Park West, city center, Port of Spain, Trinidad.

Rub elbows with the locals at the city's 200-acre centerpiece where down-town's businesspeople come to jog the 3-mile track after work, parents bring their children to stroll and eat fresh coconut from the vendors, and others come to sit quietly on park benches under shady trees. The park's north-western edge is framed by the Magnificent Seven—seven private, colonial mansions built by the well-to-do from 1904 to 1906.

Botanical Gardens★

Off Circular Rd., Port of Spain, Trinidad. 868-622-3530.

For a moment of peace in this frenetic city, head to the northwest corner of Queen's Park Savannah. Covering 62 acres, these lovely gardens, established in 1818 by the British, are laid out in a series of lawns modeled on England's famous Kew Gardens. More than 250 species of tropical trees, from acacia and flamboyant to divi-divi, flourish here.

Touring Tip: Safety First

As in any major city, stay vigilant, especially when touring side streets and local parks. The risk of being a crime victim increases if you are alone and if you are out after dark.

Aruba★, Bonaire★ and Curaçao★★★

Don't forget your ABCs—ABC Islands, that is. Sitting 404 miles west of Grenada, these three arid islands parallel the northern shore of Venezuela's Península de Paraguná. The trio shared a history of Dutch ownership dating back to the 17C, until Aruba, the westernmost of the three, gained independence in 1986. Now casinos, high-rise hotels and shops galore compete with the handsome Dutch-Colonial buildings of **Oranjestad,** Aruba's capital and port of call. Bonaire, to the east, is synonymous with spectacular dive sites. Middle island Curaçao, the largest at 38 miles long and 7 miles wide, preserves a taste of Amsterdam in its picture-perfect capital of **Willemstad★★★**, a World Heritage Site.

Papiamento

Curaçaoans are master linguists who speak four languages: Dutch, English, Spanish and Papiamento, a Creole language based on Portuguese, Spanish, Dutch and a few African dialects. Born in Curaçao, the language evolved over 300 years ago, spreading first to Bonaire, then to Aruba. Here's a little Papiamento 101 to get you by:

Bon bini – Welcome   *Dushi* – Sweetie (used by everyone all of the time)
Bon dia – Good morning   *Ayo* – Goodbye

Must-See Beaches

Cas Abao Beach★★

Northwest Curaçao. Open year-round Mon–Sun 8am–6pm. $2/car (Sun $3/car).

Coconut palms and chickee huts shade this wide beach, punctuated on each end by rocky cliffs. The outdoor bar/restaurant serves up friendliness and island-brewed Amstel beer.

Klein Curaçao★★

15mi off the southern coast of Curaçao. 2-hour one-way boat trip departs Fishermen's Pier Wed, Fri, Sun 6:45am, returns 4pm. $60 round-trip, including lunch. Mermaid Boat Trips: 5999-560-1530; www.mermaidboattrips.com.

Some say stepping on the white powder-fine beaches of this uninhabited island is a step into paradise. There's a lighthouse to explore as well, and two underwater dives from the Mermaid boat.

Palm Beach★★

West coast of Aruba, off J.E. Irausquin Blvd.

Backed by high-rise hotels, this crowd pleaser offers a long stretch of fine, white sand lined with beach bars and water-sports kiosks. It's the haunt of locals on the weekends, when Arubans set up barbecue stands and grill up hot dogs and chicken.

Baby Beach★

South tip of Aruba, east of San Nicolas.

Named for its small size, this beach is a great choice if you have kids. The waters are usually lake-calm and no more than four feet deep.

Hadicurari Beach★

Northwest coast of Aruba, off Rte. 1.

Bring your boards, or watch the action at this beach, locally called Fisherman's Hut Beach. Windsurfers love the air movement and choppy surf so much that an annual wind-surfing competition is held here.

Manchebo Beach★

West coast of Aruba, off J.E. Irausquin Blvd., south of Palm Beach.

Also known as Punta Brabo Beach, this long, wide stretch of sand where big surf rules is active with water sports. It's perfectly fine to take off your top at Punta Brabo.

Musts for Kids

Curaçao Sea Aquarium

Bapor Kibra z/n, southeast Curaçao. 5999-461-6666. www.curacao-sea-aquarium.com. Open year-round daily 8:30am–5:30pm. $15 adults, $7.50 children.

Here children can help feed sea turtles, lobsters, dolphins, nurse-shark pups and other sea critters. Kids Encounter *($45/half-day)* teaches the 4- to 12-year-old set about the marine environment.

Curaçao Ostrich & Game Farm

Groot St. Joris West z/n, Curaçao. 5999-747-2566. www.ostrichfarm.net. Open year-round daily 8am–2pm (call ahead to reserve).

With 600 ostriches and baby chicks, this farm is a hit with kids. There's even a kids' menu at the on-site Zambezi Bar and Restaurant.

Must-See Historic Sites

Willemstad★★★

Settlers from Holland arrived on the island in the early 17C. Today Curaçao's quaint capital features a stunning palette of buildings and stately homes with characteristic Dutch-style architecture, painted in all hues of pastels. Sint Annabaai divides the city's western side of **Otrobanda**, one of the most historic areas of the Caribbean, from the eastern side, known as **Punda**, a tourist hive of shops and restaurants. Stroll over the bay's **Koningin Emmabrug★** (Queen Emma Bridge), a long pontoon bridge that separates the two sections of Willemstad.

A Holiday Tradition

Every year before the Christmas season, Willemstad residents paint their homes a different color. Legend has it that Peter Castell, a former governor, got headaches when he looked at all the white houses. He convinced the islanders to paint their houses in different colors. After he died, the islanders found out that he owned a paint factory.

Also at Christmastime, islanders buy new underwear, and at midnight, make a wish as they throw their old pairs into the sea.

CURAÇAO

Noordpunt
Westpunt
Westpuntbaai
1230 △ Christoffelberg
Lagun
Boca Santa   **Christoffel**
Cruz   **National Park**
Soto ○ Barber
Boca Santa
Marta
★★**Cas Abao Beach**
Sint Willibrordus ○
Salina St. Marie
Bullenbaai
CURAÇAO
INTERNATIONAL
★★★**Museum**
Kurá Hulanda   Santa Catarina
Sint Michiel ○
Senior Curaçao
Liqueur Factory Sint Joris Baai
Otrabanda ○○ ●**Punda**   ▲**Curaçao Ostrich**
Braakeput   **& Game Farm**
★★★**WILLEMSTAD**
Curaçao Sea   Caracas   △643   **Den Paradera**
Aquarium   Baai   ●**Punt Kanon**
Nieuwpoort
Curaçao ▲
Underwater Park   ★★**Klein Curaçao** ∖

CARIBBEAN SEA

CARIBBEAN SEA

★Aruba!

0 — 5 — 10mi
0 — 10km

Hato Caves

Hotels
🏨 Avila Beach Hotel
🏨 Hotel Kurá Hulanda

Restaurants
① Gouverneur de Rouville Restaurant & Café
② Jaanchi's Restaurant
③ Old Marshe

Must-See Museums

Museum Kurá Hulanda★★★

At the Kurá Hulanda Hotel, Klipstraat, Willemstad, Curaçao. Open year-round daily 10am–5pm. $6.

Journey through the exhibits at this first-class museum, which provide an excellent overview of the cultures of Curaçao, beginning with a chronicle of the origin of mankind through modern-day Antillean art. The African slave trade, in particular, receives in-depth attention. Artifacts include examples of pre-Columbian gold and relics from Mesopotamia. Carved masks and tribal drums highlight the superb collection of African art.

Musts for Fun

Angelica's Kitchen

Hoogstraat 49, Willemstad, Curaçao. 5999-562-3699. www.angelicas-kitchen.com.

Take a cooking class in Angelique Schoop's childhood home. You'll cook up a traditional Curaçaon meal of mojitos, *funchi* (polenta), and beef with Caribbean vegetables, and then sit down on the patio with fellow students to enjoy it.

Den Paradera *(The Herb Garden)*

Fuik, Seru Grandi Kavel, 105A Banda Riba, Curaçao. 5999-767-5608. Open year-round Mon–Sat 9am–6pm.

Come visit this organic garden filled with plants used in traditional medicines. Herbal potpourris, and fruit beverages are for sale in the small shop on-site.

Senior Curaçao Liqueur Factory

Landhuis Chobolobo, Schottegatweg Oost 129, Willemstad, Curaçao. 5999-461-3526. Open year-round Mon–Fri 8am–noon & 1pm–5pm. The free tours include tastings.

For over a century, the Senior family has mixed aromatic oils and exotic spices into the peels of Valencia oranges to produce Curaçao's famed liqueur.

Touring Tip

Every morning the **Floating Market★★** in Willemstad's Punda bustles with Venezuelan fishing boats loaded with freshly caught fish and tropical produce. Come early *(8am)* to get the freshest fruits and vegetables—but be sure to wash and peel your purchases before eating them.

Musts For Outdoor Fun

Bonaire National Marine Park★★

One of the world's top dive destinations, Bonaire National Marine Park *(headquarters in Barcadera; 5999-717-8444; www.bmp.org)* encompasses the coral reef encircling the island. Most of the 86 designated sites are walk-in dives from the beach (as opposed to boat dives); numbers on roadside yellow stones match those on the park's diving map *(available at hotels, tourist offices or online at www.bmp.org)*. Here are a few great dive sites.

Touring Tip

Before entering the Marine Park, you must attend a diver orientation (unless you've dived here within the calendar year), purchase a $10 tag *(available at dive shops, from park rangers or from park headquarters.)* and attach it to your gear to dive legally in Bonaire's waters.

Bari Reef – *Sand Dollar Resort.* Amicable tarpon are the stars of this extremely popular night-dive spot in 20 feet to 100 feet of water.

Ol' Blue Reef – *Between Columbia and Karpata.* A rocky terrace quickly drops off to 80 feet for views of finger sponges and coral, including star, yellow pencil and flower. Watch for turtles in the shallows.

1,000 Steps – *South of Ol' Blue Reef.* The 64 steps down to the water lead you into a light current, where you'll probably see Hawksbill turtles—and maybe even a whale shark—amid colorful sponges and coral. It's the walk *up* the steps with your gear on that make them feel like 1,000 steps.

Weber's Joy/Witches Hut – *West side of the island.* A favorite haunt of underwater photographers, this easy shore dive in 20 feet to 100 feet of clear water spotlights massive star corals, angelfish and butterfly fish.

Klein Bonaire – *A short boat ride off the Leeward Shore.* This uninhabited islet's waters are included in the Marine Park. The isle hosts a wide range of stunning dive sites such as Carl's Hill and Sharon's Serenity.

Tour Curaçao by Car

Rent a car at Curaçao's airport and go for a scenic drive. Take Weg naar Westpunt west out of Willemstad and bear left onto Weg naar Santa Cruz through Soto to reach several isolated beaches along the northwest coastal route. On the right side of the road, **Christoffel National Park** is worth exploring *(park office in Savonet; 5999-864-0363; www.curacao-tourism.com).*

Must Be Seen: Nightlife

The night scene in **Aruba** is a lively one. Start your evening at Charlie's Bar and then move on to the gaming tables, or catch a live show at a casino. Most casinos are open from noon until dawn.

Charlie's Bar – *Main St., San Nicolas. 297-584-5086.* This island institution was opened by Dutchman Charlie Brouns in 1941 to the applause of US troops safeguarding Aruba's oil refineries during World War II; the servicemen met here to drink and strategize to defeat the Germans. Charlie visited the wounded daily and was given the Order of Knighthood for his war efforts. His memory lives on at the bar, covered in mementos, and known for its sizzling steaks and enormous shrimp.

The Alhambra Casino & Aladdin Theatre – *J.E. Irausquin Blvd 93, Manchebo Beach. 297-583-5000.* A doorman dressed as a genie grasps your hand to welcome you into this Moorish fantasy. Some 300 slots and a few gaming tables await you. The Aladdin Theatre is known for its talented singers, dancers and impersonators.

Aruban Cocktail

Locals love to sip island-manufactured Poncha crema (a rum-spiked egg nog), poured over ice and sprinkled with Angostura bitters and fresh nutmeg. Mix it with coe coe, made from the island's agave plant, and you get a "Pink Panther," a popular Aruban cocktail.

Casino at the Renaissance Aruba Beach Resort – *L.G. Smith Blvd. 82, Oranjestad. 297-583-6000. www.renaissancearubaresort.com.* Open 24/7, this casino, filled with the clanging of slot machines, is also known for its entertainment, especially Latin dance and music reviews shown in the Crystal Theater.

Copacabana Casino Bar – *Hyatt Regency Aruba Beach Resort, J.E. Irausquin Blvd. 85, Palm Beach. 297-586-1234. www.aruba.hyatt.com. Open noon–4am.* Take a peek at this stunning Rio-themed casino, where you can choose from 295 slots and 21 high-rolling gaming tables.

Royal Cabana Casino and Tropicana Showroom – *La Cabana All-Suite Beach Resort, J.E. Irausquin Blvd. 250, Eagle Beach. 297-587-9000.* Gambling crowds throng to Aruba's largest casino for some 300 slots and 30 gaming tables. Top off the evening at Tropicana's female-impersonator show.

Stellaris Casino – *Aruba Marriott Resort, L.G. Smith Blvd. 101, Palm Beach. 297-586-9000. www.marriott.com.* Nonstop action is the name of the game here in this 10,700-square-foot casino, filled with 500 slots and 32 tables for craps, blackjack and more.

The venues listed below were selected for their ambience, location and/or value for money. They are arranged by island or island group in order of price, from the most expensive to the least expensive. Rates are in US dollars and indicate the average cost of an appetizer, an entrée and a dessert for one person (not including tax, gratuity or beverages). Most restaurants are open daily (except where noted) and accept major credit cards. Call for information regarding reservations, dress code and opening hours.

$$$$	Over $50	$$	$15–$30
$$$	$30–$50	$	Under $15

The Bahamas

Sun and. . . , $$$$ Continental

Lakeview Dr., off Shirley St., east Nassau, New Providence Island. Dinner only. Closed Mon & the months of Aug & Sept. 242-393-1205. www.sun-and.com.

A haunt of celebrities since the mid-1950s, this fine-dining restaurant continues to attract famous figures with fresh-out-of-the-water dolphin, snapper and other locally caught fish. Owner since 1981, chef Ronny Deryckere pleases customers with rich conch chowder and entrées such as the Bahamian fisherman's plate of grilled lobster tail and fish, fresh conch and lump crabmeat in an herbed lemon-peel olive oil sauce.

Buena Vista Restaurant $$$ Continental

Delancey St. Nassau, New Providence Island. 242-322-2811.
www.buenavista-restaurant.com.

This pink and white Bahamian mansion, built in the late 1700s, offers gracious dining on the likes of duck liver pâté with green peppercorns in puff pastry, to start. Then proceed to filet of grouper à la Bimini (sautéed, with a curry sauce, topped with coconut), served with chutney and rice pilaf. Prix-fixe selections are available for $45.

Mangoes
$$$ Bahamian

Marsh Harbour, Great Abaco. 242-367-2366. www.mangoesabaco.com/restaurant.

The chef at this casual, cheery restaurant once cooked for Britain's House of Commons. He has pretty much aced Bahamian specialties like cracked conch and Bahamian fried chicken. And he has a way with seafood: try the mango grouper, panfried with a mango, tomato and cilantro salsa, sweet chilli compote, pickled ginger-fried hominy cake and a coconut shrimp served with grilled zucchini. There's a different vegetarian entrée each week on the menu along with a diet-friendly dish. Yacht-watching is a favorite pastime from the open-air terrace, which is perfectly positioned for toasting lipstick-red (no kidding) sunsets. After your meal, take time to browse in the gift shop.

The Poop Deck
$$$ Seafood

Yacht Haven Marina, Nassau, New Providence Island. 242-393-8175. www.thepoopdeckrestaurants.com.

Fresh seafood is king at this Nassau icon. Watch the comings and goings of celebrity yachts and mail boats in the harbor from the second-story deck. Renowned for traditional Bahamian dishes like conch (scorched to cracked), grouper fingers and lobster, this restaurant encourages you to select just-caught red or yellow snapper and have it cooked to your liking. The bar is a popular and lively hangout.

Goldies
$ Bahamian

Arawak Cay, Nassau, New Providence Island. Closed Mon. 242-326-4433.

A little bridge crosses to Arawak Cay, a manmade islet alive with conch vendors. Dining at Goldies is an authentic Bahamian food adventure, which includes lots of elbow-rubbing with the locals. This place is the most popular walk-up conch bar in the Bahamas. It's a treat to watch Goldie (or one of his bartenders) extract the meat of the mollusk from its pretty shell. Order up fresh conch salad (some islanders tout it as the capital's best) or opt for the crunchy fried fish. At night Goldies gets hopping, Nassau-style!

Jamaica

Georgian Dining Terrace $$$$ International

In the Round Hill Hotel and Villas Resort, Round Hill Bay, Montego Bay. 876-956-7050. www.roundhilljamaica.com.

Sit inside or out on the terrace with a view of the bay at this swank resort's elegant dining room. At dinnertime, Jamaican specialties complement a menu of international dishes, but the highlight is the nightly outdoor buffet ($55), a memorable event, with several themed stations serving up delicious Jamaican gourmet food, hopefully under a full moon.

The Sugar Mill $$$$ Jamaican

In Half Moon Resort, Montego Bay. 876-953-2211. www.halfmoon-resort.com.

No wonder celebrity sightings are frequent here—this restaurant epitomizes romance, and gourmet Jamaican fare. Dress up a bit and stroll into Sugar Mill's enchanting alfresco setting: an original stone terrace strung with tiny white lights and backed by the soothing sounds of water spilling over a 200-year-old waterwheel. Start with the pumpkin-coconut soup and move on to blue fin tuna, pan roasted and served on steamed callaloo (made from the leaves of the taro root), with yam pearls and mango sauce. Not in the mood for seafood? Try the curry of the day, served with island vegetables, rice and fried plaintain. Live Jamaican music sets the scene for a perfect evening.

Almond Tree Restaurant $$ Caribbean

In Hibiscus Lodge Hotel, 83 Main St., Ocho Rios. 876-974-2813. www.hibiscusjamaica.com.

A huge almond tree grows straight up and right out the roof of this two-story restaurant, so the name is appropriate, isn't it? One of Ocho Rios' most unusual dining spots, Almond Tree has a regular local following. The candlelit tables for two prompt smiles and hand-holding, while the lobster and conch dishes ignite the taste buds. Remember to hang around for a "swinging" drink in the roped chairs at the outdoor bar.

Cosmos Seafood Restaurant & Bar $$ Jamaican

Norman Manley Blvd., Negril. 876-957-4784. www.jamaicajim.com/cosmos.htm.

Have you ever eaten octopus? You can try it at Cosmos, a casual eaterie with pool tables and a television set that plays nonstop. Freshly caught lobster and shrimp are also at your disposal. Start with some Jamaican red-pea soup and, if you've had enough seafood for a while, try the curried goat or curried chicken.

Margaritaville $$ American

Norman Manley Blvd, Negril. 876-957-9180. http://margaritavillecaribbean.com.

If you're looking to party, singer Jimmy Buffett's popular venue is a sure bet. The restaurant is only one part of this sports/entertainment/shopping complex. Join the crowd of convivial patrons and enjoy a margarita (the choice is baffling—over four dozen varieties) with your meal. Menu options range from a cheeseburger-in-paradise to jerk chicken or filet mignon.

Pork Pit $ Jamaican

27 Gloucester Ave, Montego Bay (near Walter Fletcher Beach). 876-952-1046.

Looking for a laid-back, inexpensive yet authentic Jamaican culinary adventure? Join beachgoers who arrive here in swim suits and local business people escaping from the office; sit down with them outdoors at picnic tables for what many say is the best Jamaican jerk around. Jamaican jerk chicken is the most prized, but plenty order the jerk pork or fish, as well as steamed fish. Nothing complements jerk like an icy cold Red Stripe beer—a favorite island combo.

Cayman Islands

Cracked Conch by the Sea $$$ Seafood

West Bay, next to the Turtle Farm, Grand Cayman. 345-945-5217. www.crackedconch.com.ky.

This Cayman Islands' landmark serves up conch in salads, chowders and stews, and as fritters or "cracked" (panfried) as well. But there's more on the menu than just conch. You'll find main courses like blackened chicken, jerk pork, and turtle steaks in a coconut-cream sauce. Join the crowd on the patio for spectacular sunset dining.

Hemingways $$$ Seafood

In the Hyatt Regency hotel, Seven Mile Beach, Grand Cayman. 345-949-1234. http://grandcayman.hyatt.com.

Reserve in advance to enjoy a meal at this much-touted open-air restaurant. Watch the surfside parade from your table overlooking famed Seven Mile Beach, while you savor grilled snapper, grouper or another right-out-of-the-water catch. Caribbean-accented dishes, such as tenderloin seasoned with Cuban spices, or lamb accented with comino (cumin)-scented *jus*, are also good choices.

Rum Point Restaurant $$$ Seafood

Take the 30min ferry from the Hyatt Regency hotel dock (Seven Mile Beach, Grand Cayman) to Rum Point. Dinner only. Closed Sun. 345-949-1234. http://grandcayman.hyatt.com.

You'll feast on wahoo, tuna or marlin fresh from the sea at this lively Rum Point staple, palm-shaded and sitting right on the sand. The pistachio-encrusted sea bass is a perennial favorite. Dine early, though—the last ferry back to Grand Cayman departs at 9:15pm *(Fri–Sun only)*.

Puerto Rico

Il Perugino $$$$ Italian

105 Cristo St., Old San Juan (across from El Convento Hotel). Lunch Thu–Sat only. 787-722-5481. www.ilperugino.com.

Hand-painted murals and a cistern-encased wine cellar add Old World charm to this fine-dining establishment. Award-winning chef Franco Seccarelli has welcomed fellow Italians Luciano Pavarotti and Cecilia Bartoli and other celebrities to his intimate restaurant. Tease your palate with shrimp salad with marinated zucchini, then choose ravioli stuffed with chicken liver, spinach and truffle as your *piatti principali*.

La Compostela $$$$ Continental

106 Condado Ave., Condado. No lunch Sat. Closed Sun. 787-724-6088.

This award-winning gem, sitting just east of Old San Juan, has repeatedly won high honors for culinary excellence. Hearty entrées such as rabbit are seasoned with a Spanish flair. Seafood, lamb and duck courses are equally formidable, and there are two types of paella from which to choose. Attentive service and a well-stocked wine cellar (upwards of 10,000 bottles) round out a satisfying dining experience.

Su Casa Restaurant $$$$ Spanish

In the Hyatt Dorado Beach Resort, Hwy. 693, Dorado. Closed Sun. 787-796-1234. www.doradobeach.hyatt.com.

Among the eight restaurants at this north coast resort, Su Casa, housed within a weathered hacienda, ensconces patrons in Old World Spanish charm. Enter through a courtyard bursting with tropical foliage. Strolling musicians complement an array of Spanish entrées such as a roasted pork chop with achiote adobo, served with green beans and tamarind sauce. The red snapper with citrus and ginger vinaigrette should not be ignored, however. Start with a tropical green salad topped with papaya, avocado and spicy Caribbean dressing.

Bottles Gourmet Food and Wine $$$ Continental

Calle Tabonuco, Guaynabo (southwest of San Juan). 787-775-1210.

San Juan's yuppies come as they are to this casual, combination grocery store, gourmet deli, wine shop and restaurant in the lively city of Guaynabo. Go though the deli, and choose a bar stool in the wine shop or at a long table in the restaurant. Then order up some seafood pasta or the baked duck, accompanied by a French label from Bottles' extensive wine list. Don't leave without some little treat to go.

La Bombonera $ American

259 Calle San Francisco, Old San Juan. Breakfast and lunch only. 787-722-0658.

For over a century, generations of surly-looking waiters at this neighborhood icon have been waking up Old San Juan with the best jolt of Puerto Rican coffee in the city. At La Bombonera the cup of potent java is usually paired with a yummy Mallorca-style pastry from the large bakery case, or in some instances a full American breakfast from the kitchen. At lunch and dinner, the local favorite is a seafood gumbo soup called asopao.

US Virgin Islands

Craig and Sally's $$$$ International

3525 Honduras, Frenchtown, St. Thomas. Closed Mon & Tue. 340-777-9949.

There's nothing casual about the food at this laid-back, Caribbean-style cafe. Regulars keep coming back for chef Sally's innovative dishes like jumbo shrimp sautéed in papaya-rum garlic butter, served over blueberry-spiked basmati rice. Hubby Craig's wine cellar has earned the reputation as the best on the island of St. Thomas.

The Palm Garden Café $$$$ Continental

In the Ritz-Carlton resort, 6900 Great Bay, St. Thomas. 340-775-3333.
www.ritzcarlton.com.

You'll feel like royalty as you are ushered to your outdoor table, topped with a market umbrella, at this posh Mediterranean-style resort anchoring the eastern tip of the island. You'll be treated to attentive service and Caribbean-accented entrées, such as seared jerk mahi-mahi or roasted chicken in Creole sauce, fit for a monarch.

Fagioli Ristorante$$\quad$$$$ Italian

The Waterfront, Veterans Dr. (Rte. 30), Charlotte Amalie, St. Thomas. Closed Sun. No lunch Sat. 340-777-8116.

This downtown eatery, edging the waterfront, draws outdoor lovers to its cheerful courtyard for alfresco dining beneath patio umbrellas. Satisfying Italian staples such as pasta, pizza, panini and calzone share menus space with house specialties osso buco (veal) and, for dessert, tiramisu.

Bumpa's$$\quad$$$ American

38-A Waterfront Hwy. (the east end), Charlotte Amalie, St. Thomas. Breakfast and lunch only. 340-776-5674.

Look for the pink-and-white striped awning to start your day (or to take a break from shopping) with a visit to this second-story eatery. Bumpa's may not be fancy, but its hearty breakfasts and flavorful deli-style soups, salads and sandwiches bring in the crowds. Homemade pies, a harbor view and a pet iguana are added benefits, at no charge (except for the pie).

British Virgin Islands

Sugar Mill Restaurant$$\quad$$$$$ Caribbean

In the Sugar Mill Hotel, Little Apple Bay (west of Cane Garden Bay), Tortola. 284-495-4355. www.sugarmillhotel.com.

Consistently acclaimed in travel and food publications, this appealing restaurant is ensconced within a 370-year-old stone mill that formerly served as a rum distillery. Patrons savor delicious concoctions like peanut-pumpkin soup for starters, and main courses such as the Sugar Reef spicy chicken with pineapple salsa. Be sure to enjoy a cocktail at the bar on the terrace overlooking the water.

Mrs. Scatliffe's Restaurant$$\quad$$$$ West Indian

Carrot Bay, Tortola. Dinner only. 284-495-4556.

Rub shoulders with locals who come here for "de best West Indian cookin' on de island," like chicken (that's fall-off-the-bone tender) with coconut. One-time chef at Caneel Bay Resort, Mrs. S. serves up four-course dinners at one daily seating on the terrace of her home. Fruits and veggies plucked from her backyard garden go into salads and tasty treats like sour-sop sorbets and banana flambés. Sometimes a fungi band shows up, relatives who play music the old-fashioned way—on scratchboards, spoons and gourds.

Myett's Garden and Grille$$\quad$$$$ Seafood

Cane Garden Bay, Tortola. 284-495-9649. www.myettent.com.

Nature melds with island flair at Myett's. Shaded by a lush tropical garden, the casual dining space here is perfect for watching the sun melt into the ocean off one of the Caribbean's most popular beaches. Lobster, shrimp and fish are prepared on an open grill, as are landlubber standbys like steak and hamburgers. (Vegetarian dishes are always offered.) If you're hungry between lunch and dinner, fear not: snacks, soups and salads are served throughout the day, to music with a reggae beat.

Sydney's Peace and Love $$ Seafood

Little Harbour, Jost Van Dyke. 284-495-9271.

Plenty of yachts anchor in beachless Little Harbour just to take a dinghy to this quintessential Caribbean waterside hangout. It's a memorable BVI experience. Inside, T-shirts and whatever hang from the rafters. There's a self-serve honor bar where you mix your own cocktails, mark each one down and tally them up at evening's end. Sydney's grilled lobsters, which come small, medium and large, are legendary. On weekends, live bands are ferried in for dancing.

Big Bamboo $ Seafood

Loblolly Bay, Anegada. 284-495-2019.

Set upon a deserted beach that most people only dream of seeing, this beach bar has staked out a shady, open-air setting amid a grove of sea-grape trees. It's customary to place your order upon arrival, and then walk a few steps to the aqua waters for a couple hours of snorkeling, or catching rays on the sand. The famous grilled lobster dinners here are superb—your lobster is picked right out of the ocean. Barbecue chicken or grilled local fish come in a close second. Whatever you order, it's presented with laid-back, friendly service.

Pusser's Road Town Pub $ Pub Fare

Waterfront Dr., Road Town, Tortola. 284-494-3897. www.pussers.com/outposts/roadtown.

Red-roofed and accented with gingerbread trim, this joint is Road Town's perennial "in" spot. The interior mirrors a Victorian pub. The menu ranges from jerk pork to pizza, but the highlight is a lobster club sandwich washed down, of course, with Pusser's version of the famous Painkiller. The drink is made with Pusser's rum from a centuries' old recipe that the early British Navy used; seems they plied their seamen with the concoction to stiffen the men's courage.

Lesser Antilles

Saint-Martin/Sint Maarten

Le Santal $$$$ French

40 Rue Lady Fish, Sandy Ground, St-Martin. Dinner only. 590-87-53-48. www.restaurantlesantal.com.

It's worth the effort to find this intimate restaurant, situated at the eastern edge of Nettlé Bay. Inside you'll experience an evening of fine dining, with entrées such as grilled red snapper flambée with pastis, braised leeks and a white-wine butter sauce, or prawns and scallops Provençal style with crunchy noodles in a sesame-oil sauce. Start with the crêpe stuffed with lobster, mushrooms and shallots in a white-wine crayfish sauce.

Captain Oliver's $$$ Seafood

Oyster Pond, St-Martin. 590-87-40-26. www.captainolivers.com.

Popular with boaters, this open-air restaurant, situated above the waters of a lagoon, overlooks a marina filled with yachts. Oliver's chef places emphasis on fresh seafood; in fact, you can select your own lobster from the restaurant's tank. French and Creole dishes are also on the menu.

Chez Martine $$$ French

Grand-Case, St-Martin. Dinner only. 590-87-51-59.

A quality restaurant with quality food, that's what you'll find at Chez Martine. Savor house specialties such as pan-fried crayfish topped with citrus fruit, fettucine Saint-Jacques accented with tarragon, or grouper fingers sautéed in orange butter.

L'Escargot $$$ French

84 Front St., Philipsburg, Sint Maarten. 599-542-2483. www.philipsburg-info.com/escargot.

When you set eyes on this orange-colored Creole house, decorated with whimsical paintings that include snails (of course!), you'll smile even before you taste one bite of escargot. This friendly establishment has earned its reputation not only for escargot prepared seven different ways, but for appetizers like frog's legs in a light garlic sauce and main courses of filet of grouper roasted with ginger.

Da Livio Ristorante $$ Italian

189 Front St., Philipsburg, Sint Maarten. No lunch Sat. Closed Sun. 599-542-2690.
www.stmartinstmaarten.com/DaLivio.

A wall full of celebrity photos attests to the popularity of this welcoming *ristorante*. Deemed the best Italian cuisine in Sint Maarten, Da Livio's home-made manicotti *della casa*, the house specialty, comes complete with ricotta cheese and spinach in a tomato sauce. The veal scaloppini in marsala sauce with mushrooms is another good choice. Top off your meal with homemade spumoni.

Hevéa $$ Creole/French

In the Hevéa hotel, 163 Blvd. de Grand-Case, St-Martin. Closed Mon in summer.
590-87-56-85.

Part of the Grand-Case beachside lodging of the same name, this small, formal restaurant is favored locally for its excellent Creole and French cuisine. Prix-fixe and à la carte dinners focus on traditional entrées such as scallop cassoulet, or escalopes of veal with Calvados and cream. Lobster is a menu staple.

St. Barthélemy

La Mandala $$$ Thai

Rue Courbet, Gustavia. Dinner only. 590-27-96-96.

Step into this Thai-like world and you'll feel at once an atmosphere combining romance and serenity. The Asian-inspired food, from fish spring rolls dipped in tamarind sauce to Thai shrimp curry, is sure to please even the fussiest gourmand. For a most memorable experience, reserve a table set within the waters of a zen-like pond. Meals here are topped off with an old island custom—conversation, along with the slow sipping of vanilla rum.

Le Repaire $$ French

Quai de la République, Gustavia. 590-27-27-48.

The *tres délicieux* French and Creole food served at this open-air brasserie has long lured locals to gather here. They arrive early for the best authentic French breakfasts this side of Paris. Meals at lunch and dinnertime are just as popular. Le Repaire excels in seafood preparation, French pastry and views of sunsets that include the magnificent yachts docked in Gustavia harbor.

St. Kitts/Nevis

The Dining Room at The Four Seasons $$$$ Continental

In the Four Seasons Resort, Pinney's Beach, Nevis. Dinner only. 869-469-1111.
www.fourseasons.com/nevis.

Dinner in this elegant, high-ceilinged setting, with an incredible view of the sea, is always romantic. Tables topped with fresh flowers glow in candle-light. The resort's executive chef has a knack for creating memorable dishes like lobster medal-lions with pineapple carpaccio, or mahi-mahi blanketed in cashew nuts and Nevis honey. Asian-inspired entrées include pork loin with vegetable spring roll and wasabi. Soufflés reign as the dessert of choice.

Miss June's Cuisine $$$$ International

Jones Bay, Nevis. 869-469-5330. Reservations required.

Three nights a week of her choosing, Trinidad native June Mestier welcomes guests into her West Indies home for an evening of good conversation and global dishes, including, of course, a Trinidad curry. Fish is always one of the main courses. The set price covers cocktails, hors d'oeuvres, soup and two courses, as well as wine with dinner, dessert and brandy. It's a moveable feast within the various rooms of her house.

Ballahoo
$$ Caribbean

The Circus, Basseterre, St. Kitts. Closed Sun. 869-465-4197.

Located on the second floor, Ballahoo's dining room is large and pleasant, with a view of the roundabout and its dark-green clock tower, the focal point of the city. This eatery is great for a quick breakfast or lunch. At dinner, stay a while to enjoy seafood dishes like conch in garlic butter or chicken roti (an East Indian bread filled with vegetable or meat curry).

Bayembi Café
$$ American

Bank Street, Basseterre St. Kitts. Closed Sun. 869-465-5280.

Located near The Circus, this combination cafe and bar offers inside and terrace dining and three meals a day. Hearty breakfasts include fried eggs or omelets with croissants. In the evening, when the dance floor gears up to full swing, order a main course of goat water (goat stew with rum) or jerk chicken with red beans and rice.

Café des Arts
$ French

Main St. & Samuel Hunkins Dr., Charlestown, Nevis. 869-469-7098.

Tucked behind a fence and the broad green leaves of banana trees, this artsy little cafe remains pretty much a secret, except to those in the know. The menu offers light fare (delicious desserts, fresh croissants, healthy salads, fruit smoothies and yummy quiches) served within a gallery setting or outside among bright Caribbean-colored buildings. Linger and take in the creative ambience. The gallery features works of distinguished Caribbean artists.

Sunshine's Beach Bar and Grill
$ Caribbean

Pinney's Beach, Nevis. 869-469-5817. www.sunshinenevis.com.

Umbrella-shaded picnic tables sit right in the sand at this gorgeous beach. So plan a barefoot day of swimming and sunning, while sipping Sunshine's extra-rummy, blue-ribbon-winning Killer Bee punch. Choosing from the menu gets tricky: his baby-back ribs sport a secret sauce; the conch is sautéed and tender; and his shrimp and fish are sumptuous. Nightly bonfires light up the place. Be on the lookout for celebrities, dressed down, of course. Sunshine's is world famous for its New Year's Eve parties.

Antigua/Barbuda

Chez Pascal
$$$$ French

Galley Bay Hill, Five Islands, Antigua. 268-462-3232. www.chezpascal.net.

The setting is superb. This hilltop restaurant overlooks the sparkling waters of the Caribbean Sea, offering patrons magnificent views. A mélange of French flavors and Caribbean aromas, the food is artistically prepared by chef Pascal Milliat. Try the lobster medallions in basil butter. Madame Milliat (Florence) orchestrates the discreet service.

Abracadabra
$$$ Italian

Dockyard Dr., English Harbour, Antigua. Closed Jul–Sept. 268-460-2701. www.theabracadabra.com.

Expect a lively atmosphere when you dine. Located in Nelson's Dockyard, this crowded trattoria becomes a popular night spot that fills with a youthful crowd on the dance floor. For something out of the ordinary, try the *porceddu*, Chef Salvatore's roasted suckling pig, but be forewarned—it actually looks like a pig. The seared tuna is a customer favorite as well.

Catherine's Café
$$ French

English Harbour's wharf, Antiguan Slipway, Antigua. Lunch only Mon. Closed Tue & the month of Sept. 268-460-4050.

Overlooking the harbor and Nelson's Dockyard, Catherine's offers diners a menu of French classics such as *salade niçoise*, crêpes, quiches and seafood dishes. There's a great wine selection and the coffee is especially delicious.

Guadeloupe

Chez Jackye
$$$ Creole

Southern end of Pointe-Noire, Deshaies, Basse-Terre. Closed Sun evening. 590-98-06-98.

Sandwiched between the sea and the road, this renovated restaurant offers tasty Creole specialties like *lambis* (conch) cocktail or *ouassous velouté* (freshwater crayfish). At lunchtime, sandwiches and salads are available.

Côte Jardin
$$$ French

Pointe-à-Pitre marina, Grande-Terre. Dinner only Sat. Closed Sun. 590-90-91-28.

Come to this restaurant overlooking the marina off Victoria Square for food with French and Creole flair. Try, for example, the Guyana shrimp flambéed with anise, or the filet of sea bream roasted in *roucou* (a local annatto spice used primarily in roasting or broiling fish). You won't be disappointed.

Le Bon Temps
$$ Creole

Section Bontemps, Marie-Galante. In Capesterre, take N 9 toward Haut du Morne. At the intersection, turn left and drive 2mi. Closed Mon. 590-97-34-96.

On the island of Marie-Galante, you'll find typical Creole cuisine prepared with love, particularly at this restaurant of "good times." The menu changes daily according to what's available locally. The chef will be happy to suggest a selection for you.

Le Karacoli
$$ Creole

*On Grande Anse beach, Basse-Terre, Guadeloupe. 590-590-28-41-17. Lunch only.
Closed Tues.*

Named for an Amerindian jewel, this restaurant is a good address to taste typical Creole dishes like *boudin* (pork sausage) and *colombos*—spicy curries featuring goat, chicken or lamb. Seafood offerings often include conch, cod and crabs.

La Mousson
$$ Creole

In Grand-Bourg, Marie-Galante. Closed Sun. 590-97-77-97.

La Mousson (the monsoon) is the perfect restaurant for a quick bite to eat. Simple and delicious dishes like shrimp with parsley and sliced avocado, complement salads and a variety of Creole specialties.

Martinique

La Caravelle
$$$ French

On the same road to Plage Tartane. 596-58-07-32.

Enjoy crêpes and a salad for lunch on La Caravelle's beautiful terrace overlooking the sea. Evening fare here includes entrées such as grouper terrine with a basil-anise sauce, shrimp Saint-Jacques, and duck breast on a banana compote. Order the passionflower mousse for dessert.

Fatzo
$$$ Continental

11 rue Felix Eboue (beside the pharmacy), Anse d'Arlet. Dinner only. 596-68-62-79.

Located in a pretty blue and white Creole-style house, this restaurant offers superb continental cuisine. Try the grilled duck, the pork or any of the many seafood dishes.

Chez les Pêcheurs
$$ Seafood

On the beach behind the 8 à Huit supermarket, Carbet. 696-23-95-59.

Literally translated, the restaurant's name means "home of the fishermen". The star item on the menu here is, of course, locally caught fresh fish, usually grilled and served with red beans and rice.

L'Anse Noire

$ Seafood

At L'Anse Noire Beach. Lunch only. Closed Mon. 596-68-62-82.

To get to this often-crowded restaurant, you have to climb almost 150 steps. Seafood platters, grilled fish or lobster dishes are served on long wooden tables under a roof of palm fronds. You may order à la carte, for example, grilled fish with vegetables and a *chien* sauce (a Creole sauce made with local spices and hot pepper), tailored to your taste by the chef.

Le Marie-Sainte

$ Creole

160-162 Rue Victor-Hugo, Fort de France. Breakast and lunch only. Closed Sun. 596-63-82-24.

This restaurant has been a Fort de France institution for 50 years. The food is an incredible value for the price, and the atmosphere is animated and family-oriented. Try authentic area dishes such as *acras* (a crispy, salty beignet often flavored with fish), *boudin* (pork sausage), crab or crayfish, all served with local vegetables.

St. Lucia

The Great House

$$$$ French

Cap Estate in Gros Islet. Dinner only. Closed Mon. 758-450-0450.

Sitting on the site of a once-magnificent plantation manor, this restaurant has a reputation for grand and romantic dining. Impeccable service by a staff clad in traditional island dress enhances the experience. Influenced by Caribbean flavors, French entrées to savor include local crab, shrimp and chicken, often topped with a Creole sauce.

The Coal Pot

$$$ French

Vigie Marina, Castries. No lunch Sat. Closed Sun. 758-452-0284.

Overlooking the marina, this small restaurant extends a big welcome to diners at its 10 tables. You can expect imaginative sauces (mushroom, ginger or garlic butter, for example) to enhance chef Xavier's lamb or broiled fish entrées. Chicken, beef and duck are also on the menu.

The Still

$$ Creole

Still Plantation and Beach Resort, Bay St., Soufrière. 758-459-7232.

This eatery, popular with cruise-ship passengers, is situated on a working cocoa plantation located on a hillside. The two large dining rooms at the resort can seat several hundred diners. You'll feast on fish, beef or pork courses, accompanied by locally grown vegetables and fruits.

Barbados

David's Place $$$ Continental

St. Lawrence Main Rd., Christ Church Parish. Closed Mon. 246-435-9755.

Overlooking the St. Lawrence Bay, this restaurant cradles its clientele within a romantic ambience of candles and soft music. Slip into a wicker chair and prepare to savor a typical Barbados meal centered on an entrée of barracuda, mackerel, red snapper or flying fish. Shellfish and meat dishes are also available.

Mullins Beach Bar & Restaurant $$ Seafood

West coast, north of Holetown. 246-422-1878.

Located on charming Mullins Beach, this bar/restaurant offers such items as salads, marinated chicken and hamburgers for lunch. At dinnertime, patrons choose from a selection of seafood dishes.

Pisces $$ Seafood

Near the St. Lawrence church, St. Lawrence Gap, Christ Church. Dinner only.
246-435-6564.

As indicated by its name, this seaside restaurant specializes in fish and shellfish dishes. Spiny lobster, barracuda, flying fish, shrimp and other seafood are served up with locally grown vegetables and fruit. Savor your meal in the pleasant dining room, open to the sea, while listening to relaxing music and, in the background, the sound of the waves.

Waterfront Cafe $$ Caribbean

Facing Trafalgar Square, Bridgetown. Closed Sun. 246-427-0093.

A great place to watch passersby, this cafe is located on the first floor of Fisherman's Wharf restaurant. Order up a house specialty such as the fried flying-fish sandwich or the pepper pot (a highly seasoned West Indian stew with meat and vegetables). The Tuesday-night Caribbean buffet *(7pm–10pm)* is accompanied by a live band, should you care to dance.

St. Vincent and the Grenadines

The Gingerbread House

$$ Caribbean

Admiralty Bay, Port Elizabeth, Bequia. 784-458-3800.

Delicious home cooking by beloved islander Pat Mitchell is what keeps patrons coming back to this bayside cafe. Trimmed with gingerbread and sitting in the shade of an old almond tree, the house sports a veranda and the hung-sash windows typical of Caribbean homes. Butterflies glide by and the laughter of local children fills the air. Expect freshly squeezed fruit juices, morning-baked Bequian cakes and pies and homemade sweet-potato pudding. Dinner brings scrumptious seafood and steaks as well as spicy curries. For dessert? Warm gingerbread drizzled with lemon sauce, of course.

The Porthole

$$ Caribbean

Front St., Port Elizabeth, Bequia. Closed Sun. 784-458-3458.

Lined with windows open to the breezes of Admiralty Bay, this beachfront eatery pulls in islanders for Bequia native Noeline Taylor's hearty home-cooked food. Her three-course meals at dinnertime focus on a choice of seafood, steak, chicken or lamb. Try the grilled fish Creole-style or the curried ginger chicken, two local favorites. Then enjoy coffee in the reading area Noeline created as a book exchange.

De Reef

$ Caribbean

Lower Bay, Bequia. 784-458-3484.

A popular beach bar for lunch at Lower Bay's enticing stretch of sand, De Reef also draws the locals and tourists for breakfast, dinner, cocktails, and on Sunday afternoons, live music. You should definitely reserve in advance for dinner. But at both midday and evening meals, fresh seafood dishes featuring conch, shrimp or lobster with a West Indies flair are sure to please.

Mac's Pizzeria

$ Creole

Belmont Walkway, Admiralty Bay, Bequia. 784-458-3474.

When in Bequia, you must go to Mac's to savor the pizzeria's world-famous lobster pizza out on the porch overlooking beautiful Admiralty Bay. Other house specialties include Mac's Conch McNuggets, and an extra-heavenly homemade key lime pie made with a shortbread crust. Follow the aromas of banana bread baking in the oven, and you'll stumble upon this favorite "yachtie" eatery that never breaks the bank, even if you order some of the Creole specialties.

Grenada

Morne Fendue Plantation House $$ Creole

Near Sauters, St. Patrick's Parish. Closed Sun. 473-442-9330.

This two-story 18C house, constructed with river stones and reputedly a lime-and-molasses mortar, regularly attracts islanders for its spicy West Indian buffet. Served on the veranda, traditional dishes include callaloo soup, pepper-pot stew, pigeon peas and rice, chicken and fish. If you prefer to eat indoors, the airy dining room is set with dark-wood chairs, and tables are covered with lace cloths.

Patrick's Homestyle Cooking $$ Grenadian

Lagoon Rd. (opposite bottom entrance to Grenada Yacht Services), St. George's. 473-440-0364. www.grenadaguide.com/patrick.

A meal here is one of the most unique—and authentic—dining experiences in the Caribbean. Patrick himself is as much a draw as is his banquet of home-cooked Grenadian dishes. For a set price, you get 20 tapas-size plates of soups (callaloo—made from the leaves of the taro root—vegetable or pumpkin), salads (crab, potato, lobster, breadfruit) and meats such as stir-fried rabbit, curried mutton, beef casserole and ginger pork. Patrick cooks the food fresh each day.

Trinidad and Tobago

The Blue Crab $$$ Caribbean

Main & Robinson Sts., Scarborough, Tobago. 868-639-2737.

Miss Allison, as the locals call her, embraces all who enter this restaurant as if they're family; she is as big a draw as the traditional cuisine she cooks. The specialty here is curried crab and dumplings, but the combination platters of flying fish and shark bites are just as popular. She makes up pitchers of steeped sorrel, and serves ginger beer—perfect drinks for the screened porch.

La Tartaruga $$$ Italian

Buccoo Bay Rd., Buccoo Bay, Tobago. Dinner only. Closed Tue, Thu & Sun. 868-639-0940. www.latartarugatobago.com.

Take a seat on the bougainvillea-entwined patio, choose a bottle of Italian wine from the restaurant's 200-plus stock, and begin a culinary journey that will leave you feeling as if you're in a grand restaurant in Rome. Gabriele De Gaetano, the sincere, highly animated owner, imports oils, cheeses and olives directly from Italy; he buys organic herbs, produce and fish locally from the islanders. Every day he bakes bread. Try his homemade pastas, fresh lobster or fresh fish. Then linger under the stars over cappuccino and a gelato or cheesecake.

Tamnak Thai $$ Thai

13 Queen's Park East, Port of Spain, Trinidad. No lunch Sat–Mon. 868-625-9715. www.tamnakthai.co.tt.

Looking for exotic and spicy food? Here you'll find classical Thai cuisine cooked up by specially trained chefs. The menu is filled with fiery salads, soups, curries, stir frys and plenty of fish, including dishes with cuttlefish and with mussels. Duck, lamb, chicken beef and pork are presented as main courses as well. Enjoy your meal outdoors on the patio, or inside in individually styled rooms accented with Asian paintings and artifacts.

ABC Islands

Papiamento Restaurant $$$$ Continental

Washington 61, Noord, Aruba. Dinner only. Closed Mon. 297-86-45-44.
www.papiamentorestaurant.com.

Long ago, the Ellis family transformed this 175-year-old manor into one of the best restaurants on the island. Three Ellis children trained in Holland. Today they are award-winning chefs, who adhere to traditional stone and coal-pot cooking methods to turn out exceptional flavors. Savor Eduardo's Seafood Pot, a mix of seafood, vegetables and herbs (picked from his herb garden), slow-cooked in a terra-cotta pot. Be sure to tour the house before leaving.

El Gaucho Argentine Grill $$$ Argentine

80 Wilheminastreet, Aruba. Closed Sun. 297-582-3677. www.elgaucho-aruba.com.

This first Argentine steak house on Aruba is now legendary. Nearly 30 years of serving high-quality, fork-tender-and-juicy Argentine beef, grilled to perfection, has made this restaurant renowned. If you don't fancy a steak, another top contender is the Pincho Torro Caliente (a spicy beef shish kabob). The decor is pure macho gaucho, but strolling musicians add a touch of *l'amour* as they strum tangos and boleros on their guitars. Even the wines are from Argentina.

Gouverneur De Rouville Restaurant & Café $$$ International

De Rouvilleweg 9, Otrobanda Waterfront, Willemstad, Curaçao. 5999-462-5999.
www.de-gouverneur.com.

Handsomely restored and painted a bold red with white trim, this 18C three-story building is a popular spot to watch the busy waters of Sint Annabaai. The restaurant includes an interior bar and an inner courtyard; seating on the second-story veranda is coveted for its views of the historic architecture of the Handelskade section across the bay. The menu offers a great variety of dishes, from fish stew to lamb shanks.

Jaanchi's Restaurant $$ Caribbean

Westpunt 15, Westpunt, Curaçao. 5999-864-0126.

Hundreds of bright yellow birds are lured to the feeders in front of this open-air restaurant to serenade diners with their cheery chatter. Meanwhile Jaanchi, a local character, sings his menu to you and offers his recommendations. Combination platters might include a Curaçaoan version of conch, shrimp, fish and goat or iguana stew. Enjoy coffee and cookies in the rocking chairs outside.

Old Marshe (Old Market) $ Caribbean

At Konigin Wilhelminabrug (Queen Wilhelmina Bridge), Willemstad, Curaçao.

Picnic tables fill up with locals at lunchtime in this historic building that once served as the old market-place. Regular vendors serve up extra-generous portions of traditional Curaçaoan foods like *funchi* (polenta), *piska hasa* (red snapper), *komkomber stoba* (cucumber stew) and Gouda cheese stuffed with meat or fish.

The properties listed below were selected for their ambience, location and/or value for money. They are arranged in order of price, from the most expensive to the least expensive. Prices are in US dollars and reflect the average cost for a standard double room for two people (not including applicable taxes) in high season. High season in the Caribbean is in the winter and spring (mid-December to mid-April); rates are usually lower in summer and fall. Price ranges quoted do not reflect the hotel tax, which varies by country.

$$$$$	Over $350	$$	$100–$175
$$$$	$250–$350	$	Under $100
$$$	$175–$250		

The Bahamas

Compass Point $$$$ 18 cottages

West Bay St., Nassau, New Providence Island. 242-237-4500 or 800-633-3284.
www.compasspointbahamas.com.

Celebrities frequent this colorful 1.5-acre boutique resort, secluded near Gambier Village. Centered on two pretty coves, upscale "huts," painted in primary colors, offer the perfect hideaway within cool tropical gardens. The pleasant guest room interiors mix batik fabrics and washed woods. There's an on-site restaurant, and the oceanfront bar is ideal for lingering over a Bahama mama cocktail.

British Colonial Hilton $$$ 291 rooms

1 Bay St., Nassau, New Providence Island. 242-322-3301 or 800-445-8667.
www.nassua.hilton.com.

When a 1922 fire destroyed the hotel railroad magnate Henry Flagler built on this spot, the government constructed a new one. Now a Hilton property, the 7-story hostelry fronts its own beach. Rooms are decorated in cheerful Caribbean colors. Five restaurants, a fitness center and a swimming pool are on-site.

Dillet's Guest House
$$ 6 suites

Dunmore Ave. & Strachan St., Chippingham (1mi west of downtown Nassau), New Providence Island. 242-325-1133. www.islandeaze.com/dillets.

This 1928 house exudes Bahamian charm within a tropical garden. From the moment you arrive, you'll be embraced in the welcome of the Bahamian family who owns it. The comfortable rooms are accented with the art of a relative, whose studio is next door. Five of the rooms come with kitchenettes. Your day starts off with a home-cooked breakfast, included in the rate.

Nassau Beach Hotel
$$ 400 rooms

Cable Beach, New Providence Island. 242-327-7711 or 888-627-7282. www.nassaubeachhotel.com.

Overlooking a wide beach, this hotel offers its guests plenty of activities. There are two pools, six tennis courts, a fitness center and equipment for water sports such as kayaking. Choose to dine in one of five restaurants, and you can catch up on the latest news at hotel's Internet cafe. Tastefully furnished, all guest rooms have a balcony or patio.

Peace & Plenty
$$ 32 rooms

George Town, Exuma. 242-345-5555 or 800-525-2210. www.peaceandplenty.com.

Sitting in the middle of George Town, off the calm waters of Elizabeth Harbour, this pale-pink, Colonial-style inn is both famous and popular. The hotel rooms flank a swimming pool that lies steps away from the ocean. Guest quarters sport fabrics in soft pastels or warm oranges and yellows. Complimentary ferries take patrons to Peace & Plenty's Stocking Island Beach Club.

Sivananda Ashram Yoga Retreat
$$ 54 cabins

Paradise Island. 242-363-2902. www.sivanada.org.

Sure to soothe the souls of off-the-beaten-path travelers, this serene retreat is nestled between the neon-bright turquoise waters of the Atlantic and deep-blue Nassau Bay. Opt for a small, sea-breeze-cooled, no-frills cabin on the beach; a semiprivate oean-view room; or a tent pitched amid coconut palms. There are no private baths, only shared facilities. Two vegetarian meals, two yoga classes and two meditation sessions are included each day of your stay.

Turks and Caicos

Grace Bay Club $$$$$ 21 suites

Grace Bay, Providenciales. 649-946-5050 or 800-946-5757. www.gracebayclub.com.

Set on the edge of one of the world's prettiest beaches, this luxury resort caters to well-heeled clientele who come to de-stress or get plenty of exercise. There are opportunities to cycle, play tennis and kayak or simply laze on the beach. Guest quarters are decorated with a Spanish flair; the Egyptian cotton linens and a 27-inch flat-screen TV will no doubt enhance your comfort. A continental breakfast and afternoon tea are included in the rate.

Parrot Cay Resort $$$$$ 51 units

Parrot Cay, off the western shore of North Caicos. 649-946-7788. www.parrotcay.com.

People come to this private 1,000-acre island to unwind on the posh resort's three miles of powdery sand facing a green-blue sea. Ocean- and garden-view rooms soothe guests with the elegant simplicity of four-poster beds draped with white muslin and sleek rattan or teak furniture. Each room has its own veranda. Hire one of Parrot Cay's butlers and be waited on hand and foot. Enjoy Mediterranean cuisine in the resort's Terrace (**$$$$**) restaurant.

Caribbean Paradise Inn $$ 16 rooms

Grace Bay, Providenciales. 649-946-5020 or 866-946-5020. www.paradise.tc.

Three salmon-colored Bermuda-style buildings surrounded by tropical foliage comprise this charming inn. Situated around the corner from the Grace Bay Club, the inn offers rooms awash in soothingly soft pastels; all quarters have a refrigerator and a ceiling fan, and either a balcony or a patio. Partake of the complimentary breakfast buffet on the cheerful, open-air terrace.

Sibonné Beach Hotel $$ 29 rooms

Grace Bay, Providenciales. 649-946-5547 or 800-528-1905. www.sibonne.com.

This low-rise complex proudly proclaims it was the first lodging on Grace Bay. It picked the best location—right on the bay's white-sand beach. Wander the footpaths within the resort's impressive palm and bougainvillea gardens as you head to the swimming pool, the restaurant or the beach. Each pleasantly appointed room has a ceiling fan, a mini-refrigerator and a courtyard patio. A stay at the Sibonné is a good value for the money.

Jamaica

Grand Lido Negril Resort & Spa $$$$$ 210 suites
Seven Mile Beach, Negril. 876-957-5010 or 877-467-8737. www.superclubs.com.

This all-inclusive resort attracts couples, singles and adult families. Grand Lido is set on 22 acres of rambling gardens just off a secluded cove; part of the beach is reserved for those who want to bare it all. Activity reigns here, from tennis and volleyball to windsurfing to diving, but the sunset cruise aboard the resort's 147-foot yacht is a must. Suites come with a Jacuzzi and your own balcony. Champagne, yoga sessions and other goodies are included in the rate.

Half Moon Resort $$$$$ 419 units
Montego Bay. 876-953-2211 or 866-648-6951. www.halfmoon-resort.com.

Long a host to royalty, this island icon marries Colonial charm with tropical beauty. Whitewashed Georgian-style buildings anchor 400 acres of gardens, recreational fields and a shopping village. Choose from two dreamy beaches: Sunrise (to the east) and Sunset (to the west), both overseen by lifeguards. Diversions include an 18-hole championship golf course, world-class tennis and squash facilities, an equestrian center, a spa and six restaurants. Thankfully, the famed resort has banned motorized water sports in the bay.

Round Hill Hotel and Villas $$$$$ 63 units
Rte. A1, Montego Bay. 876-956-7050 or 800-972-2159. www.roundhilljamaica.com.

Understated elegance reigns at this 110-acre resort built along the sea and into the hillsides of a former pineapple plantation. Some of the rental cottages here are owned by Ralph Lauren and other celebrities. The private, gold-sand beach is reserved exclusively for guests. Spacious rooms shine with fabrics and wall treatments coordinated in soft blue or other palettes. A restored 18C plantation  house makes the perfect location for Round Hill's spa, which offers soothing treatments using indigenous island oils.

Sandals Ocho Rios Resort & Golf Club $$$$$ 529 rooms
Main St., Ocho Rios. 876-974-5691 or 888-726-3257. www.sandals.com.

This huge and widely popular all-inclusive resort stretches out between the green St. Ann Mountains and the biggest beach in Ocho Rios. Stay here if you like nightly parties with live music and dancing. The suites are pleasantly decorated and include a four-poster bed and a sitting area. Just about everything for a fun getaway is in-  cluded in the rate, from tips and water sports to gourmet dining and snacks. Spa treatments are extra.

Cayman Islands

Southern Cross Club

$$$$ 10 bungalows

Little Cayman. 345-948-1099 or 800-899-2582. www.southerncrossclub.com.

Rated consistently as a top dive resort worldwide, this small club makes for grand memories on an island that time has passed by. Four-poster beds and island colors enliven the bungalows, which front a fantastic beach. Landlubber activities range from horseshoes and badminton to swaying in hammocks. Meals (included in the rate) are tasty and healthy. A tiki bar on the beach draws a crowd, but diving is king here—the club has two custom dive boats and offers lessons at all levels of ability.

Divi Tiara Beach Resort

$$$ 71 rooms

Cayman Brac. 345-948-1553 or 800-367-3484. www.divitiara.com.

Catering especially to divers, this complex consists of two-story apartment-like buildings, painted in pale yellow or pink and overlooking a beautiful beach. A respected dive operation and a Nikon School of Underwater Photography are added draws; special-needs divers can be accommodated in every way. Rooms are tropical in color and newly renovated. Diversions include a swimming pool, tennis courts, kayaks, nature trails, a water trampoline and a spirited beach bar.

Puerto Rico

Hotel El Convento

$$$$$ 58 rooms

100 Cristo St., Old San Juan. 787-723-9020 or 800-468-2779. www.elconvento.com.

This former 350-year-old convent now houses an enchanting place to stay in Old San Juan. Rich furnishings, highly polished floors and arched windows greet guests upon arrival. Rooms are equally well appointed with handcrafted furniture and marble bathrooms. Have breakfast in the garden terrace overlooking San Juan Cathedral or relax with a book in the library. Added amenities include a rooftop pool and a fitness center. Enjoy salads and sandwiches for lunch at **Patio del Nispero ($$)**, the hotel's courtyard restaurant.

Hyatt Dorado Beach Resort

$$$$$ 289 rooms

Hwy. 693, Dorado. 787-796-1234 or 800-233-1234. www.doradobeach.hyatt.com.

The 1,000 palm-dotted acres of this resort were once a grapefruit plantation. In the 1950s Laurance Rockefeller constructed an oceanfront hotel here, and needless to say, it soon became a magnet for celebrities, royalty and heads of state. It still draws worldly guests to its championship golf course, spa, casino, tennis courts and nature trails—to say nothing of a river pool longer than the Empire State Building laid end-to-end. Rooms are handsomely furnished and come with a patio or balcony. Of the eight on-site restaurants, be sure to dine on Puerto Rican cuisine in historic **Su Casa** *(see Must Eat)*.

Caribe Hilton

$$$$ 646 rooms

Las Rosales St., San Geronimo Grounds, San Juan. 787-721-0303 or 800-445-8667.
www.hiltoncaribbean.com/sanjuan.

A San Juan landmark built in 1949, this recently renovated luxury hotel once lured the stars of Hollywood's Golden Era. Anchoring a peninsula, 17 acres of tropical gardens growing between Old San Juan and the pulsing neighborhood of Condado set the scene. Individual accommodations are comfortable and bright. Oceanfront swimming pools come equipped with a swim-up bar; hammocks line the secluded beach; and the spa and fitness center make tension vanish. Five on-site restaurants offer guests a variety of cuisine and settings.

Wyndham El Conquistador Resort

$$$$ 750 rooms

1000 Conquistador Ave., Fajardo. 787-863-1000 or 877-999-3223.
http://el-conquistador.wyndham-hotels.com.

Themed as an Old-World Spanish village, this mammoth resort boasts elevated views not only of the Caribbean but also of the Atlantic. Spacious rooms include a sitting area, a refrigerator and sizable bathrooms. Opportunities for scuba diving, windsurfing, wave running and fishing lie at your doorstep. If you're a landlubber, try horseback riding, playing a round of golf at the resort's championship course or swimming in one of its six pools. Then you'll be ready for relaxing at the on-site Golden Door Spa.

US Virgin Islands

Caneel Bay Resort $$$$$ 166 rooms

Caneel Bay, St. John. 340-776-6111 or 888-767-3966. www.caneelbay.com.

Rimming seven white-sand beaches, this dreamy 170-acre vacation retreat lies within St. John's untrammeled national park. Remaining loyal to Laurance Rockefeller's preservation creed, the exclusive resort designed its guest quarters to blend into the natural landscape. Each room is an island-style sanctuary decked out in wood and stone and furnished with rattan and wicker. Guests can choose between two on-site restaurants, and find mind-body refuge at the Self Centre *(see p73).*

The Buccaneer $$$$ 138 rooms

Gallows Bay, east of Christiansted, St. Croix. 340-712-2100 or 800-255-3881. www.thebuccaneer.com.

Opened in 1948, this well-known hotel—one of the first in the Caribbean—sits amid 340 acres on the site of a former indigo plantation. The vast resort boasts world-class golf and tennis facilities, four restaurants, three beaches, two pools, a spa and a fitness center—almost a town unto itself. The free kids' camp encourages families to stay here. Appointed with pastel fabrics and wicker furniture, the comfortable guestrooms include a patio or balcony. Be as active, or inactive, as you like. Try yoga on the beach or walk the nature trail.

Hotel 1829 $$ 15 rooms

Kongens Gade, Charlotte Amalie, St. Thomas. 340-776-1829 or 800-524-2002. www.hotel1829.com.

Celebrities, literati and the artsy flock to this boutique inn, which resembles a Mediterranean-style villa. Built in 1829 by a wealthy Frenchman for his bride, the house was one of the largest residences in the King's Quarter. Today it's a treasure trove of antiques throughout, including centuries-old Italian chess pieces as tall as a person, a Tiffany stained-glass window and Moroccan-glazed floor tiles. Cedar-ceiling rooms enclose bamboo platform beds draped with mosquito netting. The on-site bar was once the kitchen of the historic house.

Maho Bay Camps $$ 114 tent cottages

US Virgin Islands National Park, Cruz Bay, St. John. 340-715-0501 or 800-392-9004. www.maho.org.

This globally famous eco-resort offers nature-loving travelers a place to settle in and connect with the land. Constructed in the 1970s of recycled materials, the spacious tent cottages are secreted within lush hillside vegetation and cooled by trade winds. Built on platforms to safeguard the flora, the dwellings are linked by boardwalks. Massage, yoga, park presentations and glassblowing demonstrations in the Trash to Treasure Art Center are popular pastimes here. Two outdoor restaurants serve healthy meals, and bathhouses are conveniently located.

British Virgin Islands

Bitter End Yacht Club $$$$$ 85 units

On the North Sound, northeast Virgin Gorda. Accessible only by boat or ferry.
284-494-2746 or 800-872-2392. www.beyc.com.

Billing itself as a "rollicking nautical village," this South Seas-style resort offers loads of fun, yet is ideal for those looking to hang out and do nothing. Cooling trade winds, stunning water views and a mile of sandy beach seduce landlubbers as much as yachties. Among the water sports offered here, sailing reigns, be it lessons at the club's sailing school or regattas starting from Bitter End's marina. The restaurant is widely acclaimed for its generous buffets. Watching movies under the stars after dinner is a favorite activity.

Peter Island Resort $$$$$ 56 units

Peter Island. Accessible only by boat or helicopter. 284-495-2000 or 800-346-4451.
www.peterisland.com.

About as exclusive as they come, this eye-popping property is the stuff dreams are made of: a resort on a private island. You won't have all 1,200 acres to yourself, but there's plenty of seclusion, thank you. Walk along the beach—one of five—or take a trail up the hillside. Handsomely appointed with rich fabrics and overstuffed chairs, the spacious guest rooms come with a balcony or patio. Savor Caribbean cuisine at the **Tradewinds Restaurant** (**$$$$**), overlooking the blue waters of the Sir Francis Drake Channel—a memorable event.

Anegada Reef Hotel $$$$ 20 rooms

Setting Point, southwest Anegada. 284-495-8002. www.anegadareef.com.

Definitely for off-the-beaten-path travelers hoping to get away from it all, this no-frills hotel sports an island decor and sits on spacious grounds affording spectacular views of the neon-bright sea. It's an ultra-casual, ultra-laid-back kind of place that's ultra-quiet. Simply appointed rooms are reminiscent of motel units. Rates include three meals a day, enjoyed outside on the beach or in the Garden Restaurant. Yet, depending on the length of your stay, you might want to eat a meal or two at a couple of the beach bars on the island.

Long Bay Beach Resort & Villas $$$ 123 units

Long Bay, Tortola. 954-481-8787 or 800-345-0356. www.longbay.com.

A 52-acre hillside estate is home to this resort, which offers lodgings in casual and airy beachfront cabanas, family villas and estate homes. The mile-long sandy beach is a glorious one, with great vistas of the island. Rooms are outfitted with blond furnishings, floral-patterned bedspreads and pastel-painted walls; some rooms include a Jacuzzi. You won't be bored: spa treatments, workouts in the fitness center, tennis and water sports of all kinds are yours for the asking.

Mongoose Apartments
$$ 6 units

Cane Garden Bay, Tortola. 284-495-4421. www.mongooseapartments.com.

It feels like a home away from home in these just-off-the-main-road, tropical-colored apartments. The innkeepers go out of their way to make your stay as rewarding as can be. A private balcony graces each apartment, and a three-minute stroll through a coconut palm grove puts you in the heart of the village of Cane Garden Bay, with its famous beach and popular restaurants. At night, as the breeze cools your apartment, expect a serenade by Caribbean tree frogs.

The Moorings–Mariner Inn
$$ 40 rooms

Wickhams Cay II Rd., off Waterfront Dr., Road Town, Tortola. 284-494-2332 or 888-952-8420. www.moorings.com.

For those satisfied with modest simplicity, this clean, two-story inn sits in the middle of a first-class marina, energized with the comings and goings of watercraft. Built in 1979, the Moorings complex centers on an 80-slip marina that provides yacht charters and water sports. With balconied views of Drake's Channel and a laid-back appeal, the inn attracts landlubbers as well as seamen. Rooms are sizable; refrigerators and showers (no tub) come standard. The open-air restaurant serves up great rotis (an East Indian bread, filled with vegetable or meat curry) and the two bars buzz with sailors' yarns.

Lesser Antilles
Anguilla
Cap Juluca
$$$$$ 116 units

Maundays Bay (southwest coast). 264-497-6666 or 888-858-5822. www.capjuluca.com.

Ritzy and glitzy, this lap-of-luxury resort, with views of Sint Maarten's mountains, keeps the accolades coming. The posh 179-acre property centers on a row of whitewashed Moorish-style villas fringing two miles of gorgeous beach. The ambience here is one of exclusivity and romance—you're meant to feel pampered. All rooms have marble bathrooms and terraces facing the sea. Diversions include croquet, tennis, reading in the library, spa treatments and wellness rituals, and heavenly cuisine at the resort's restaurant.

CuisinArt Resort & Spa
$$$$$ 93 rooms

Rendezvous Bay. 264-498-2000 or 800-943-3210. www.cuisinartresort.com.

The emphasis here is on savoring grand cuisine, participating in a cooking class or two and touring the edible gardens (including a hydroponic one), where tropical fruit, vegetables and herbs are harvested for the day's gourmet meals. Themed dinners are a highlight here. Light-filled suites in multistory Mediterranean-style buildings feature an oceanside terrace, a mini-refrigerator and a walk-in closet. The on-site spa focuses exclusively on the well-being of resort guests. Cooking classes are open to non-guests by reservation.

Lesser Antilles
Saint-Martin/Sint Maarten

Privilege Resort and Spa
$$$$$ 22 units

Anse Marcel, St-Martin. 590-87-38-38 or 800-874-8541. www.privilege-spa.com.

Backdropped by lush green hills, Privilege Resort hugs a sheltered bay with a yacht-filled marina. Bedrooms and suites come with marble bathrooms, and a terrace or balcony for gazing at the water. Come here and be content with lazing about in a hammock, or enjoy a game of tennis or squash, swim in the pool and even pump iron in the gym. The staff will organize a cruise for you in one of those long motorboats called a cigarette. Save time for a late-afternoon seaweed wrap in the on-site spa, though.

Le Meridien
$$$$ 233 rooms

L'Habitation de Lonvilliers, Anse Marcel, St-Martin. 590-87-67-00 or 800-543-4300. www.stmartin.lemeridien.com.

As you walk into the stately Colonial-style reception building to check in, you'll find yourself immersed in a palette of bold oranges and olive greens—colors reflected in the property's setting. The tropical plantation gardens here brim with palm trees, hibiscus, oleander and bougainvillea. The decor of the guest rooms marries these bold colors with hand-crafted Malaysian furniture. From your own terrace or balcony, you can bask in the sun, but the beach lies just steps away. Four restaurants, a fitness center and a swimming pool are on the grounds.

Princess Heights
$$$$ 15 suites

156 Oyster Pond Rd., above Dawn Beach, Sint Maarten. 599-543-6906 or 800-441-7227.

Rising into the hillsides of Sint Maarten, these condominium-style accommodations are just right for travelers with an independent bent. The lodgings have the feel of your own apartment, but come with the amenities of a hotel. Each unit consists of a beautifully furnished one- or two-bedroom suite with marble floors, a kitchen and a balcony overlooking the sea. Princess Heights sits across the road from Dawn Beach, and there's a swimming pool on the premises for your enjoyment.

Mary's Boon Beach Plantation
$$$ 32 units

117 Simpson Bay Rd., Sint Maarten. 599-545-7000. www.marysboon.com.

In business here for over 30 years, this favored Sint Maarten lodging sits right on Simpson Bay Beach. Guests who return year after year like its convenient location just south of the airport and close to shops, restaurants and casinos. They also like the atmosphere and the charming rooms, complete with a terrace; newer units sport four-poster beds. If you like to cook, book a garden studio or an apartment, which have kitchenettes.

Hévéa $ 9 units

163 Blvd. de Grand Case, St-Martin. 590-87-56-85.

Hévéa is well situated. All you have to do is cross the street to take advantage of lovely Grand-Case beach. The establishment is housed within a large Creole dwelling, restored and tastefully decorated. Accommodations are comfortable, and there's an excellent French restaurant, also called Hévéa, on the premises *(see Must Eat)*. You'll definitely find tranquillity in this corner of the island: especially in the off season, the place is almost deserted in the evening.

Lesser Antilles
St. Barthélemy

Eden Rock Hotel $$$$$ 16 units

Baie St. Jean. 590-29-79-99. www.edenrockhotel.com.

Anchoring a rocky promontory surrounded on three sides by the brilliant-blue waters of St. Jean Bay, this famed hotel is a St. Barts' legend. Topless sunbathing on its two picturesque beaches is de rigeur. Newly renovated, along with its recently acquired neighbor, Filao Beach, the hotel shows off inventive decor in its public spaces, laced with Caribbean charm. Suites are done up in muted blues and yellows, with added touches like colorful wall art and vessel basins. Le Tapas Bar is a happening place, with wooden decks cascading down the hillside.

Hôtel Guanahani $$$$$ 69 units

Grand Cul de Sac. 590-27-66-60. www.leguanahani.com.

This St. Barts' icon, sitting on its own 16-acre peninsula, offers a perfect blend of the famous French joie de vivre and West Indian Creole-style architecture. Each intimate cottage offers laid-back but high-styled comfort done up in rare island wood and Caribbean colors. Private patios offer terrific views of the Caribbean Sea. Be sure to experience the delicious French-style breakfast buffet in the open-air restaurant overlooking the beach. The beauty salon offers *très chic* coiffures—some stylists are Paris-trained.

Lesser Antilles
St. Kitts/Nevis

The Hermitage $$$$$ 15 cottages

St. John's Parish, Nevis. 869-469-3477 or 800-682-4025. www.hermitagenevis.com.

Slip into the relaxed feel of this elegant plantation inn, perched 800 feet above sea level. Because the property edges a rain forest, you can expect sightings, around sunrise, of the elusive green-velvet monkey. The breeze-cooled, West Indian cottages, decked out with canopy beds and antiques, dot flowery acres of cashew and mango trees. Guests are invited to cocktails and canapés with the innkeepers in the 340-year-old Great House, before dining in the on-site restaurant. Horse-drawn carriage rides, history hikes, nature walks, afternoon tea and a farmyard encounter with peacocks and sheep are a few of the activities here.

Golden Lemon Inn & Villas $$$$ 25 units

At the northern point of Dieppe Bay, St. Kitts. 869-465-7260 or 800-633-7411.
www.goldenlemon.com.

This beautiful property has West-Indian pizzazz written all over it. Expansive
grounds filled with tropical flora set the stage for the handsome two-story 17C
Great House, painted a pale yellow and sporting a wraparound veranda. Bedrooms are individually appointed with mahogany four-poster or antique metal
beds and all feature sizable bathrooms with modern amenities. Attention to
detail is evident throughout. A black-sand beach lies steps away.

Ottley's Plantation Inn $$$$ 25 units

Between Cayon Town and Lodge (east coast), St. Kitts. 869-465-7234 or 800-772-3039.
www.ottleys.com.

You'll think you're back in the 19C when
you arrive at this elegant plantation. The
estate's manor, or great house, dates to the
1830s; guests fortunate to stay here will
find the lodgings especially delightful.
Wicker and mahogany furnishings plus
floral-patterned chintzes in the guest
rooms convey English Colonial charm. The

Caribbean-style cottage rooms, as well as the grand villa, offer modern amenities such as Jacuzzis. Don't miss the champagne brunch on Sundays in the
Royal Palm Restaurant ($$$).

Montpelier Plantation Inn $$$ 17 rooms

In St. John Parish, four miles east of Charlestown, Nevis. 869-469-3462.
www.montpeliernevis.com.

The atmosphere of this highly touted hillside retreat is pure elegance. Encompassing stunning gardens and a 60-foot mosaic-tiled pool, the inn sits amid the
ruins of a former sugar plantation. White-painted walls and white bedspreads
are accented with soft green or blue accessories in the guest rooms, each
opening onto a veranda. Partake of English scones at afternoon tea, and in the
morning, a bountiful breakfast *(both included in the rate)* is highlighted by
mangoes and oranges grown on the plantation. Evenings bring drinks, hors
d'oeuvres and chats with the innkeepers prior to alfresco dining.

Ocean Terrace Inn $$$ 71 rooms

Basseterre Bay, Fortlands, St. Kitts. 869-465-2754 or 800-524-0512.
www.oceanterraceinn.com.

The highlight of this hotel, which overlooks Basseterre Bay, is its lagoon-like
fantasy pool that's sure to soothe frayed nerves with the sound of a waterfall.
Take your pick of three pools, and end your swim in the outdoor Jacuzzi. All
standard rooms, pleasantly decorated, have balconies from which the bay can
be seen. Be sure to try the West Indian buffet (Fri; **$$**) in the on-site restaurant
named, appropriately, **The Waterfalls**. When you're ready for sand and surf,
take the free shuttle to Turtle Beach.

Lesser Antilles
Antigua/Barbuda

Curtain Bluff $$$$$ 72 rooms

Old Road Village, Antigua. 268-462-8400 or 888-289-9898. www.curtainbluff.com.

A haven for bon vivants, this clubby resort caters especially to families with children *(in Feb, no children under 12 years)*. Kids will enjoy activities from sailing to fishing; twice a year the resort holds a two-week youth camp. Graced with fresh flowers, well-appointed rooms come equipped with balconies that overlook the golden sands and blue waters of Morris Bay and Grace Bay. Rates include three meals a day and afternoon tea. Keep fit with Pilates or yoga sessions; then treat yourself to a seaweed wrap in the resort's spa.

Hawksbill Beach Resort $$$$ 112 units

Five Islands Village, St. John's, Antigua. 268-462-0301. www.hawksbill.com.

Hawksbill edges no less than four powdery beaches, one designated clothing-optional. The resort attracts honeymooners and families seeking an active stay. Recreational options are plentiful—from snorkeling and shopping to enjoying massages in the wellness center. There's a barbecue each week and entertainment nightly. Pleasantly furnished rooms come with a balcony.

Admiral's Inn $$ 14 rooms

English Harbour, St. John's, Antigua. 268-460-1027. www.admiralsantigua.com.

This three-story brick building, a former warehouse in Nelson's Dockyard, was completed in 1788. The ceilings in the upstairs rooms retain their original timbers; some rooms are furnished with canopied four-poster beds. An apartment called the Joiner's Loft overlooks the harbor. In the ground-floor restaurant, you can see the names of frigates early seamen carved on the workbench that now serves as the bar top.

Guadeloupe

Bungalow Grand Palm $$ 4 units

Pointes des Basses, between Grand-Bourg and the airport on Marie-Galante. 590-97-70-34.

A quiet place to stay, this lodging consists of four well-kept cottages, each with one bedroom (twin beds), a sitting room, a kitchenette and a terrace. A short path leads to the sea, but the best beaches for a swim are Petite Anse or Feuillère, each about 4 miles away.

Le Domaine de Malendure $$ 50 units

Morne Tarare, Basse-Terre. Closed Sept-early Oct. 590-98-92-12.

Located close to the black sands of Malendure Beach, this hotel, which sits offshore from the Bouillante Nature Reserve *(see p110)*, draws diving enthusiasts. Occupying a terraced slope, some two dozen bungalows offer great views of the Pigeon islets. Breakfast in the on-site restaurant is included in the rate.

Martinique

Sofitel Bakoua $$$ 139 rooms

Point de Bout. 596-66-02-02 or 800-221-4542. www.sofitel.com.

This luxurious hotel sits near the beach facing Fort de France Bay. Comfortable guest rooms feature a pastel color scheme, a bed with mosquito netting and a private bath. Take advantage of the the swimming pool overlooking the sea. You can play billiards and table tennis, as well as participate in water sports. There are three restaurants on-site, and a continental breakfast comes with your stay.

Hôtel Diamant les Bains $$ 28 units

92 Rue Justin-Roc, in the heart of le Diamant. Closed Sept. 596-76-40-14.

This family-oriented establishment has direct access to a beach lined with coconut trees. There's a swimming pool on-site, surrounded by a tropical garden. Some of the guest rooms overlook the sea, and there are bungalows lining the shore. A continental breakfast is served in the huge dining room, which specializes in Creole dishes at lunch and dinner.

Manoir de Beauregard $$ 11 rooms

Route des Salines, south of Ste-Anne. 596-76-73-40.

Come stay in one of the three rooms upstairs in this 18C manor house, built in the Creole style. Other rooms are located in a newer addition. All guest quarters are sizable and have a private bathroom. This historic manor boasts some modern amenities, such as a swimming pool on the grounds. There is a restaurant as well, offering French and Creole meals. The best beach, though not the closest, is Salines Beach, a short drive away.

Squash Hotel $$ 107 rooms

3 Blvd. de la Marne, Fort-de-France (toward Schoeler). 596-72-80-80.

Located just 10 minutes from the airport, this well-maintained, high-rise hotel offers good value for your money if you are more interested in seeing the sights than staying in resort-style accommodations. Rooms are air-conditioned and come with a television and a mini bar; some rooms face the sea. Breakfast at the hotel's open-air restaurant is included in the rate.

Saint Aubin Hôtel $ 15 units

Rte. 1, between la Trinité and Ste-Marie, on the east coast. 596-69-34-77.

Sporting wraparound verandas, this charming two-story dwelling sits in the heart of a sugarcane and banana plantation. The hilltop house offers amazing views of the island. You'll enjoy absolute tranquillity here in sizable and comfortable rooms. Linger by the swimming pool or take the small trail that leads to the beach *(about a mile from the hotel)*. Reserved for hotel clients, the on-site restaurant serves breakfast only *(included in the rate)*.

Saint Lucia

Anse Chastenet
$$$$$ 49 units

*Anse Chastanet Beach, Soufrière, on the southwest coast. 758-459-7000 or
800-223-1108. www.ansechastenet.com.*

Rave reviews repeatedly characterize this lodging as one of the most exotic, most
romantic in the world. Sitting on 600 acres of tropical jungle edging a fabulous
beach, the resort cascades down a hillside, offering mouth-dropping views of the
sea and the Piton peaks. Wrapped in balconies, the gazebo-shaped cottages are
filled with elegant furnishings and colorful madras plaids. Whole walls (or half a
wall) have been eliminated so you feel you're living within nature at tree-top
height. Diversions include diving, snorkeling, tennis, biking and spa treatments.

LeSPORT
$$$$$ 155 rooms

Cariblue Beach, Cap Estate. 800-544-2883. www.thebodyholiday.com.

Come here to tone up and tune out. Set within
an especially pretty part of the island, this
secluded, upscale resort focuses on a combination of fun, fitness and well-being. All meals and
activities (except certain spa treatments) are
included in the rate. Upon arrival, put on your
white cotton robe and head out each day for stress-management classes ranging
from meditation to tai chi, as well as a spa treatment. Body "guards" ensure a good
time (and help single travelers feel at ease), while body "guides" plot your fitness
program. The on-site restaurant offers a variety of light, healthy meals.

Windjammer Landing Villa Beach Resort
$$$$ 237 units

Labrelotte Bay, Castries. 758-456-9000 or 800-958-7376. www.windjammer-landing.com.

White-stucco Mediterranean-style villas with red-tile
roofs snuggle within tropical gardens on the hillside of
Labrelotte Bay. The 55-acre resort accommodates families
and newlyweds who opt for activities galore, or a romantic hideaway. Parents love the fun club for children,
and there's a program for teens as well. Spacious guest
quarters include a kitchen and a terrace. There are four restaurants and four swimming pools to choose from, as well as a fitness center and tennis courts.

Ti Kaye Village Resort
$$$ 33 rooms

Anse Cochon, Vieux Fort, north of Soufriere. 758-456-8101. www.tikaye.com.

Ti Kaye is St. Lucian patois for "small house,"
and that's exactly what's nestled within the
cliffs of Anse Cochon—colorful gingerbread-
trimmed West Indian guest cottages. Extra
perks include a private outdoor shower, and
a porch where a hammock gently sways in the breeze. Some 166 steps lead
down to a wide, sandy beach protected in a cove. A full breakfast is included
in the rate.

Barbados

Sandy Lane Hotel and Golf Club $$$$$ 112 units

Hwy. 1, Sandy Lane Bay, St. James. 246-444-2000. www.sandylane.com.

You'll see why royalty and celebrities favor this posh, pricey resort for their getaways. The place is dripping with luxury and style. White urns and fountains dot the well-landscaped, palm-studded grounds. A handsome Palladian-style mansion made of coral sets the standard for the other structures. Sea views or garden vistas greet you at every turn. Safeguarding privacy and increasing the level of comfort, accommodating staff members cater to your wants. Richly appointed, generous-sized rooms with white walls and bedspreads are accessorized in soft pastels and equipped with plasma TVs, DVD players and other high-tech perks. Walk out your door to golf courses, tennis courts, a spa, four restaurants and the beach, of course, where a multitude of water sports awaits you.

Tamarind Cove Hotel $$$$$ 110 rooms

Paynes Bay, St James. 246-432-1332 or 800-326-6898. www.eleganthotels.com.

You may not want to leave this oasis of white sand and tropical gardens spreading along the blue-green waters of Paynes Bay. Your haven at this Mediterranean-style resort is a spacious room with off-white walls, cream-colored wicker furniture and a bed draped with mosquito netting. Diversions include four swimming pools, three restaurants, tennis courts, a fitness room and a beauty salon, not to mention a host of water sports at the sea's shore. A member of the Elegant Hotels group, Tamarind Cove is one of Barbados' most distinctive vacation properties.

The Crane $$$$ 68 units

Crane Bay, St. Philip. 246-423-6220 or 800-223-9815. www.thecrane.com.

The oldest resort in the Caribbean, The Crane opened in 1887. Back then, the resort had its pick of the beaches, and it chose a beautiful one: Crane Beach, where pinkish sands edge turquoise waters. Renovated and updated with modern amenities, The Crane accommodates guests in spacious apartments handsomely appointed with rich wood furnishings, including four-poster beds; 12-foot ceilings, hardwood floors and balconies add to the allure. You may want to request a unit with a kitchen or a Jacuzzi. Luxuriate at the much photographed swimming pool perched picturesquely above the beach.

St. Vincent and the Grenadines

The Cotton House $$$$$ 20 rooms

West coast of Mustique. 784-456-4777. www.cottonhouse.net.

Hobnob with the rich and famous at this refined plantation-style inn. Seclusion and privacy are its hallmarks. The rooms, suites and cottages of the hilltop estate exude a sophisticated Caribbean charm. Cool whites or creams dominate the color scheme; furnishings are plush, and beds are draped in mosquito netting. In the great room of the main house, you'll partake of cocktails and appetizers preceding a candlelit dinner. The gift shop in the old sugar mill offers a selection of savvy souvenirs. Expect sterling service, breathtaking views and a great little spa.

Raffles Resort $$$$$ 156 units

Canouan Island. 784-458-8000. www.raffles-canouanisland.com.

This upscale resort chain might even trump The Donald in showing off its spare-no-expense, 300-acre mecca of Caribbean luxury. Everything from the spa treatment rooms to the extra-long swimming pool has high style written all over it. Fresh flowers grace large guest rooms ensconced within vibrant orange or cooling white walls. You'll even have your own golf cart while you're here. Seven restaurants serve culinary feasts. The Donald? He's playing right along with his Trump Club Privée, an elegant casino, and Trump International Golf Club, a gorgeous, challenging 18-hole course that excites even the most jaded golfers.

Ocean View Inn $$ 6 rooms

Grand Bay, Canouan Island. 784-482-0477. www.oceanview-can.com.

Sailors looking for a good night's sleep on dry land, and vacationers seeking a simple, out-of-the-way spot just steps from a lovely beach, are drawn to this inn, which sits close to a full-service marina. The two stories of the modest hotel are wrapped in verandas offering sea views or hillside vistas. Rooms are airy and roomy; all have a ceiling fan and a private bath. Breakfast is included in the rate.

Frangipani Hotel $ 15 units

Belmont Walkway, Port Elizabeth, Bequia. 784-458-3255. www.frangipanibequia.com.

Built by a local sea captain, this century-old, shingle-sided house offers modest rooms with a shared bath in the second story, or charming garden units built of local stone and hard wood with a private bath. A great place for yacht ogling, the beach bar serves up Hairoun (Bequia-brewed beer) and creative cocktails; the outdoor restaurant is known for Thursday night barbecues and jump-ups.

Grenada

Laluna
$$$$$ 16 units

Morne Rouge, St. George's. 473-439-0001 or 866-452-5862. www.laluna.com.

While some resorts excel in excess, Laluna embodies the philosophy that "less is more" (except in its rates). Just 16 thatched-roofed cottages incorporate personal touches. Each one individually decorated, guest quarters blend Eastern, Mediterranean and Caribbean styles. Bamboo furnishings and cotton fabrics complement the beauty of the setting, while private terraces and open-air bathrooms encourage you to feel at one with the natural landscape. Plunge pools and yoga sessions add to the feeling of tranquillity. A stay at Laluna is sure to refresh even the weariest tourist.

LaSource
$$$$$ 100 units

Pink Gin Beach, south of St. George's. 473-444-2556 or 888-527-0044. www.lasourcegrenada.com.

This health-focused, all-inclusive resort sits on 40 beachfront acres. Embracing the estate, the gardens are extensive *(guided garden tours are offered)*, culminating in a waterfall. One spa treatment per day is included in the rate. Also part of the price are relaxation therapies like yoga and tai chi, as well as water sports, fencing and archery. Rooms feature four-poster beds, marble floors and ceiling fans. The staff is among the friendliest in the Caribbean; bodyguards will make sure you're never left alone at mealtimes, unless you want to be.

Trinidad and Tobago

The Villas at Stonehaven
$$$$$ 14 villas

Stonehaven Bay, Tobago. 868-639-0361. www.stonehavenvillas.com. Not child-friendly for children under 7 years of age (low balconies and infinity pools).

Perched on a hillside, these 18C French Colonial-style villas boast stunning views of the sea. When you step into your villa's foyer, you'll feel as if you're coming home. Each villa is equipped with four bedrooms decked out in elegant furnishings, a full kitchen, a private pool, multiple balconies and a veranda. You're even assigned a housekeeper who, upon your request, prepares breakfast and dinner and serves you drinks on the shady terrace.

Blue Haven Hotel
$$$$ 55 rooms

Bacolet Bay, Scarborough, Tobago. 868-660-7400. www.bluehavenhotel.com.

Legend has it that this is the site where Robinson Crusoe was stranded in 1659; his ship's anchor is a favorite curio among the guests. Movie stars and royalty have hidden out here, too, within the 15 seaside acres that overlook Bacolet Bay. The hotel's Colonial-style villa houses a great restaurant and terrace bar. In season guests are entertained by folklore shows, calypso music and steel bands.

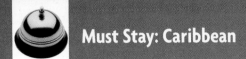

Coblentz Inn
$$ 16 rooms

44 Coblentz Ave, Port of Spain, Trinidad. 868-621-0541. www.coblentzinn.com.

A feng shui master was consulted in order to bring a sense of balance and tranquillity to this boutique hotel, which sits a short walk from Port of Spain's Queen's Park Savannah. Rooms are bright and cheery, with yellow drapes and bedspreads. Spend some time in the quiet library if you want to be alone. At **Battimamzelle ($$)**, the inn's sunny rooftop cafe, the chef aims to please, whether it's a simple sandwich kicked up a notch by a new sauce or a full-course gourmet dinner. A continental breakfast is included in the rate.

The Pax Guest House
$ 9 rooms

St. Johns Rd., Tunapuna, Trinidad. 868-662-4084 or 800-869-0639. www.paxguesthouse.com.

Serenity-seeking eco-travelers love this 1916 country inn, a unique lodging be-cause it resides on the grounds of a Benedictine monastery. Surrounded by 600 forested acres within Trinidad's lush Northern Range, the monastery sits 800 feet above sea level. Rooms are modest and simple; from your balcony you'll enjoy views of the forest-covered mountains. Be sure to take one of the inn's guided birding excursions, which are popular with those who stay here.

ABC Islands

Avila Beach Hotel
$$$ 108 rooms

Penstraat 130, Willemstad, Curaçao. 5999-461-4377 or 800-747-8162. www.avilahotel.com.

Surround yourself in history at this colorful hotel. The lobby of this beachfront property sits in an 18C Dutch Colonial mansion that once housed British and Dutch governors. New wings the flank the mansion. Rooms in both the west and east wings are done up in white with bamboo furnishings; they have balco-nies offering views of the sea. The west wing is connected by a walkway to the beach pier, where there's a jazz bar and an outdoor restaurant located right over the water. A spa has recently opened on the premises.

Kurá Hulanda Hotel
$$$ 80 rooms

Langestraat 8, Willemstad, Curaçao. 5999-434-7700 or 877-264-3106. www.kurahulanda.com.

Looking for an artsy accommodation with European elegance? Then come to this village of restored, pastel-painted 18C and 19C Dutch-Colonial buildings that wrap around several European-style courtyards. Each one-of-a-kind room is furnished with antiques and hand-carved mahogany and teak furniture. There's a natural rock grotto that's a sun-'n-swim dream complete with a soothing waterfall. The grounds are accented with museum-quality sculpture; the hotel's interior shows off art from around the globe. On the hotel's square, Jacob's Bar is a favorite spot for sipping wine. As the sun goes down, **Jaipur ($$)** serves tasty Indian cuisine, and the fine-dining **Astrolab Observatory ($$$$)** restau-rant prepares first-rate continental dishes.

Index

Index

Index

Index

Photo Credits